ISBN 0-942604-93-8

Published by
Madison Square Press
10 East 23rd Street
New York, NY 10010
Phone: (212) 505-0950, Fax (212) 979-2207
E-mail: MadisonSqPress@aol.com
Printed in Hong Kong

FRED OTNES

COLLAGE PAINTINGS

Jill Bossert

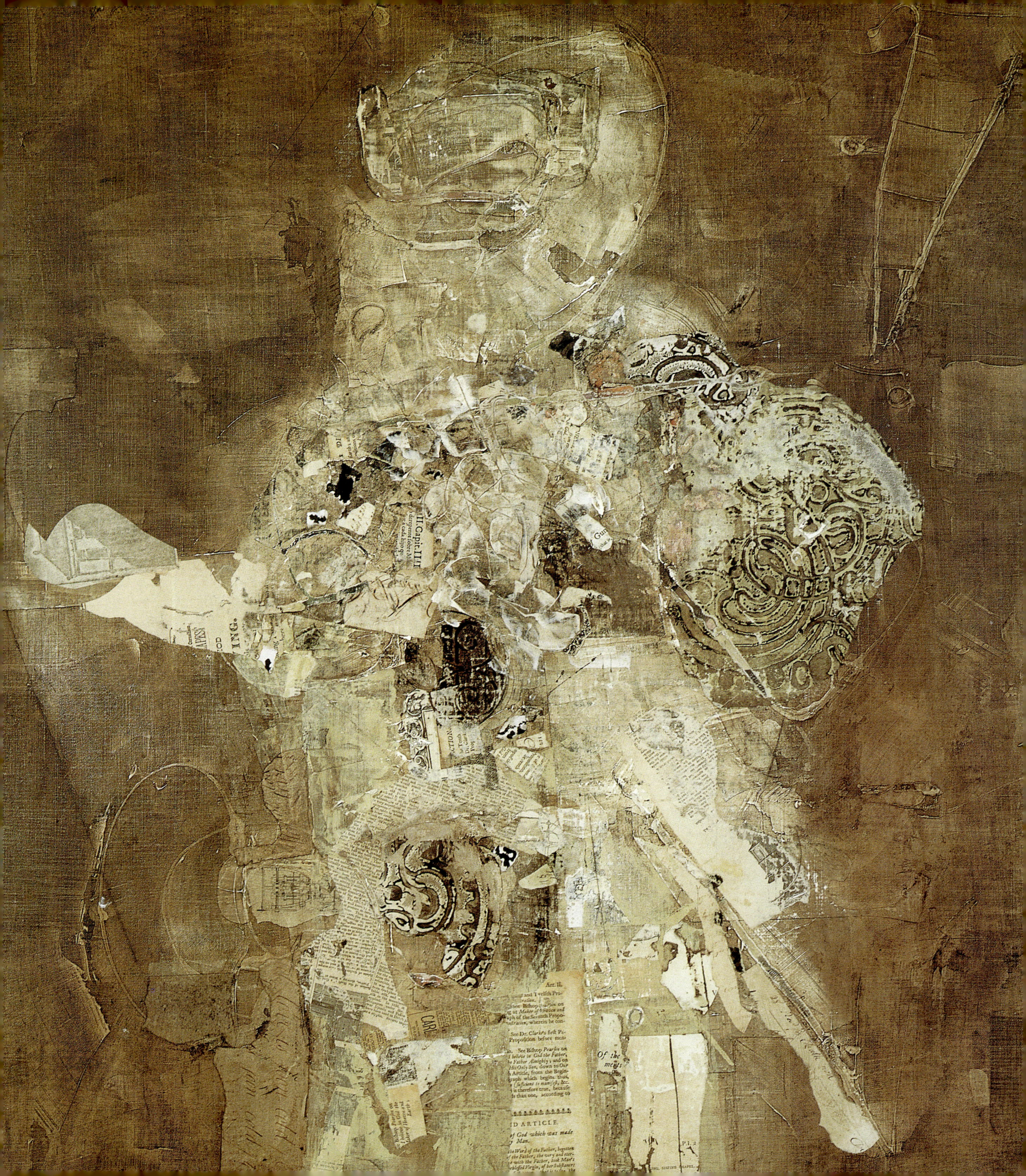

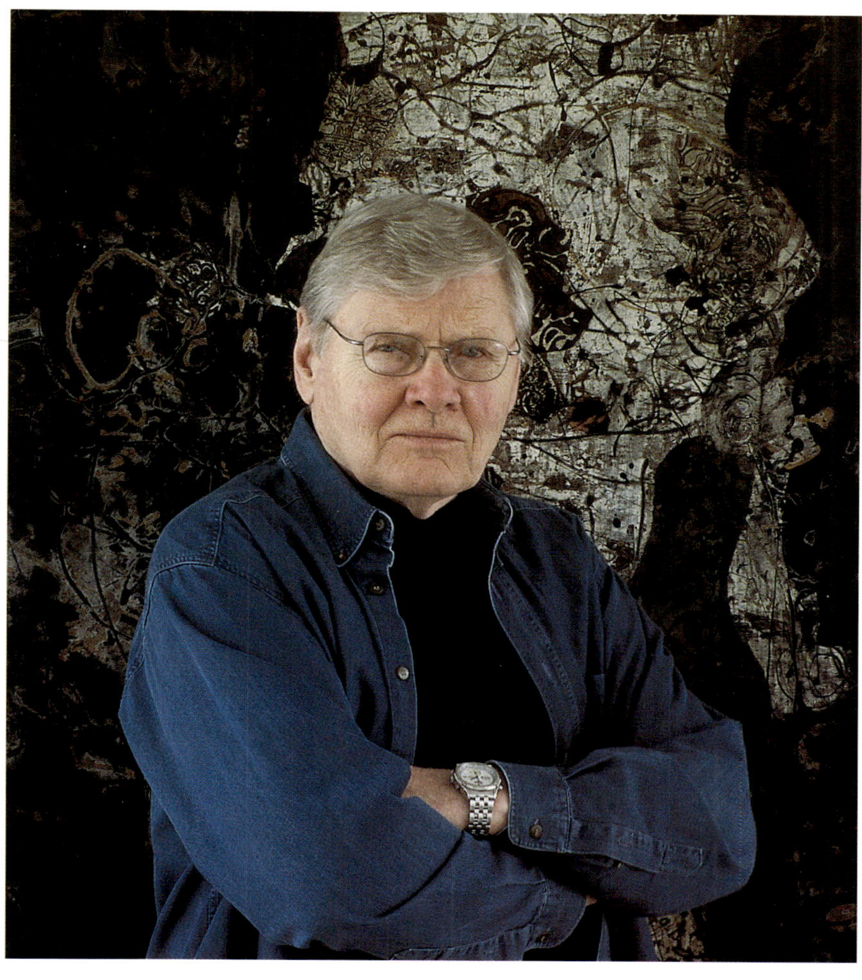

1
Umber Figure
1994

2
Fred Otnes
2003

The art of collage relies on chance, the felicitous arrangement of unrelated objects and oddments: an interesting edge of torn paper, printers' type, the scale on a slide rule, an anatomical engraving, a swatch of patterned cloth from India, a reproduction of a quattrocento Madonna, a feather. Left to chance alone, such elements are intrinsic to themselves and their relation to one another remains discrete. In the hands of the artist Fred Otnes control merges with chance to create works of subtle, refined beauty that are designed with such assurance as to appear inevitable, works that are infused with a mystery that is both fleeting and eternal. The subtle tension between control (frames within frames, architectural and mathematical elements, arches and figures) and chance (endless variations of torn shapes layered and scattered, multitudes of textured surfaces) creates a mesmerizing whole.

Throughout the work are far-ranging art historical references that include the ancient Greeks, the Renaissance, the Dutch masters, and Victoriana, as well as the many elements of Modernism, from Cubism to Abstract Expressionism. These historical appropriations are juxtaposed against more universal symbolism such as birds and trees, which in turn play against the sheer abstraction of torn paper and areas of raw linen canvas. Dreamlike, even fantastic, yet grounded, the subtle delicacy and complexity of the surface is held by the eloquent strength of the overall design.

Although Otnes concedes that all collage artists owe a debt to Joseph Cornell, for whom his admiration is great, Otnes marks his early exposure to Cubism as the starting point of his fascination with the flat dimensionality and formal cues that have remained constant in his collage work. Although his initial endeavors as an artist began far more conventionally, those perspectiveless planes in sepias, browns, and blacks, with their scraps of imbedded ephemera, have endured.

Born on December 3, 1930, in Junction City, Kansas, a place that claimed to be the geographic center of the United States, Otnes's Midwestern roots are evident in his reticence, his lack of pretension, and his practical and disciplined work ethic. His Norwegian-born paternal grandfather was a civil engineer who moved to Junction City

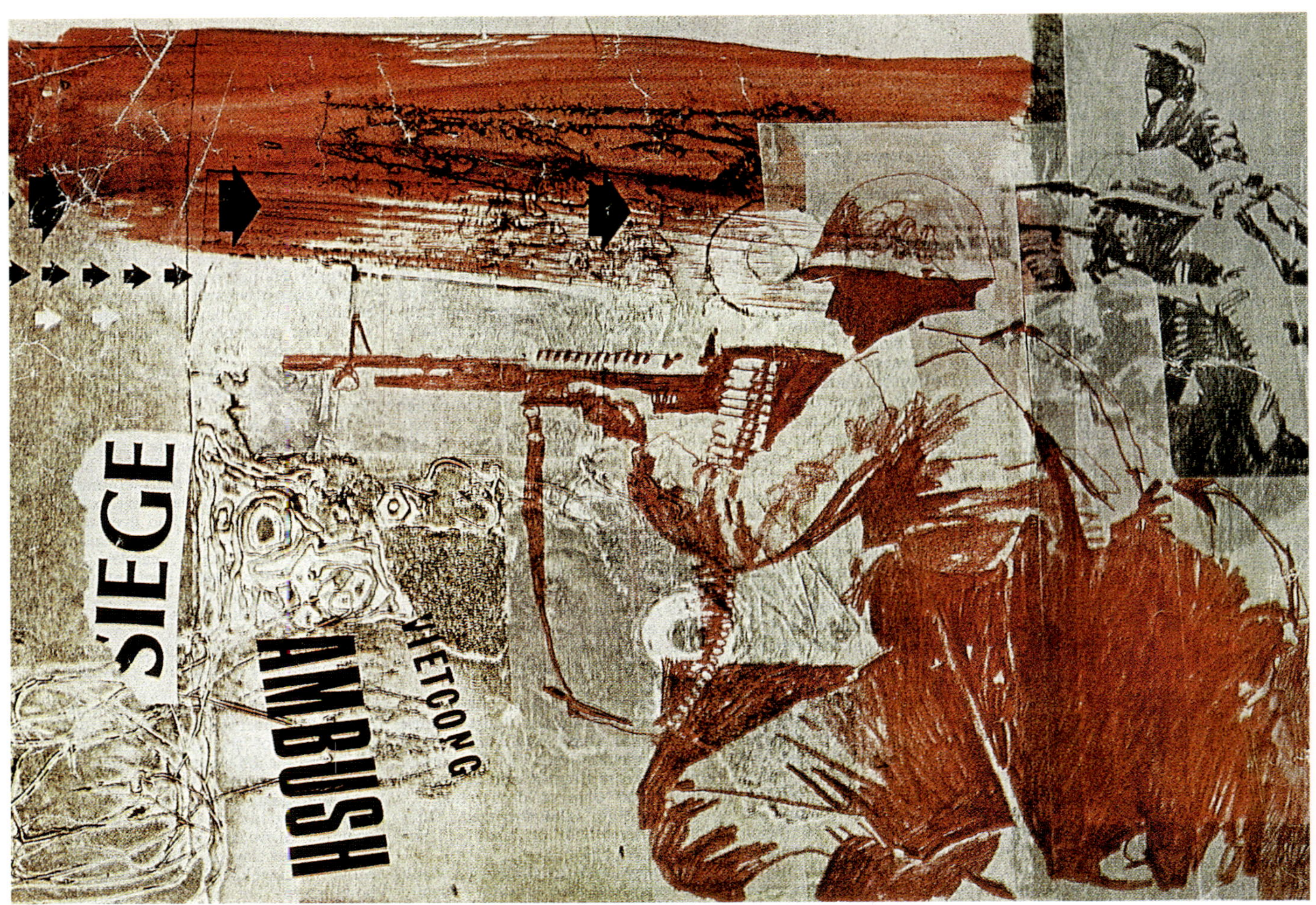

3
Saturday Evening Post
1960's

to work at Ft. Riley, a nearby military base. On his mother Dorthea's side, the Flower family, of English, Irish, and Scots heritage, had been in the country for generations. His maternal grandfather, a carpenter and contractor, was responsible for a number of buildings that stand in the city to this day.

Otnes's father, Frederick, was employed as a sales manager for various companies, including Folger's Coffee and Nabisco, which necessitated frequent relocation for the family throughout the region. Even when settled in one town, the Otneses and their three boys moved from house to house, which often meant a change of schools as well. This lack of roots made making friends difficult for the admittedly shy Otnes, who to some extent credits the development of his very strong sense of independence to his peripatetic youth. And, he points out, growing up in the Depression made clear to him the necessity of making a living.

To add to his sense of isolation, Otnes lost his brother Donald, who died at the age of nine; nor was he particularly close to his younger brother Robert, when they were children. In adulthood, however, Robert would become his best friend and one of the most important and influential relationships in the artist's life.

Otnes's ability was evident from an early age when, like many youngsters, he imitated his favorite cartoonists and comic book artists. His father, who had some artistic talent, was very encouraging, though he died at age 45 and would not witness his son's great success. Otnes's skills improved to the point that his high school art teacher, who recognized his talent, arranged for him to visit the local newspaper, *The Lincoln Journal*, where he was hired to work after school and then throughout the summer. He spent time in various departments doing pasteup, cartoons, hand lettering, photography, and some drawing. But his most important apprenticeship was to be in the engraving department. For Otnes the experience was life altering: the practical education was invaluable, but more important, the work made sense of everything he had been doing with paper and pencil up to that point and allowed him to imagine a future in art.

After high school he continued at the *Journal* until 1947, when he joined the Marine Corps. Stationed in Hawaii, he was assigned to the Fleet Marine Force Mapping and

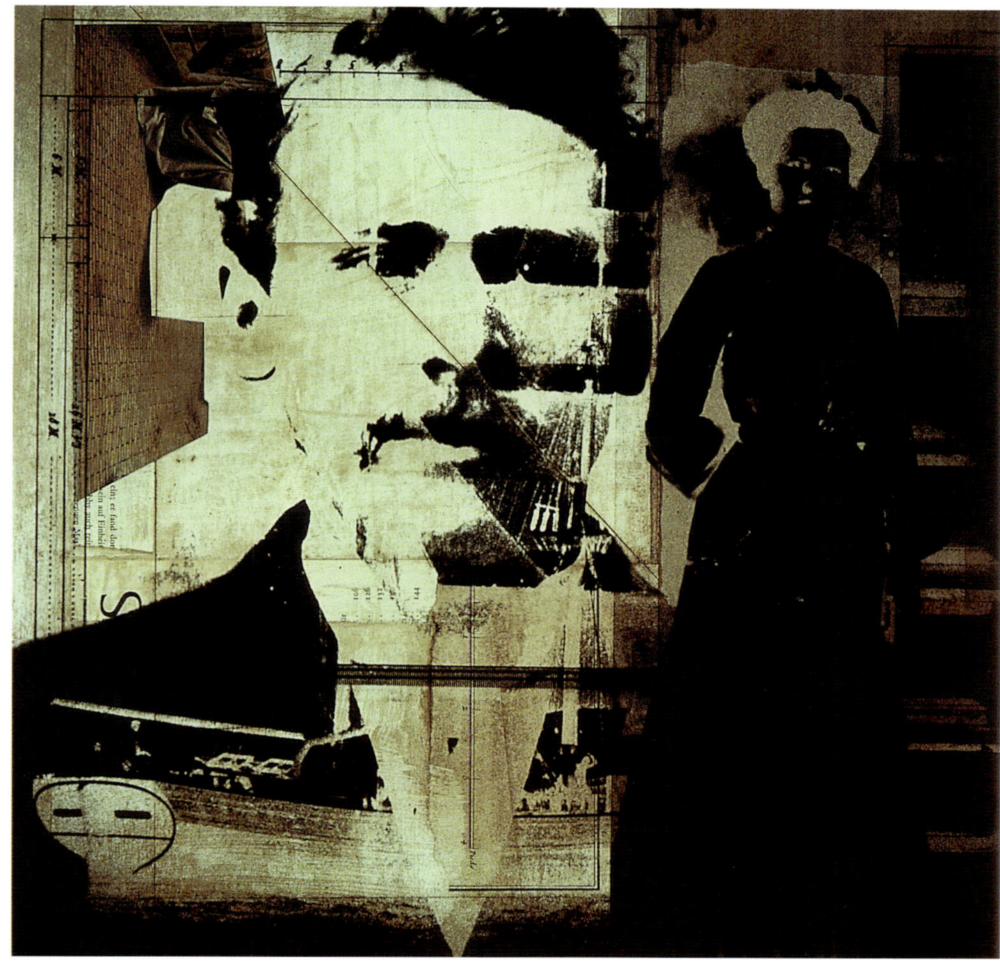

4
Eugene O'Neil Plays, Franklin Library
1960's

Reproduction Unit. His newspaper experience proved invaluable to his work producing illustrations for brochures and other printed materials. In 1949 Otnes returned to the *Journal* briefly before enrolling at the Art Institute of Chicago. Exposure to the Institute's fine art collection, he says, was more important to his art education than his classes. To support himself, he worked as an illustrator at the Illustrators Studio in Chicago and found it, too, to be more meaningful than his formal education. Otnes says, "Art history classes were a punishment; it wasn't what I liked about art. I liked looking at art and doing art. I got more out of seeing the works in the museum." Although he appreciated the Old Masters, he was particularly drawn to modern artists, especially paintings by Braque and Picasso. At the time, Cubism, with its pictorial flatness, was completely unfamiliar to him, and he knew no particular reason why he should identify with it. Yet Cubism was to have a great and lasting impact on him: it was the beginning of his love of Modernism, with its commitment to form without the illusion of depth.

Otnes dropped out of the Institute after one year, and though he attended painting classes at the Academy of Art at night, he concentrated on his job at Whitaker-Guernsey, one of Chicago's top studios. There he turned out illustrations for major advertising clients such as Abbott Laboratories and United Airlines. He identified with, and his work reflected his admiration for, such artists as Al Parker, Robert Fawcett, Austin Briggs, and Noel Sickles, among others, all of whom were expert draftsmen.

The artist's somewhat chaotic bachelor existence ended in 1953, when he met Fran McCaughan, to whom he was immediately drawn. From southern Illinois, she was both gentle and remarkably efficient and created order in Otnes's life, helping him schedule his work, pay the bills, and create a comfortable home. As he puts it, "I did the art; she did everything else." But more important and from the very start, the couple did everything together, forging a uniquely close and equal partnership that endured until Fran's death, in 1995. Otnes's admiration remains boundless, and he considers their relationship the best thing that ever happened to him.

By 1953, having conquered Chicago, Otnes went to New York with a portfolio of new samples and a letter of

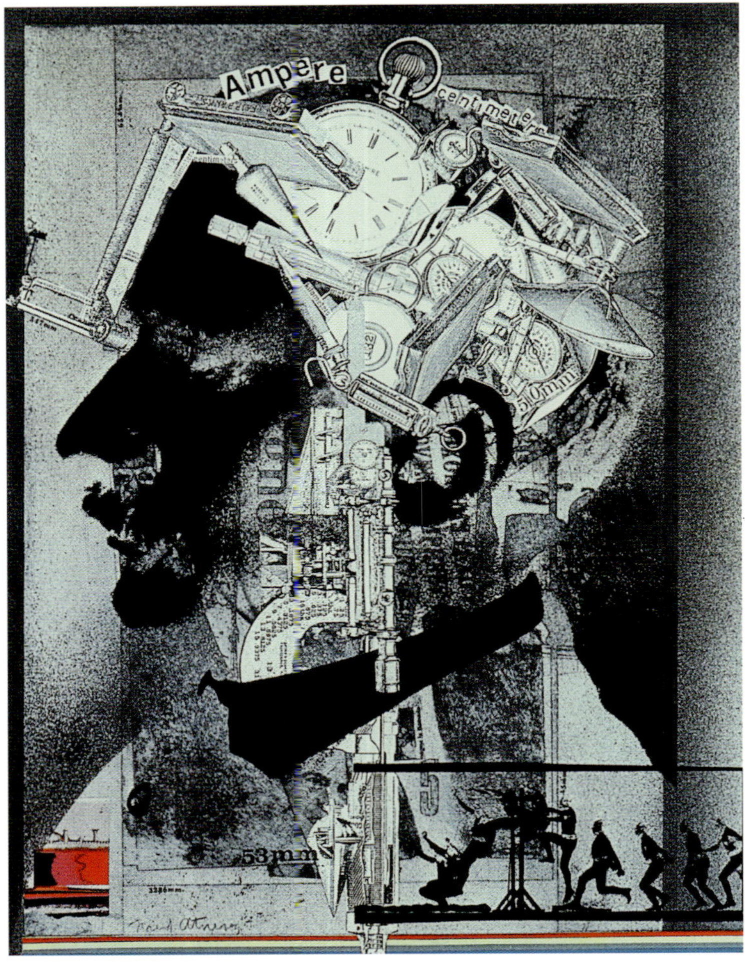

5
Lithopinion
Magazine
1960's

recommendation from Whitaker-Guernsey. Within a week he had secured a position at the prestigious Rahl Studios and rented a house in suburban Westport, Connecticut, home to many famous illustrators. For more than ten years Otnes worked successfully as an illustrator in a representational style for many advertising clients and for such publications as *The Saturday Evening Post*, *True*, and *Collier's*, specializing in the more masculine themes—adventure stories, mysteries, westerns, hunting, and fishing.

In 1963 the Otneses built a house in West Redding, Connecticut, designed by the architect John Johansen in the International style. It is magnificently situated at the top of seven acres, which included a limestone quarry that they converted into a dramatic swimming pool. The house, where Otnes still resides and which he credits in part with his development as an artist, is a Modernist gem with pristine lines and a preponderance of glass walls. The décor, in whites, grays, and blacks, is in perfect keeping with the structure, as are the furnishings, held in a mid-twentieth-century time warp: an Eames chair and ottoman, a glass coffee table placed between a black leather sofa and a pair of Barcelona chairs, a white marble pedestal dining table, all complemented by perfectly placed, graphically compelling objects. And it is an ideal setting for Otnes's art. To him the house is, by design, meticulous and extremely well organized, in contrast to the transparency that lets in great washes of light and the random complexity of the natural world.

In this house, which Fran ran superbly and with grace, the Otneses shared a rich life of work, travel, and friends, including such top illustrators as Bernie Fuchs, Robert Heindel, Alan E. Cober, and Mark English, with whom Otnes played chess every week until 1977, when English moved to Kansas City. The men remain close to this day, discussing art long distance and, when English comes east, visiting galleries and museums together. As English says, "I think it's funny that Fred and I, more than anyone else, are of the same mind. When we look at shows, we like the same things, we buy the same books. It's amazing. Though our work's very different, we both have admiration for each other and respect each other."

Another neighbor was the renowned illustrator Austin Briggs, with whom Otnes shared a love of modern art

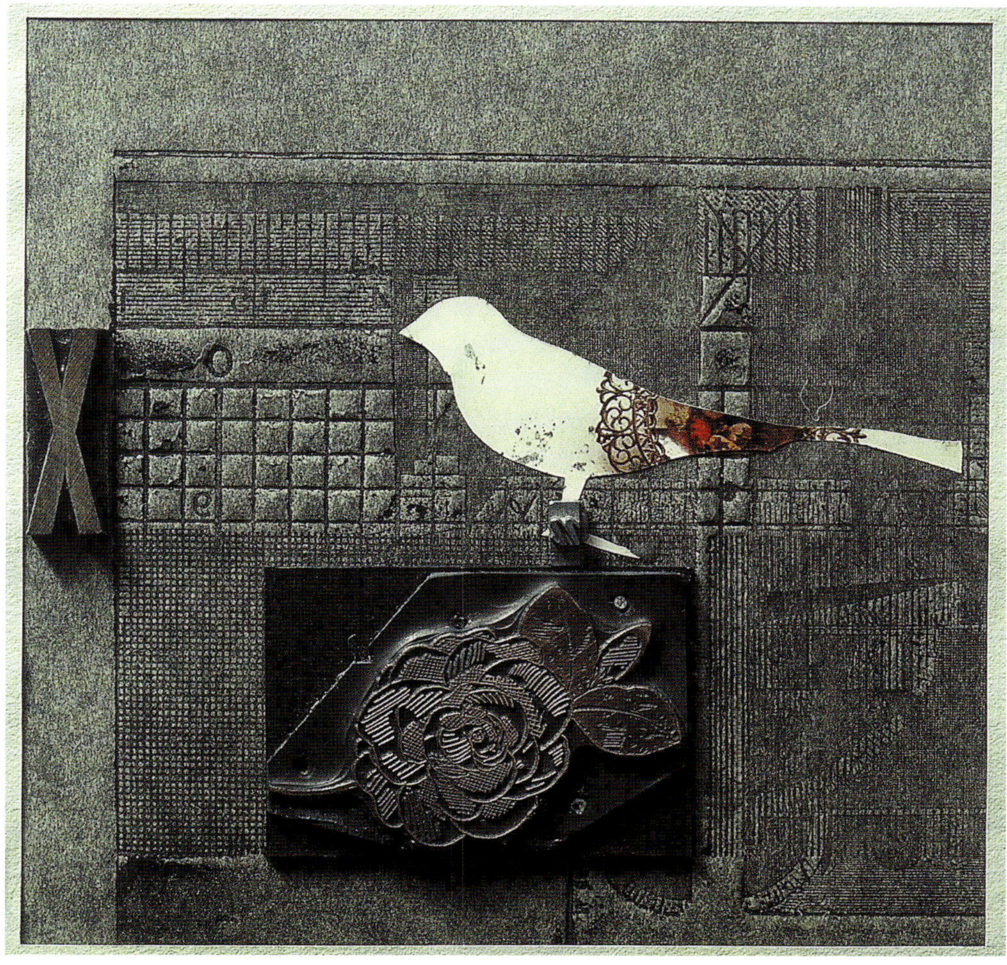

6
Annual Report
Cover
1980's

and architecture. (Not unexpectedly, Otnes especially admires the work of the Bauhaus masters Walter Gropius and Mies Van der Rohe; Le Corbusier; and contemporaries Richard Meier and Charles Gwathmey.) He credits Briggs with helping him recognize what constitutes a good artist and what one had to do to become one.

In 1962, Otnes signed with the highly respected art representative Bill Erlacher, of Artists Associates. Thus began a special partnership, rarely achieved between artist and rep, that lasted more than thirty years. Erlacher, a patient, gentle man, would often be the "voice of reason" between Otnes and his clients and was invaluable in forging the artist's successful career, both in acquiring work and demanding commensurate fees.

By the early 1960s the publishing world, which had been the arena where illustrators became well known, even famous, was in a state of flux; the major weekly magazines were losing advertising revenue to television, and the fiction market, which had always relied heavily on illustration, was also being overtaken by soap operas and drama shows on television. As periodicals began to specialize, narrowing their markets and relying more and more on photography, there was less call for traditional illustration. Otnes, though working steadily, could see a dwindling demand for his kind of narrative approach and decided it was time to make a change.

An avid museum and gallery visitor, Otnes's primary interest throughout the years had been fine art rather than illustration. If he was going to develop a new approach, he felt he would concentrate on the kind of artwork to which he'd been attracted but which, until then, the illustration market had not allowed. The actual transition took place one weekend in 1964, when Nelson Pollock, an art director and friend, came to visit and brought some books and magazines related to award-winning graphic designs of that year. Looking through the pages, Otnes recalled the days when he was involved in graphics at the *Lincoln Journal* and in the Marine Crops—the kind of imagery that had fascinated him for the last twenty years. That weekend he put into action what he had been considering doing for some time: to completely change his style of working.

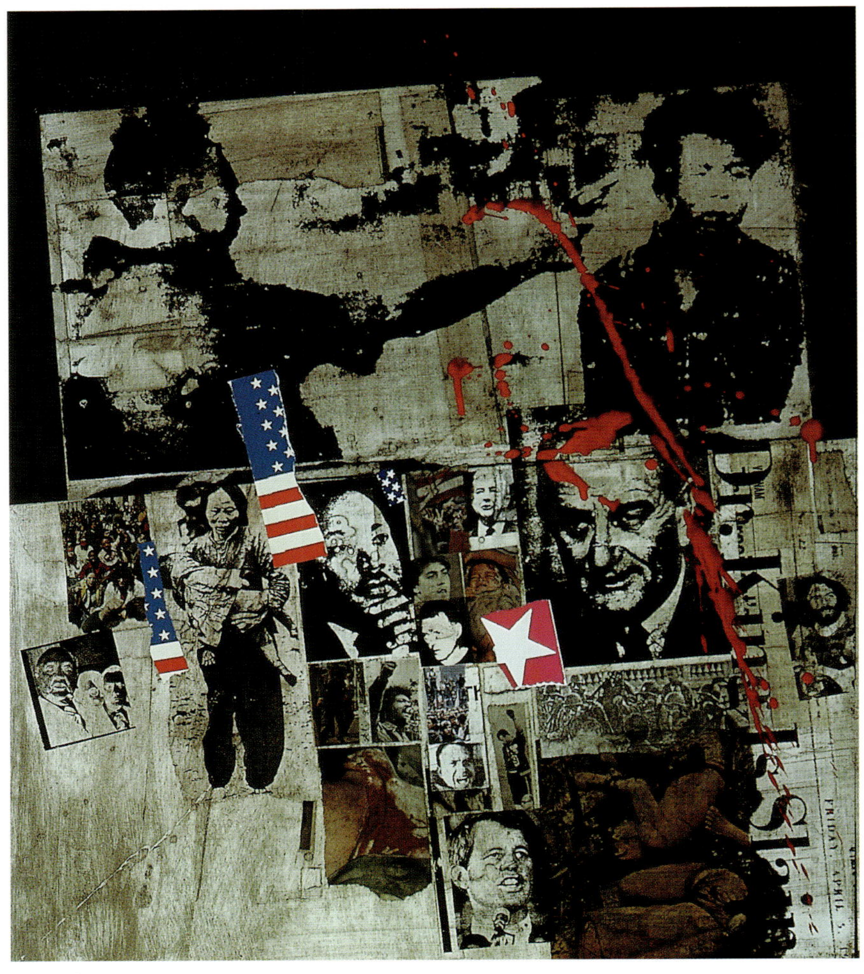

He called a contractor and had a studio added to the house, ordered an etching press out of Chicago (one he still uses), and hired a printmaking specialist to set up the studio and instruct him on a variety of printing techniques. Professionally, the transition—what Mark English calls his "metamorphosis"—was abrupt. After building his new studio, Otnes stopped producing traditional illustration, and things fell into place almost immediately. Robert Hallock, art director of *Lithopinion*, the highly sophisticated and beautifully produced trade publication of the Amalgamated Lithographers Union of America, saw Otnes's new works as something that would fit well into his magazine and quickly and frequently published them (Figure 5). Otnes began with printmaking alone but quickly added collage elements to the work. He then employed photographic images within the collage, using his own photography or adapting imagery from other sources, such as old family photos.

7
Cover Magazine Section
Washington Post
1970's

8
Illustration,
Franklin Library
1990

An invaluable help to her husband in his work, Fran was responsible for managing what would become an enormous collection of scrap material, keeping track of photographs, and cutting and filing a variety of ephemera from books and magazines. Although she had no formal art training, she found she had a talent for decoupage, and for a brief time she was represented by Artists Associates.

The appearance of Otnes's work in Hallock's prestigious magazine quickly led to general acceptance of his new style. A piece on Vietnam (Figure 3), the first of his new work to appear in a national magazine, combined collage elements and figures drawn on tissue and ran in *The Saturday Evening Post*. Early in this transitional phase, the Franklin Library, publisher of finely made illustrated books, asked Otnes to illustrate a collection of plays by Eugene O'Neill (Figure 4), the first of many projects for the publisher. It was the first piece that combined collage and transfer photographic elements—in this case a photo of Otnes's grandfather—to depict the content of the stories, a departure from the client's conventional use of narrative illustration.

The 1960s and 1970s was a period of political and social upheaval in the country: the war in Southeast Asia and its attendant protests, the fights for civil rights for African Americans and for women's rights, assassinations, ecological destruction, and the drug culture were all fertile ground for

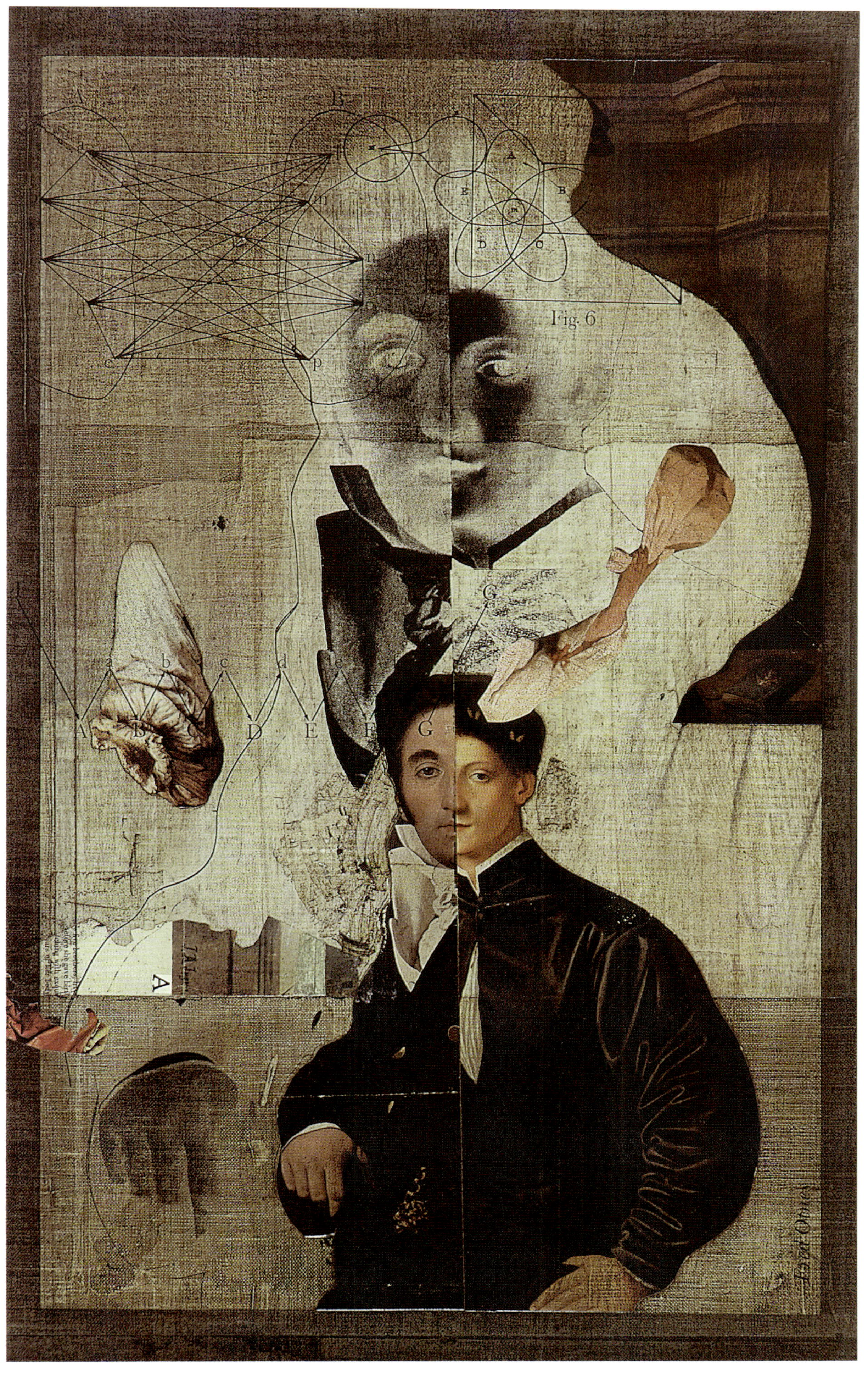
Fig. 6

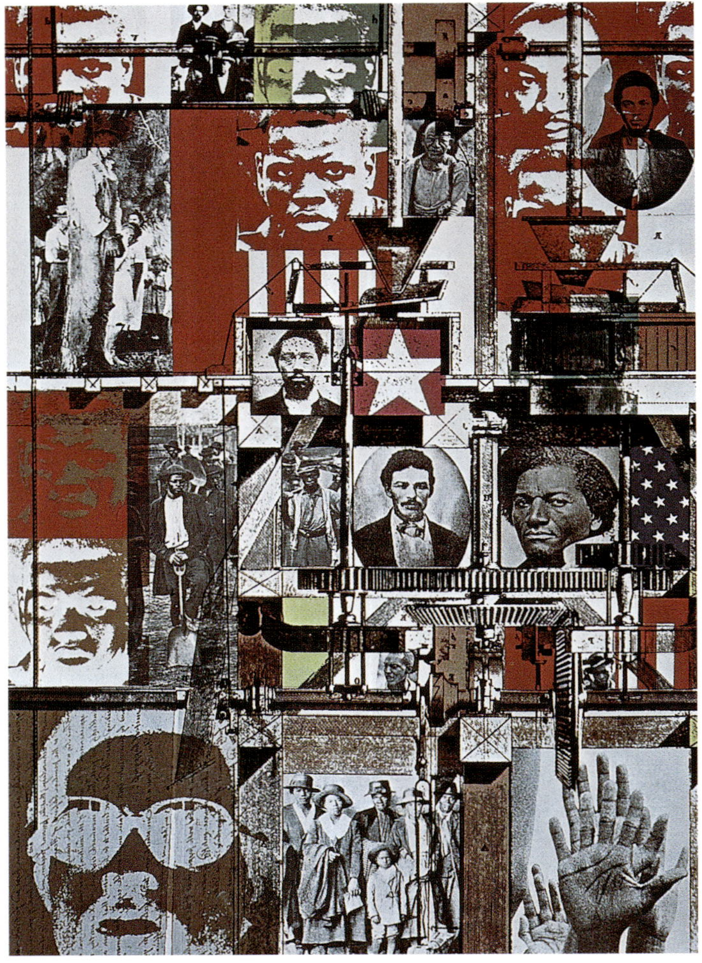

9
Cover
Pocket Books
1970's

editorial debate and deliberation. The complex and abstract nature of such debate was difficult to render in traditional illustration methods but very well served by Otnes's collages, which almost immediately became more significant in his work than the straight printmaking. A defining image for Otnes was a work by Robert Rauschenberg that appeared in *Life* magazine. Depicting contemporary upheavals, its crowded juxtaposition of silk-screened images was a technique Otnes felt perfectly illustrated the subject matter; further, it directly related to the work he was exploring.

To Otnes it was clear that television had accustomed his audience to viewing repeated images and to taking in enormous amounts of content. His illustrations, with their numerous and varied elements, encompassed entire events and the atmosphere around them—it was storytelling in a different way, such as his cover for *The Washington Post* depicting the decade of the 1960s (Figure 7).

For thirty years Otnes's illustrations appeared in *Penthouse* magazine, where his technique was ideally suited for wide-ranging or somewhat abstract features on current affairs, such as the collapse of liberty in America (Figure 10). In the same vein, Otnes did a series for *The Atlantic Monthly*, which dealt with the historical view of the life of Christ (Figure 15). At the time Otnes was very aware of the structural nature of Richard Diebenkorn's work and found the strong horizontals and verticals symbolically perfect for the subject.

For assignments with less pointed agendas, Otnes produced many works with a nostalgic, dreamy atmosphere, combining old photographs rendered with the photo-transfer technique, paint, antique collage elements, and even flowers Fran had pressed, as in a cover for the graphic arts magazine *Print* (Figure 16). The bird and the open window, Otnes says, should imply creativity to the viewer.

At this time Otnes was also constructing assemblages for illustration assignments. Attracted by the work of Louise Nevelson and other sculptors working with the form (with the overarching precedent of Joseph Cornell's boxes), Otnes considered this structural work as an extension of his collages. During his travels with Fran to antique shops and renovation supply houses, he sought out old woods and objects that had intrinsic beauty as well as adding meaning to the theme of the piece. By now Otnes was submitting

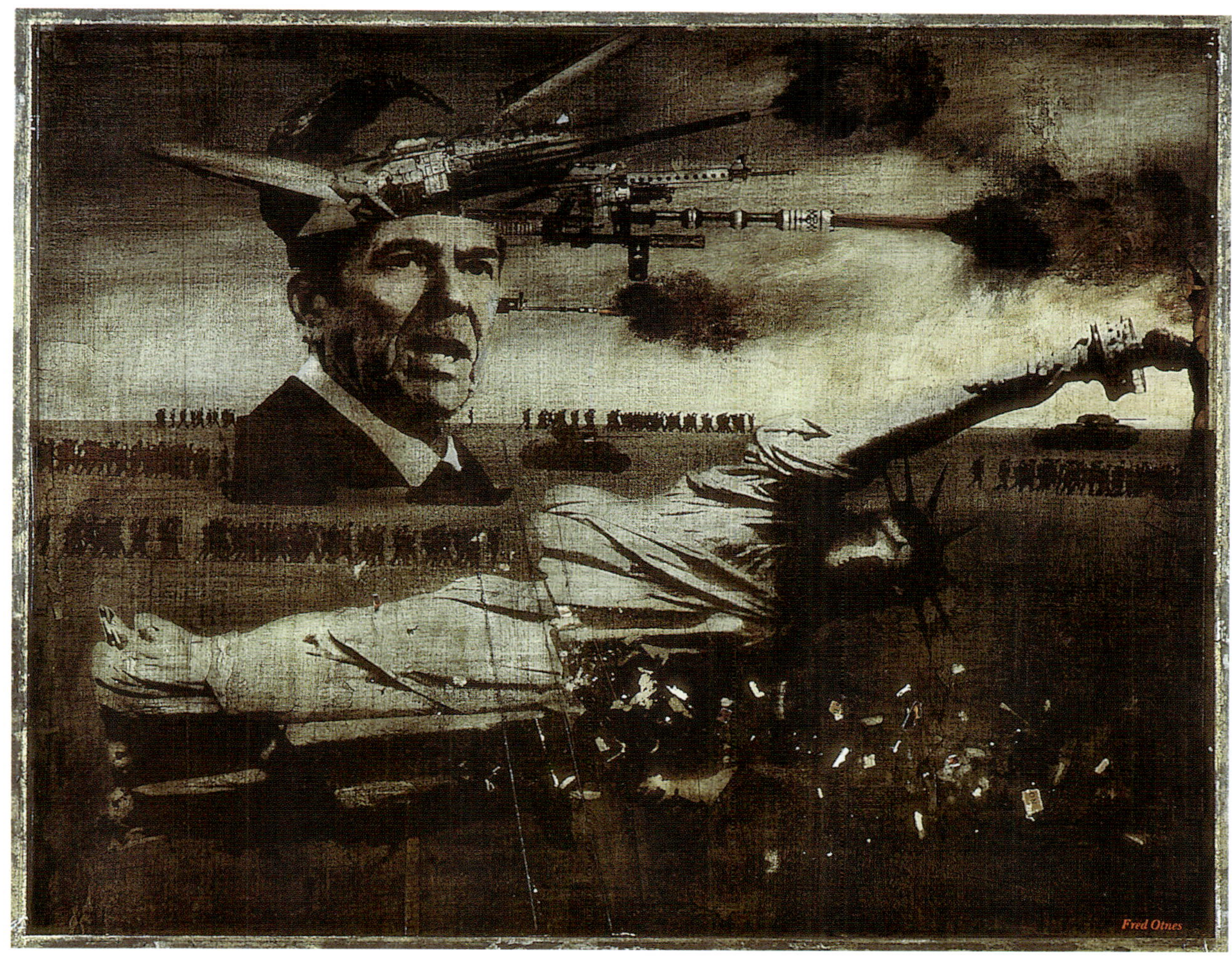

10
Penthouse
Magazine
1980's

photographs of the works to the client so that he could control how light and shadow interacted with the dimensionality of the assemblages, as seen in an early, simple piece utilizing collage elements and type blocks for an annual report (Figure 6).

In the early days of the personal computer and other emerging technologies, Otnes's work was sought after by companies desperate for symbolic visuals to project a high-tech look for their products and services. Influenced by the work of Eduardo Paolozzi, Otnes photographed the programming symbols off the screen of a small computer he used primarily for playing chess. He made a plate from which he was able to create infinite variations, utilizing his photo-transfer technique for clients nationwide, from the giant IBM to now defunct dot coms (Figure 17). The high-tech look was also effective for a variety of pharmaceutical giants and large conglomerates, companies with no single product to represent, who wished to express the intangible benefits of their holdings. For five years Otnes worked for many of the major firms (Figure 20).

When working with clients, Otnes found there were those who saw the collage artist simply as someone who assembled multiple fragments that defined the content of the illustration. Otnes himself approached collage as a means of creating an image that solved a problem. The first approach was, he has said with not so gentle sarcasm, "the literal mind at work." He found literalness a hindrance to creativity, and though at times it took some convincing, most clients let him have free rein. For nearly thirty years Otnes enjoyed extraordinary success working for editorial and advertising clients, designing stamps for the U.S. Postal Service, and creating posters for thirty-four movies and a mural for the Ronald Reagan Library.

His poster for the Smithsonian National Air and Space Museum was also blown up to be a dramatic wall-sized mural (Figure 19). Like many of his illustrations, the clean design and sheer beauty of Otnes's multilayered work belies its difficulty. The complexity of working with linear patterns, multiple shapes and values, forces the artist to think "like a three-dimensional chess game." After careful research to get the appropriate elements—both subjectwise and graphically—he must set up each layer and transfer it one color at a time.

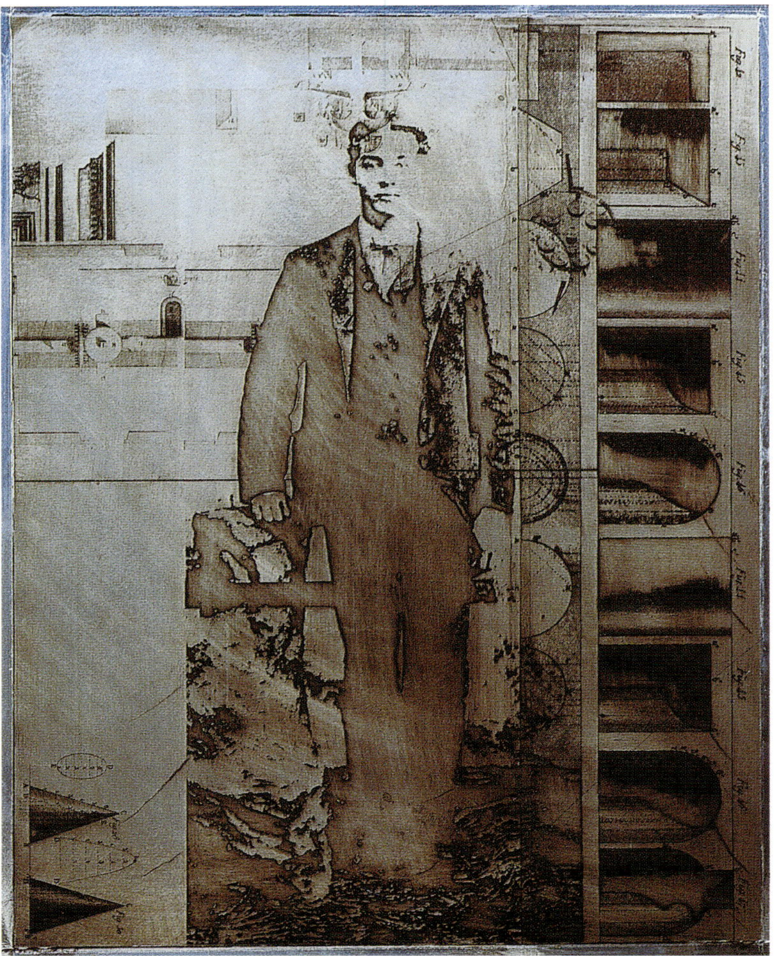

One of Otnes's great skills is his ability to visualize in advance how every shape and value is going to relate to all the others when the piece is complete.

With his unique approach, Otnes was one of the agents of change in the field of illustration, among the forces that moved illustration away from the traditional, representational narrative, providing clients an alternative interpretation of text or concept. His beautifully elegant solutions to countless illustration problems garnered Otnes more than two hundred awards from such prestigious organizations as the Art Directors Club of New York and the Society of Illustrators, which honored him with Gold and Silver Medals and its Hamilton King Award.

By the mid-1980s the sophistication of graphic design software, as well as a proliferation of stock illustration and photography, caught up with advertisers' needs—art directors could create adequate, if not inspiring layouts, and bypass the illustrator. Otnes saw it was time to consider another change. "I didn't know if I intellectualized this or if it was intuitive, but I knew that something created by hand was going to be the way to go," he says of that time, a period when he had begun to show his work at universities and colleges where he lectured and in galleries nationwide as well as in Paris, Japan, and Korea. In 1993 he had his first show at the Reece Gallery in New York, where he has exhibited ever since.

THE WORK

Otnes's method of working is a labor-intensive and lengthy process that requires extensive preparation and many steps to complete. His assistant, Roger Mudre, prepares the materials and organizes the studio, but when Otnes works, he works alone. Deeply focused, his level of concentration places the artist in what he describes as a strange, nearly hypnotic state as he reacts to the material before him, feeling his way through it.

Beyond the daunting technical aspects, it is a complicated process that can vary piece to piece, day to day. There are times when Otnes consciously places limitations on himself, when he might, for example, restrict his use of color: "You have to decide not to use everything on the palette. You try something with two values or two colors." Or he might

11
Illustration
1960's

12
Early
Experimental
Collage
1960's

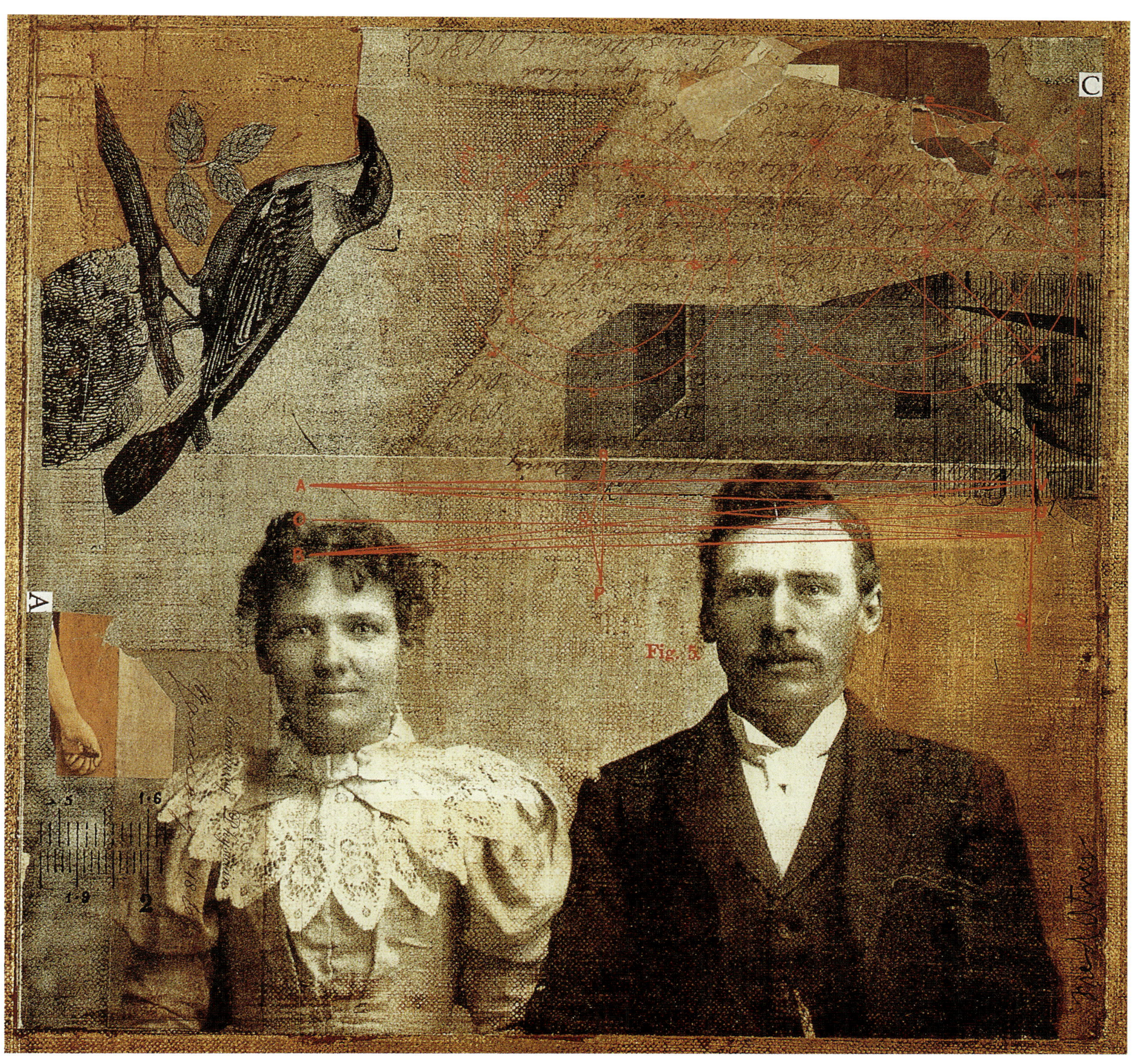
C
A
Fig. 5

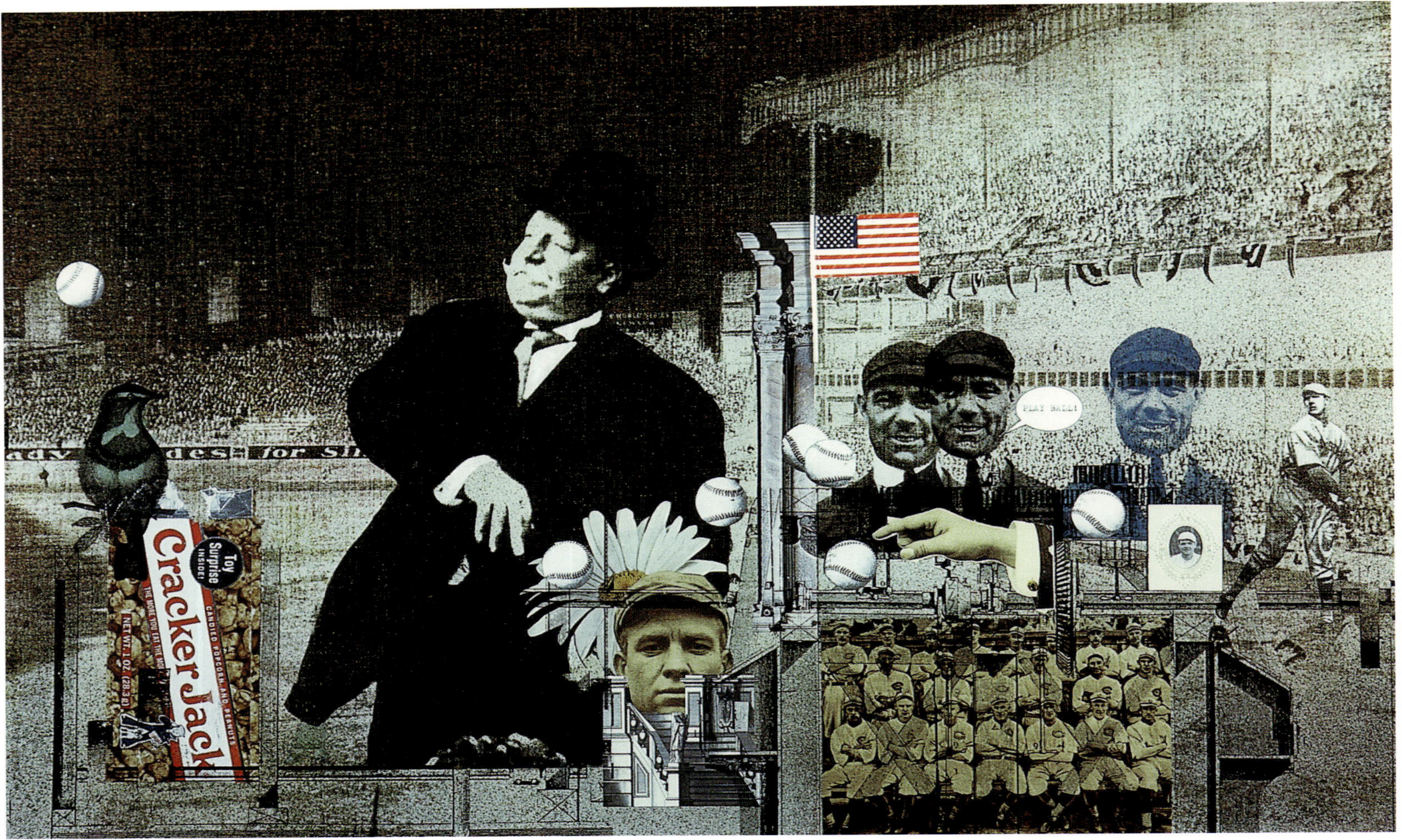

13
Sports Illustrated
1970's

limit his subject matter, deciding if the composition will be centered or off balance, highly structured or loose, low keyed or highly contrasted. Sometimes he comes to a general idea by way of outside influences, considering the problems examined by artists he esteems. For example, after having looked at a work by Richard Diebenkorn and admiring its simplicity, he might take that as a starting point—to do something simple in form and make it his. It may be only a single element of a reproduction he's just seen—the color or the balance—that motivates him. ("It's not that I get a Picasso and decide I'm going to do a Picasso.")

On the other hand, it may be that his last work relates to the next work thematically, tonally, or compositionally. Then again, "sometimes it depends on how much energy I have in the morning. In fact, sometimes *nothing* motivates me. I arrive at the studio and look at the blank piece and start doing things. Also, I'm very good at 'leftovers,' where something I've tried has hit the dust but two months later it's become fresh to me. Then I do something drastic to it, like paint over it and sand it down, and things begin to happen."

Although he knows others may not see collage in this light, Otnes believes that all art is an extension of drawing. "Most people think of art in terms of the tools you use—they have categories in their minds related to the *instruments* the artist uses rather than the *action*. They think if you're using a pencil or a pen, you're making a drawing, and when you pick up a brush, a drawing becomes a painting. But in reality, it's the same damn thing. If you pick up an airbrush, it's still a drawing. If you pick up a stick instead of a brush, it's a drawing. If you're doing a collage figure, you use the same mental processes to determine how you're going to represent the body. It's an image out of your head going onto a surface."

Attracted to great drawing and great design, Otnes's influences and inspirations are exceptionally broad and continuously expanding. Gerrit Henry, consulting editor for *Art News* and *Art in America*, has noted some of Otnes's fine-arts inspirations as "of course, the Picasso of Three Musicians, that cup-paper bombadier Kurt Schwitters, the evocative, ticket-and-wine-label issuances of Robert Motherwell." In addition to the Modernists, Otnes admires

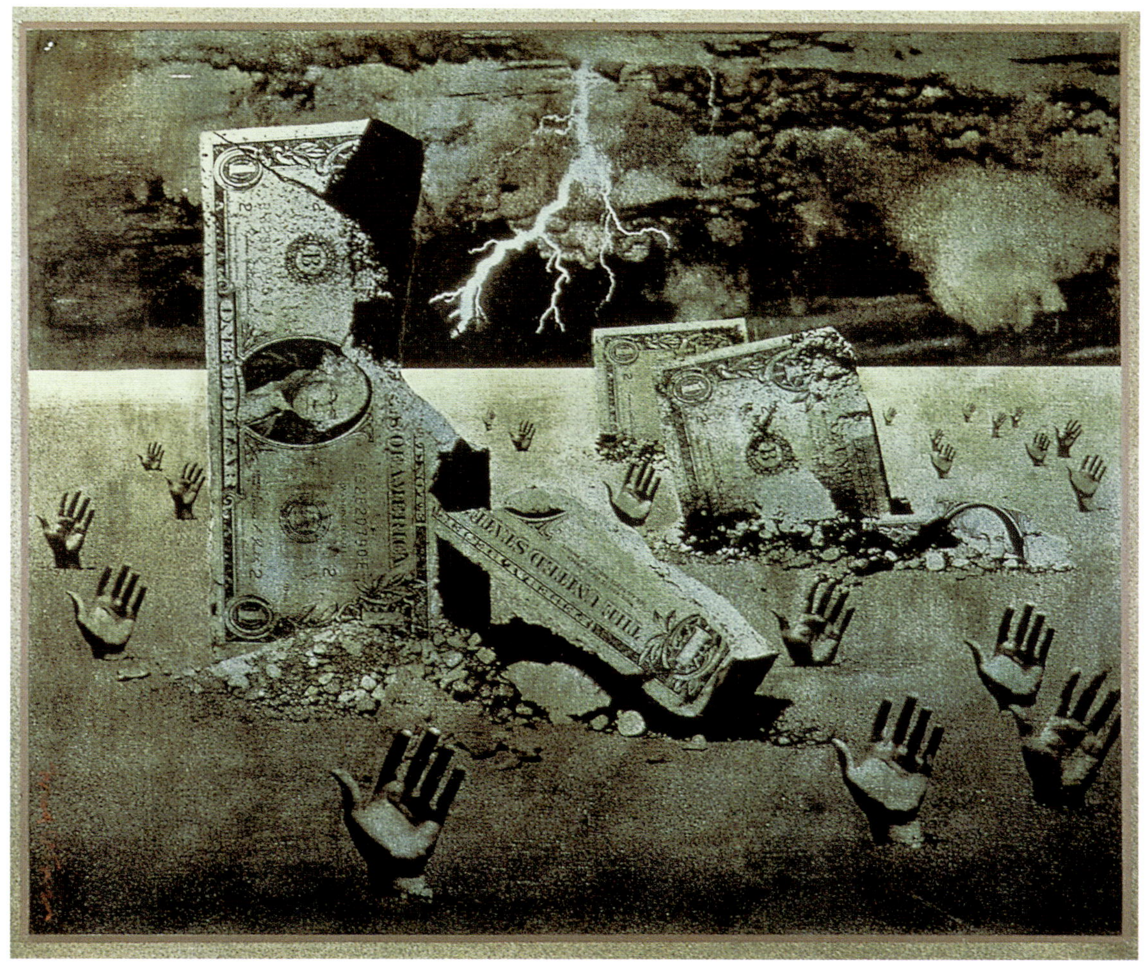

14
Penthouse
Magazine
1980's

the skill of certain Renaissance painters, noting, in particular, Piero della Francesco, whom he considers a great designer because he "worked in flat terms with no light or volume, and no horizon or perspective."

A partial list of artists Otnes admires would have to include luminaries such as Jean Dubuffet, Paul Klee, Juan Miró, Marcel Duchamp, Man Ray, Ben Nicholson, Romare Bearden, and Larry Rivers, and contemporaries such as Frank Stella, Antonio Tapies, Conrad Marca-Relli, Manolo Valdéz, and Anselm Kiefer. He is also impressed with works by younger artists such as the Starn Twins and Chris Ofili, about whom he says, "It's not the content that I care for, but I admire how well it's done. I like to think I'm open to any kind of art, but there's a line that when they've crossed it, they've lost me."

With some exceptions, what is common to nearly all these artists is their dedication to the flatness of the picture plane. Whether it is the subtle lyricism of a Marca-Relli or the juicy exuberance of one of Valdéz's appropriations, to Otnes, surface, texture, and drawing are paramount.

In apparent contrast to these artists trained in the Western tradition, Otnes is also drawn to African art, with its powerful sense of design and attention to form, as well as to Art Brut and Outsider Art. Of these naïfs and mystics, he says, "They've loosened everything up, and in most cases they're unaware that's what they're doing, so you admire what they did and how they stylized it. They put it down and they're happy with it. That's what I like about it. I even like the color in their stuff, though it doesn't mean I want it in mine."

Echoes of the Victorian steel engravings used by Max Ernst, coupled with the use of eighteenth- and nineteenth-century printed matter are important, if not essential, to much of Otnes's work. A major source of this printed imagery comes from books the artist's brother has given him over the years. Robert, a retired engineer whose intelligence and far-reaching knowledge Otnes deeply admires, is editor of the *Journal of the Oughtred Society*, an arcane and learned publication devoted to the slide rule. It is also another source of collage material, with its engravings of measuring devices that Otnes finds "beautiful in their way."

Through the years, Otnes's visits to Robert on the

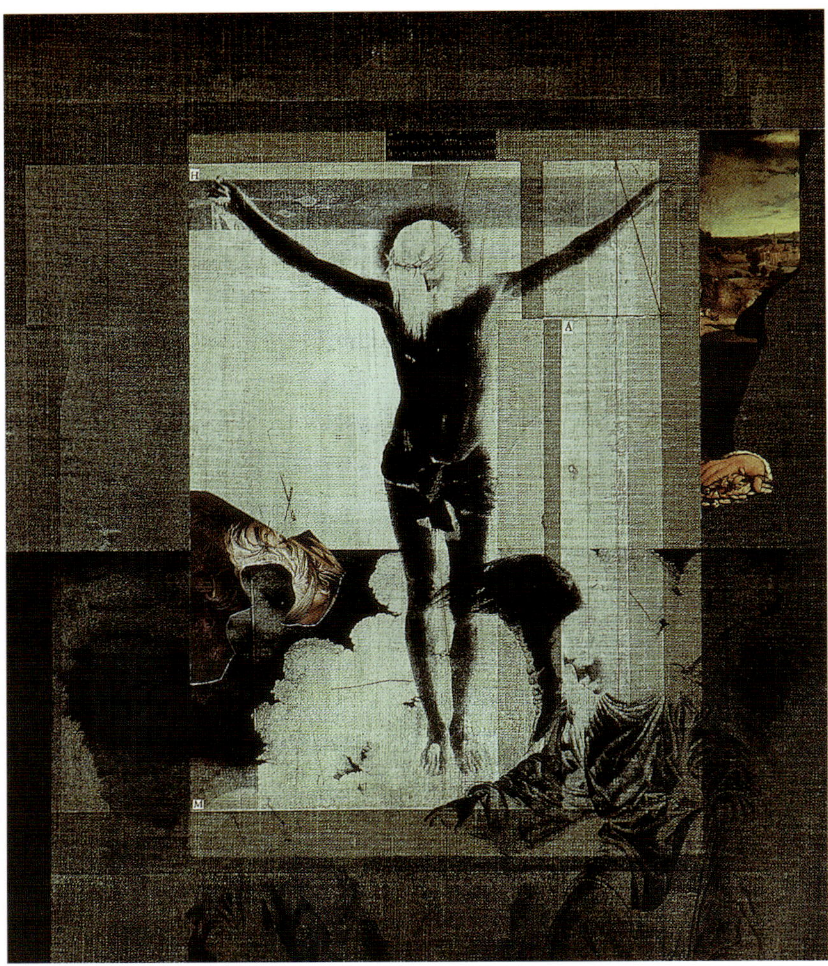

West Coast have been influential in his work. The brothers have explored all the major museums and galleries from Los Angeles to San Francisco. There Otnes was introduced to the Northern California artists he came to admire, such as Nathan Olivera, Manuel Neri, David Parks, and, of course, Richard Diebenkorn.

While appreciating an extensive array of artists, Otnes remains critical, with some exceptions: "When I look at one of Diebenkorn's *Ocean Park* series, there's nothing I could move on the picture. It's perfectly put together, it's in perfect taste, it's perfect in just about every way that I identify with."

15
Atlantic Magazine
1992

Otnes's own work, even at its most exuberant, is always in exquisite taste. This is due in part to his palette, much of which he describes as monochromatic, though in fact one which displays innumerable gradations in tone (and unexpected dashes of paint), belying the term. This chromatic reticence is also reflected in Otnes's home and wardrobe, a part of his personality which he explains to some degree as a reaction to childhood memories of home. His mother, he notes, displayed cheap Japanese toys and Mexican art from Woolworth's that even as a youngster Otnes felt was too bright and colorful. "There was no taste growing up in the Midwest; I had a lot of reaction *against* things, rather than having any positive influences from them." Later, as his exposure to art grew, he was unimpressed by artists known for being colorists, nor did he feel he had a gift for it himself, which he offers up as further explanation regarding his attraction to a limited palette. "I don't like what you'd call pretty or beautiful things. I like handsome things. I like African sculpture, not rainbows or sunsets. I don't necessarily dislike it if someone else does it well, but not in my own work. In fact, I can't do it at all."

16
Cover for Print magazine
1974

As expected, Otnes admires Rembrandt's and other European masters' use of blacks and dark browns, of objects or figures emerging out of the background, a quality found in some of his work, as in *Night Fear* (Figure 57)—though he's quick to point out he is just as apt to create a piece with barely a change in value, or one that goes from a medium to light value, or any variation thereof. Otnes began the darkly disturbing *Night Fear* by working from a neutral, monochromatic background and then adding elements

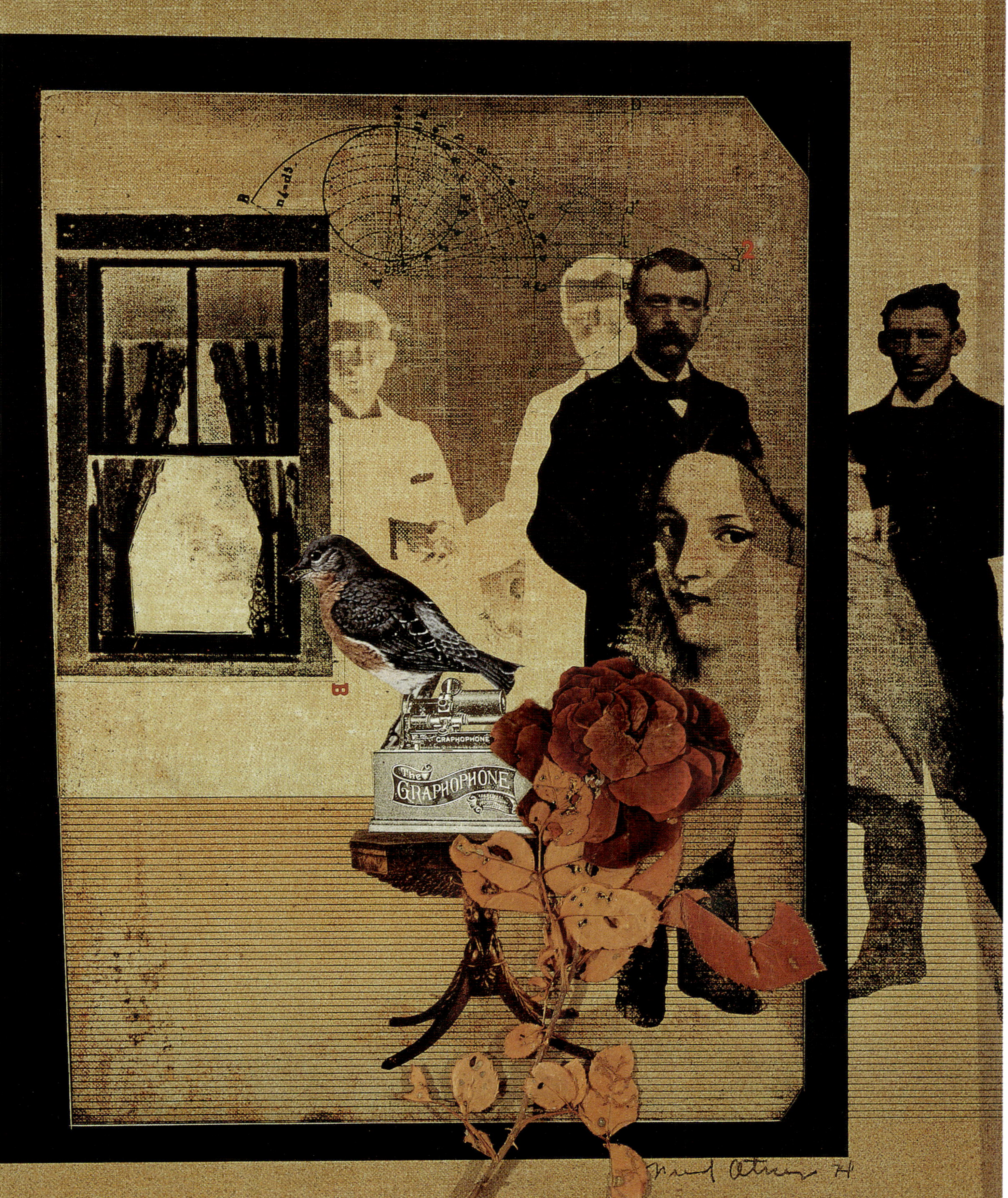
GRAPHOPHONE
The GRAPHOPHONE

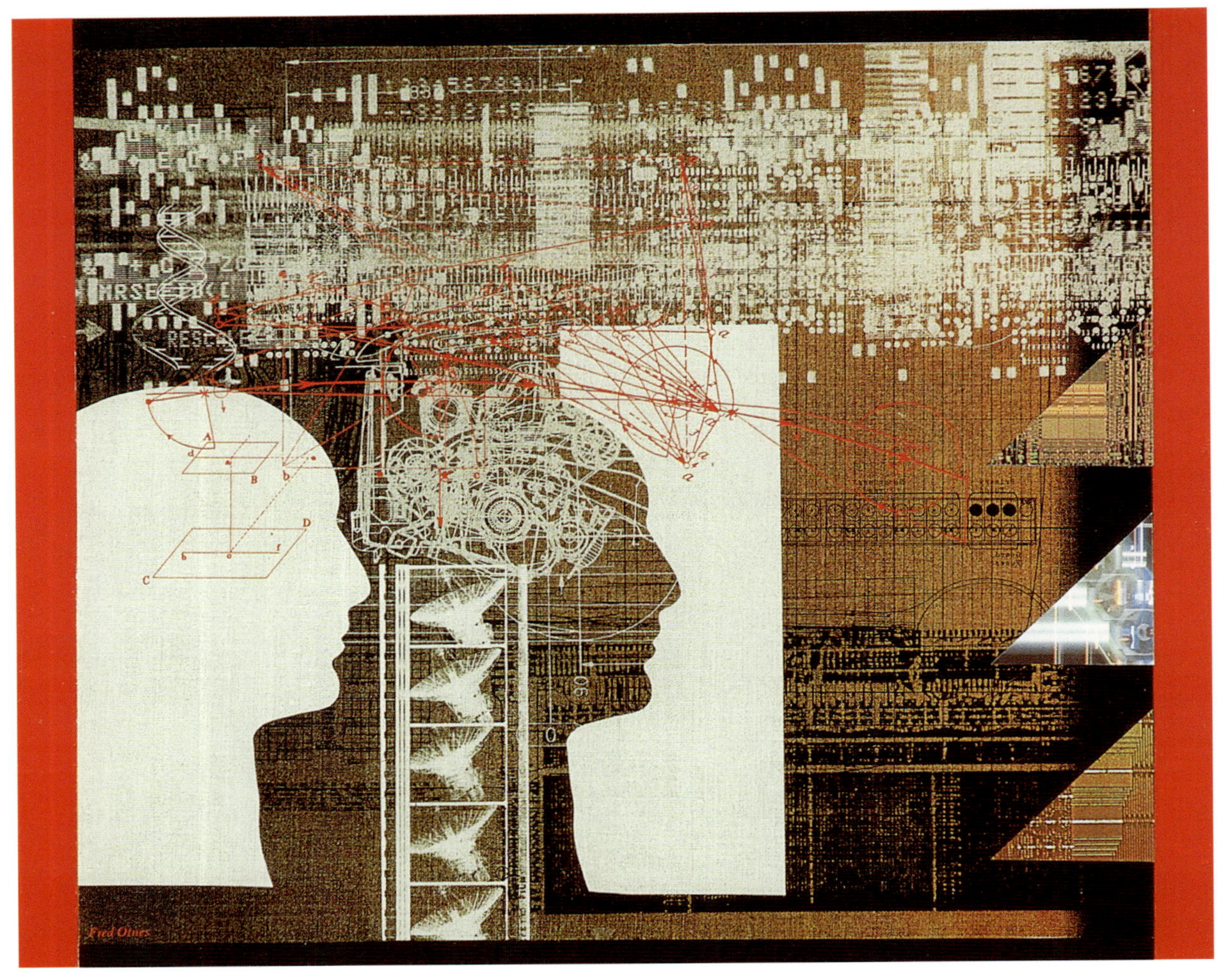

17
High Tech
Software Company
1987

chosen for their graphic interest—such as a favorite leaf pattern taken from an Old Master painting. It is, he says, "a version of Surrealism—almost a place, but not a real place—a poetic interpretation of a scene. There is a certain amount of relief in the collage that happens over and over in what I do. Some of it's almost invisible, pieces and fragments, subtle underlying structures that give it depth and interest beyond the first impact. There's a sense that something's going on beneath what is apparently visible. The buried elements and obscurities involve the viewer, and my interest is in the subtleties of the tones, textures, and structures that are emerging out of the background. This kind of mystery is important in what I do."

Another work with dense areas of darkness with emerging imagery is *Little Kimble* (Figure 58), though its intention is radically different from that of *Night Fear*. As in a number of works, which he describes as nostalgic, Otnes explores ways to create a sense of time. "It's as if it were done a century ago and had been sitting undisturbed in a room for a hundred years." This is achieved not only by the charm of the old fashioned cigarette card but by distressing the surface, fading the color, as if it had been coated with dust. For Otnes, it has the appeal of the older works found in museums. The other attraction in the piece is the use of raw umber. "I could live with raw umber and black for the rest of my life. It has infinite possibilities, gradations, subtleties—it has tonal variations that are very beautiful."

Soldier Boy (Figure 100) falls into this nostalgic realm, its source material from a book of bicycle patent diagrams, imagery Otnes has used repeatedly. In his hands, nostalgia is never sentimental; rather, in their sophistication and dark grace, his works are testaments to time passing. They show an attachment and respect for that which went before, or for how we imagine or even wish those times past had been—a certain innocence we harbor for earlier eras, which are infused with a somber melancholy of time lost. That said, Otnes confesses that having fully explored this approach, he is progressing away from it.

The evocative title of *The Fathom or the Chain* (Figure 116), as with many works, is taken from a collage element: a fragment of a page torn from a book. Formally structured, the work relates to architecture, one of Otnes's

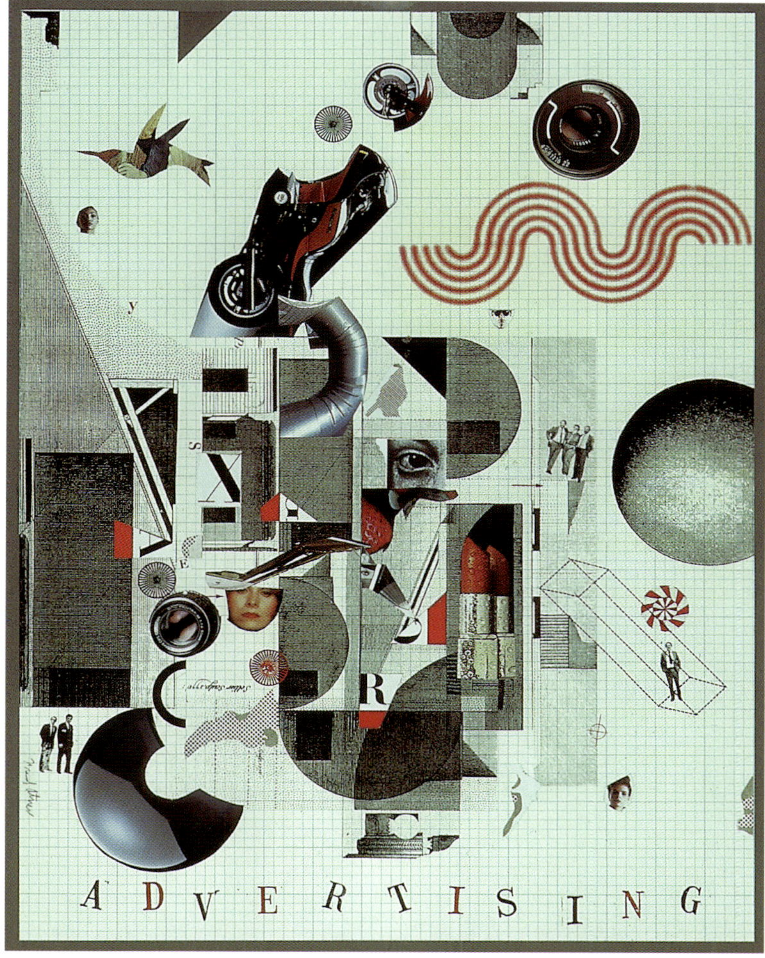

great interests. The central image is a kind of abstract building, and the Renaissance-style frame is consistent with the portrait emerging from a window shape—itself made up of torn engravings of building elements. Otnes describes this portrait as "perfect" for the work, an adjective he often uses to describe how certain elements fit in certain places. Of all the collage elements from which he could choose, its perfection is evident to him—and ultimately to the viewer.

In addition to his appropriative use of works by artists such as Rembrandt, Titian, Caravaggio, and other masters, Otnes uses favorite symbolic images, most frequently trees and birds. In *Silver Bird* (Figure 50) he wanted an object—not a figure—to be the center of the picture. To him the bird, universally understood as a representation of freedom, is first and foremost beautiful. "A bird is a beautiful thing collaged up this way, the feathers go in a certain way that pleases me. Because I over-painted the surface in white, then scraped it off, there was a halation that was unplanned but evolved." Otnes resists any interpretation of subject—that, for example, there is constraint against the bird, a containment that is in apposition to the tree because of the white halo surrounding it. He allows that the viewer is welcome to take whatever he or she wishes from the work, and that something may be going on about which he, the artist, is not aware. Nonetheless, for him the textural changes and interesting interaction of shapes are more important than interpretation.

Long after a work is complete, Otnes recalls the mystery in its fabrication, as in *The Day of the Fourteenth* (Figure 59), which incorporates a figure, its source unknown, which has been nearly scraped away. Fragments of tree leaves from an Old Master work and the suggestion of an horizon line made up of a slender line of type. Otnes's attraction to type, coming from Old Latin, Middle German, and old English texts is not literal. Rather, it is the look of it, the graphic progression of satisfying black shapes on a light background, which he then isolates by cutting or tearing, sometimes putting in reverse or placing upside down. With a kind of visceral intensity, Otnes describes the area where an ancient playing card has been laid down over other elements: "Shapes on shapes on shapes again, you can see something was cut out and laid down and scraped off, peeled off, distressed. And the color, the pinks, are interesting, and where

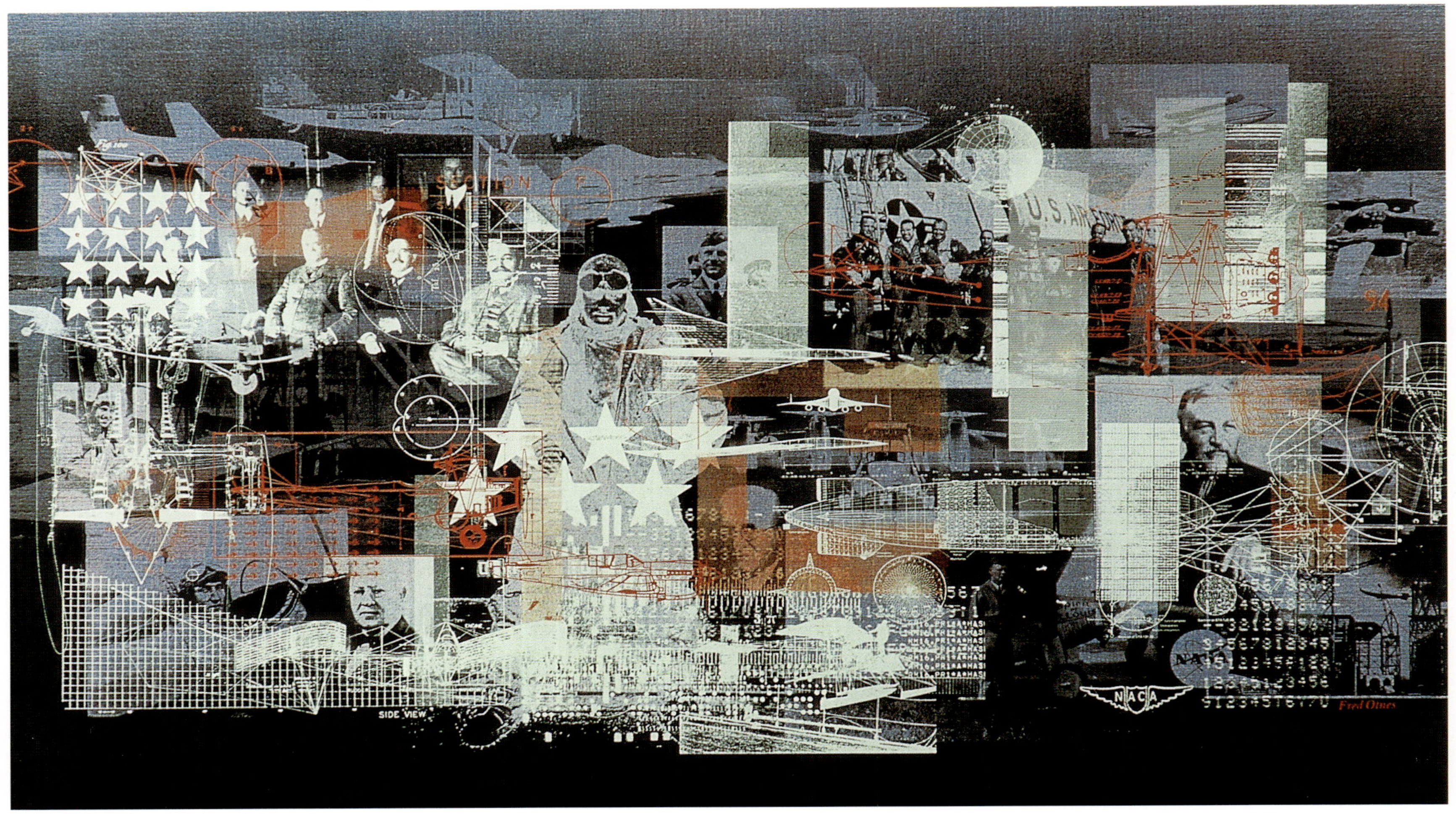

19
Poster and Mural
National Air and
Space Museum
1990

everything is peeled away the surface of the raw board itself absorbed more of the red. Like an old antique, showing the stress it experienced."

For Otnes the appeal of the collage form resides in its freedom. Working flat on a table, he moves the elements around and, as he says, "looks for things," shapes and sizes, without commitment, a design that's happening as he's doing it. In the work *Maybe Lisa* (Figure 70) he laid out elements and textures that formed a figure—but not absolutely. "Although I think about and try to visualize something to start with, there is enormous flexibility once I'm into it. In fact, I can take an image just so far, then put a coat of paint over the whole thing, sand it down and what's left is terrific, something to build other images on top of." As to the title of this or other works, they are sometimes as obscure as the pictures themselves. In addition to the printed fragments within the work that become titles, they can also be, as Otnes somewhat cryptically puts it, "funny combinations of words. I don't know any Lisa, but maybe it's like Lisa? Maybe it describes Lisa?"

Otnes's collage technique makes large-scale works difficult, but he has been pushing the limits, as with *Rauch* (Figure 51), which at 60" x 48" is one of his largest works. A precise, quiet figure, the piece is very low key, the change in value from the background to the foreground undramatic. The whole idea, the artist says, is "to be laid back. My natural inclination with color is minimalist, with very subtle arrangements of values and colors." Some of the elements come from reprints of the old mathematical books from his brother, steel engravings created during the Age of Reason, a formal, controlled period of time attractive to Otnes, who notes, not surprisingly, that you won't find the flamboyance of Romantic or Baroque imagery in his work.

Otnes describes *Liagre* (Figure 68) as being nearly opposite to *Rauch* in that the figure shape is almost falling apart, fragmenting and dissolving. Beneath it an image has been sanded down, creating a complex textural surface with the somewhat chaotic (to the extent an Otnes work can be chaotic) rhythm, in contrast to the contained and almost golden serenity of *Rauch*. Another work that Otnes has tried for extreme value changes is *Partners* (Figure 47), pure whites

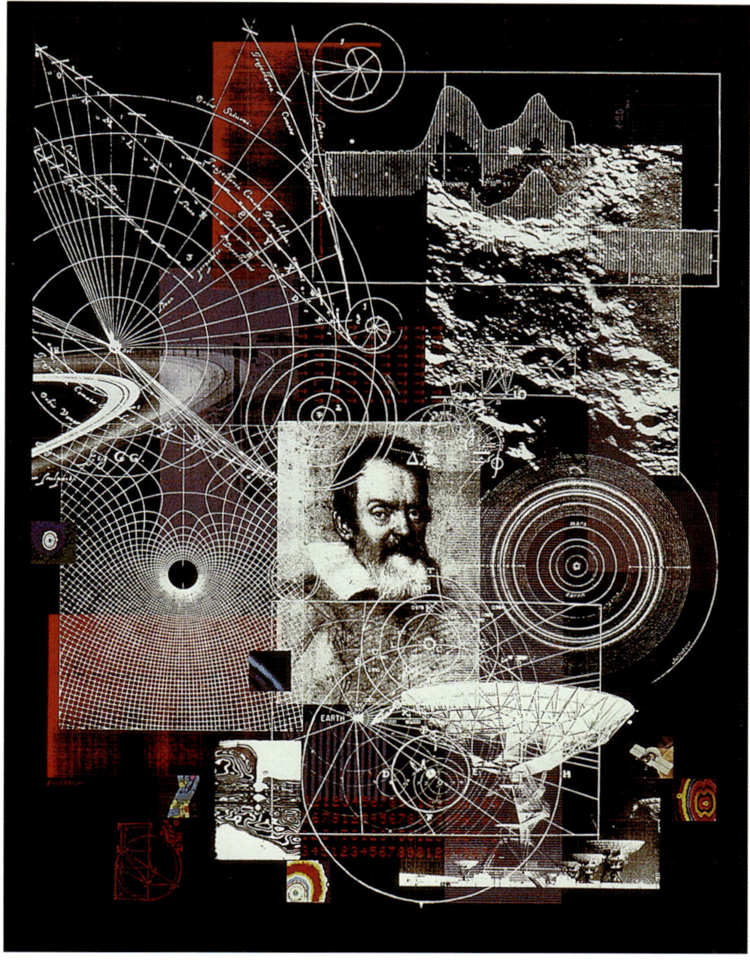

20
Software Poster
1992

and light colors of two figures on their own collage ground enclosed in a pure black background. The rhythm of the figures themselves and the vibrant patterns—bold stripes, accents of red and orange—and seemingly tossed-off pieces of patterned paper, give the work a lightness of gesture, a visual buoyancy.

In even Otnes's most abstracted works, such as *Oldwel* (Figure 107), the elements often pull themselves together into figures, grounding them into the particular. He says, "There's a plan, but there's not a plan. I don't know why a figure starts to appear. I just like it, it's some kind of intuitive thing." Within the context of the figurative, Otnes continues to move further away from realism, attempting to keep literalness at bay. For inspiration Otnes looks to those artists he admires to see how they avoid the literal. The Abstract Expressionist Marca-Relli has said, "The figure is an ideal, a point of reference.... It is never meant to be intended realistically; it is a resource which, like the 'gesture' contributes to the creation of a compositional space in the painting."

Rarely do Otnes's figures become female or male: "I don't even want that; it interrupts the abstract quality if you start identifying them by gender." There are exceptions, such as *The Times Man* (Figure 90), so named because of a torn masthead that makes up the crown of his hat. This bold image manages to be both demonic and comic, a somewhat broad example of simultaneity so often found in Otnes's work.

In 2001 a devastating fire in Otnes's studio destroyed many paintings, his vast scrap file of ephemera collected over thirty years, his photo-engraving equipment and plates, his enormous library of art books, and his collection of graphics periodicals (which Otnes credits as helping him "get a sense of putting things together in a certain organized state"). Only the etching press survived, and a few "experiments" he had been making the day of the fire using a piece of tapestry from India with "beautiful little shapes in it." While rebuilding the damaged area of his house, Otnes made his studio in his garage and began to create a new set of imagery, starting by running the Indian tapestry patterns through the press onto different papers. *Pollai* (Figure 81) contains these patterns worked in raw umber, black, and grays. A powerful image, the

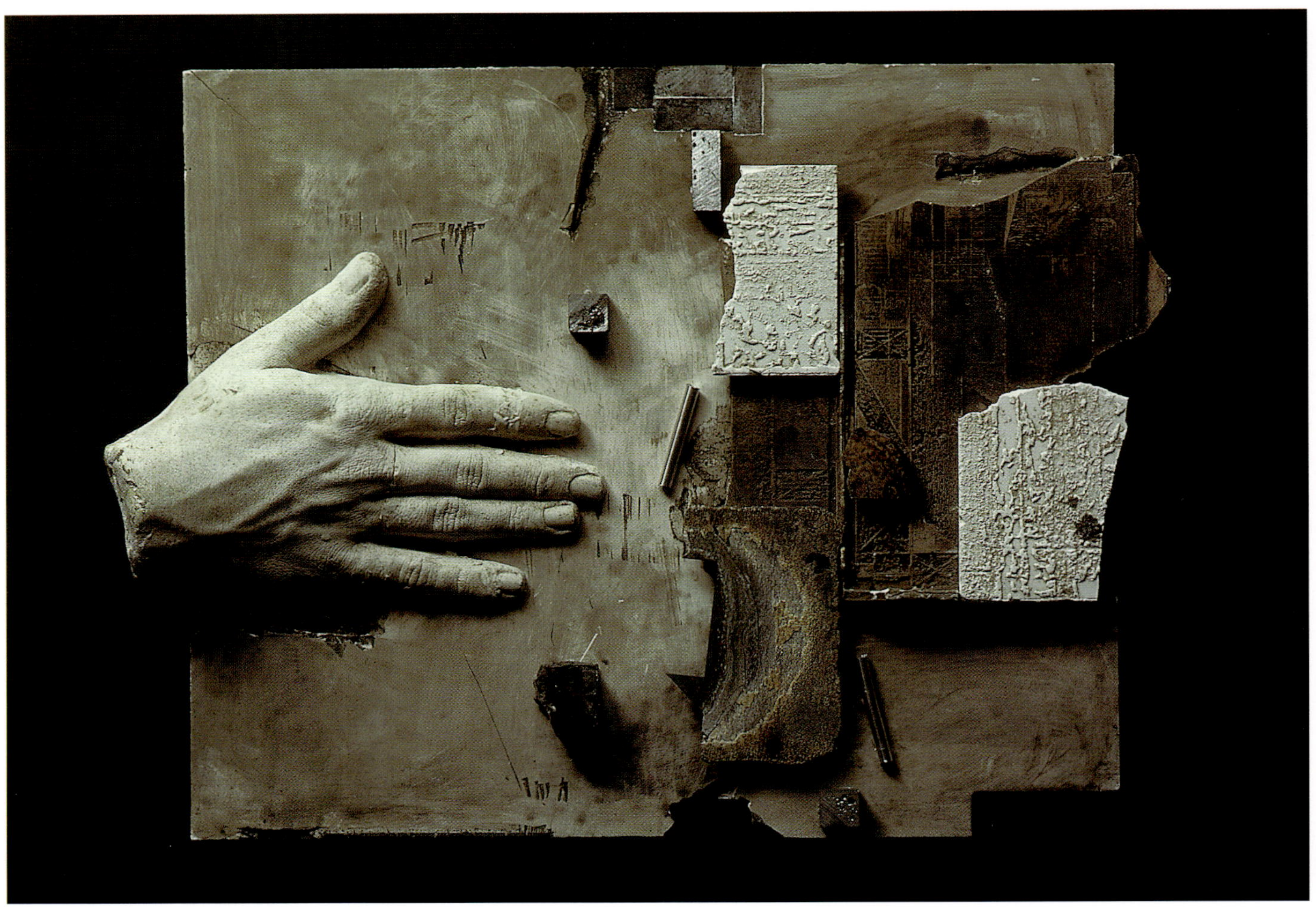

massive figurehead reflects Otnes's fascination with Art Brut and Outsider Art, and, as with much of his work, the layers of influence are manifold, referring as well to Dubuffet and African art.

Gerrit Henry has said, "Otnes shares with other modern collagists the mad conceit that chance is a mainstay of composition, and that chaos can be a matter of most sublime order." The artist agrees and finds it to the point. In every work Otnes makes choices that bring together disparate elements, but there are degrees to Otnes's control by virtue of the medium. His technique of scraping away, for example, produces a texture somewhat in the way weather affects a building over time, making it sublime. His control is intuitive, born of experience, as is the recognition of successful "accidents." For Otnes the simple assessment that the work "looks good" is sufficient.

If randomness and chance were all, however, every work Otnes began would be a success, but he finds that despite finding areas in a piece that work ("a beautiful chunk"), if the whole piece is not successful, he rejects it and therein lies another form of control. "All great art has strength in its organization and intuition in equal measure. If it's too rigorously rational, there's a lack of life to it, too much on the other side and it's like monkeys smearing paint."

Otnes admits that having lost all his collage material has given him a certain freedom in the post-fire works. Without the predominance of colonnades and borders, rulers and circles, frames and historical references, the work has become less constructed. Where there may be a lack of ephemera or appropriated images, the surfaces are all the more compellingly complex, every inch interesting to the eye. And for all its flatness, the intricate layering—where a patterned paper is pressed against a scraped away area or a passage of tinted linen—gives the viewer a strange feeling of dimension and a desire to touch the textured plane.

Mark English says of Otnes, "I've watched his work grow and become more abstract. It's gorgeous, the textures he works with, the patterns. All the things I like are there in the work—they're very powerful images." Yet Otnes is not completely comfortable working in pure abstraction. He qualifies his reticence as not being sure of himself in that area *yet*, and he sees total abstraction not as a goal per se but as a

21
Assemblage for High Tech Company
1993

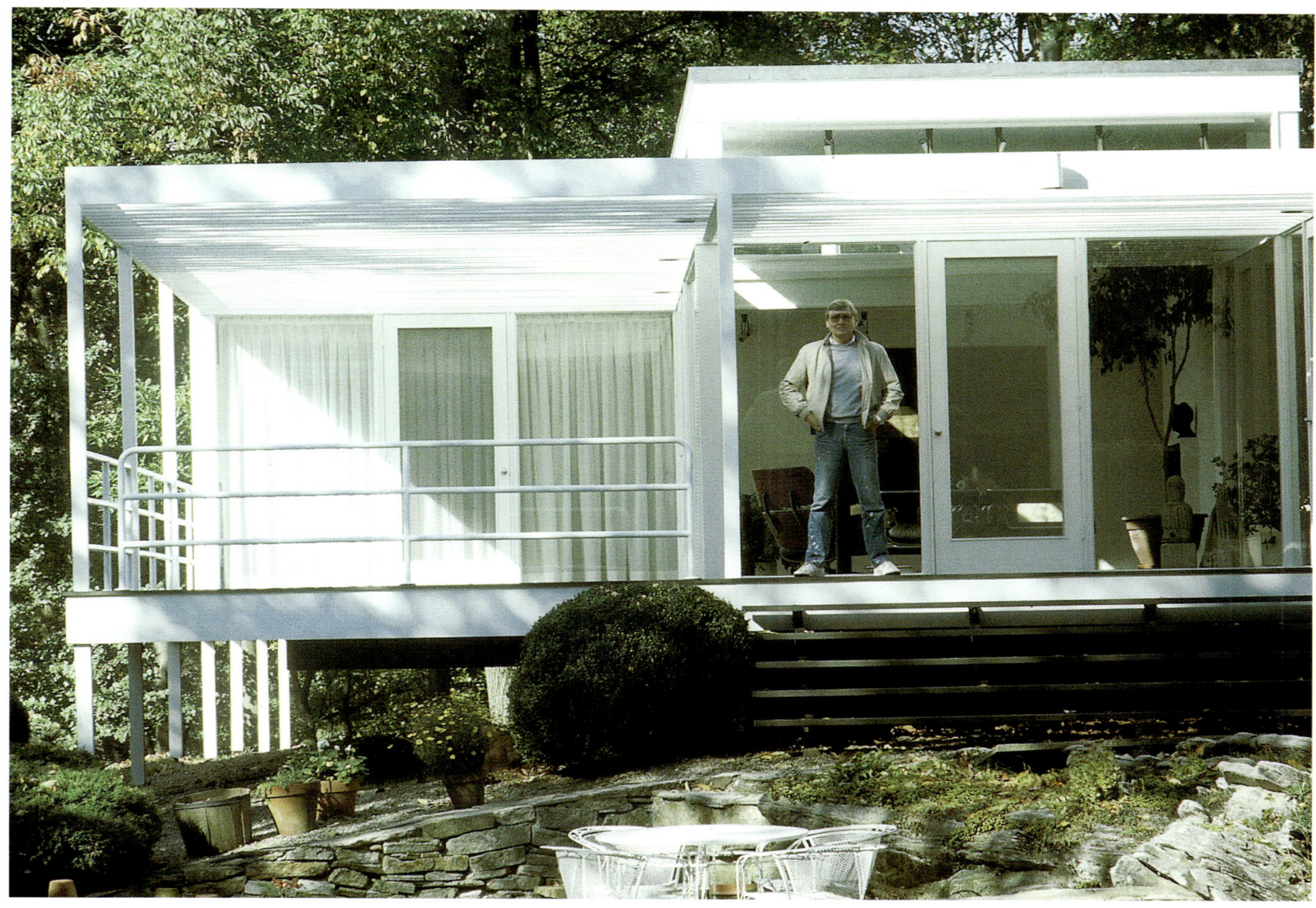

22
Fred Otnes
Studio and Home

scenario: one day he will wake up and think, "I won't do a figurative piece. I'll do an abstraction. It will be fun that day, a little more interesting."

Reflecting upon Otnes's artistic life, one can see his work evolve in stages that parallel the mores and concerns of the culture in which he's lived. As a part of, and in response to the shifting art movements over the years, Otnes feels he's been a man of his time. His dedication to art—its progression and endless variation—has always been the focus: "It is the art, the idea, the intellectual and visual process that's most important."

Unwilling to remain static, despite his success, he continues to push himself, all too aware of the persistent challenges. "You always have the idea that at some point in your career you'll have worked out all the problems, that you'll be in total control and wonderful things will happen when you wake up each day. But it's almost always the opposite of that. There's chaos, where you have areas that you don't understand, where you're uncertain about where things have come from and where they're going." Forever dealing with intangibles, the work remains a struggle. "You're always in trouble as you try to progress from where you've been, always searching for a newness. If you're not in trouble, the work looks tired and staid and without energy. Maybe I even force myself into great trouble, making myself work through it, resolving it into something a little bit better and different. It certainly hasn't gotten easier."

Otnes's trouble—his ongoing effort to create exciting imagery—becomes the viewer's reward. The artist's long experience and unflagging desire is manifest in each successive work as he intensifies the levels of sophistication, the subtlety of design, and the complexity of surface texture. It is a mysterious process, this rendering of order from chaos, one that the eye can see but that the literal part of the brain cannot explain. It is where Fred Otnes's work resides, the place where viewer and artist communicate most deeply.

23 | UNTITLED 2003

Collage painting, 48" x 48"

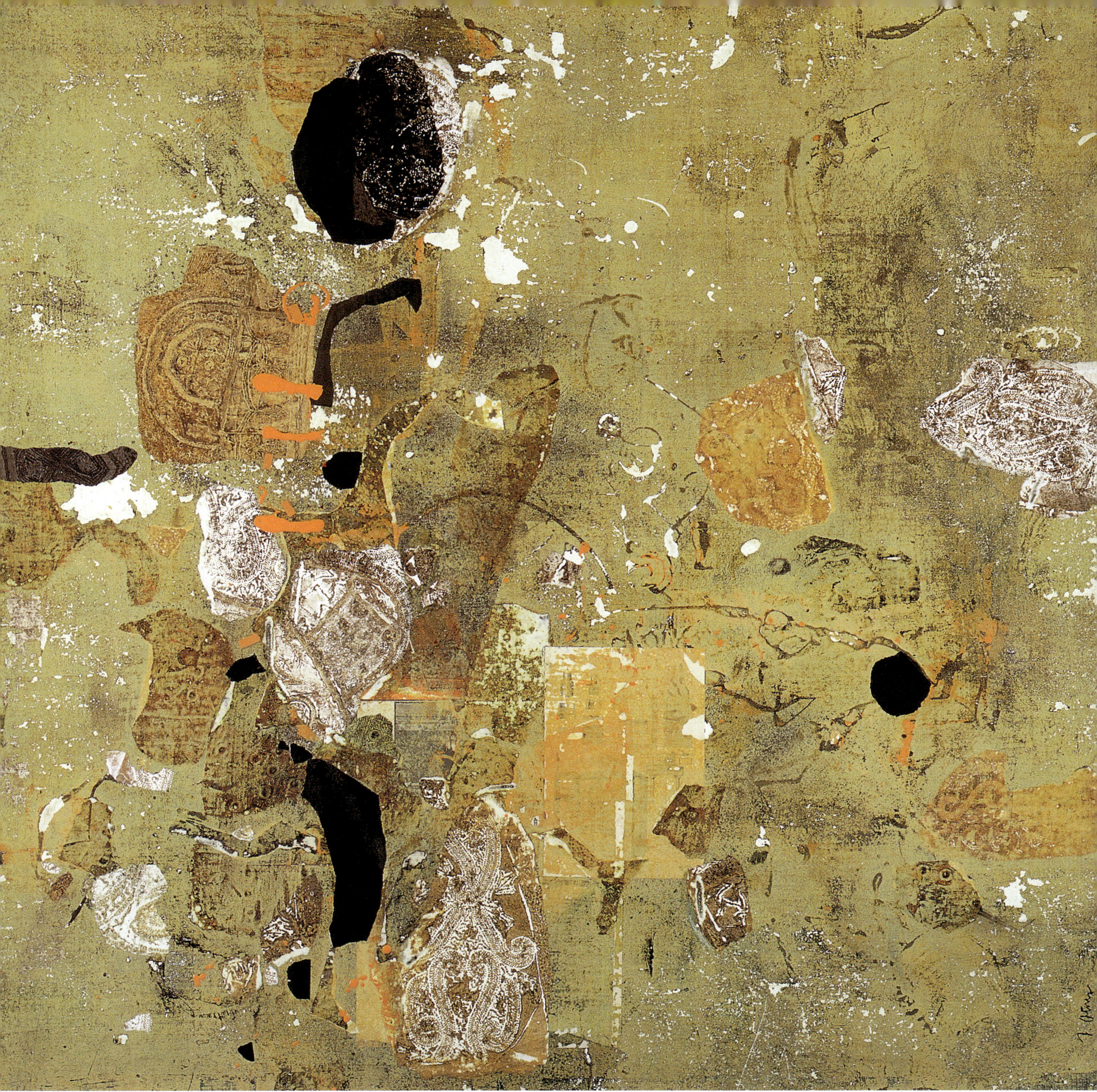

24 | DARK WARRIOR 2003

Collage painting, 34" x 27 1/2"

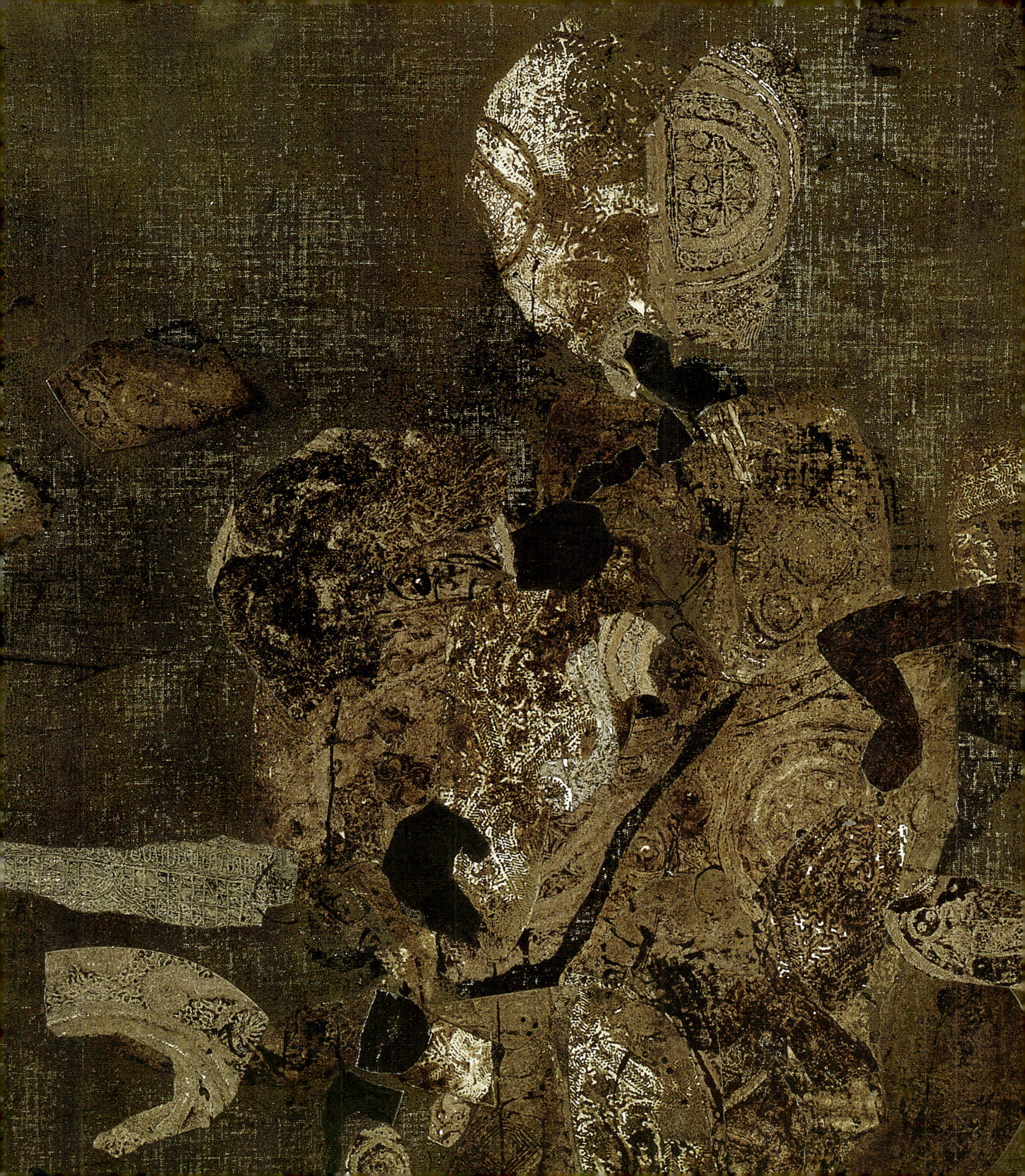

25 | UNTITLED 1987

Mixed media collage, 18" x 26"

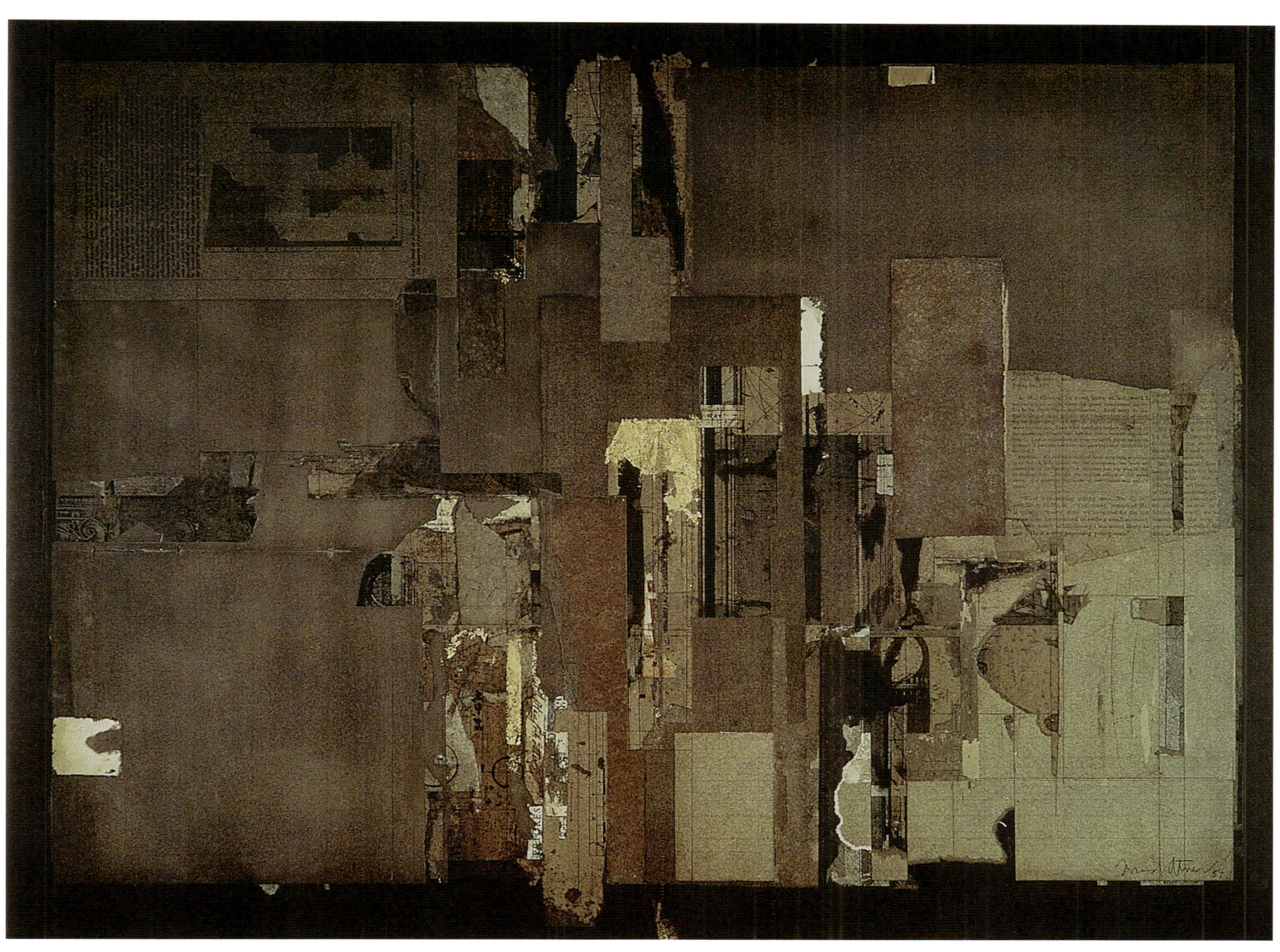

26 | EDRA 2002

Collage painting on linen, 23" x 22"

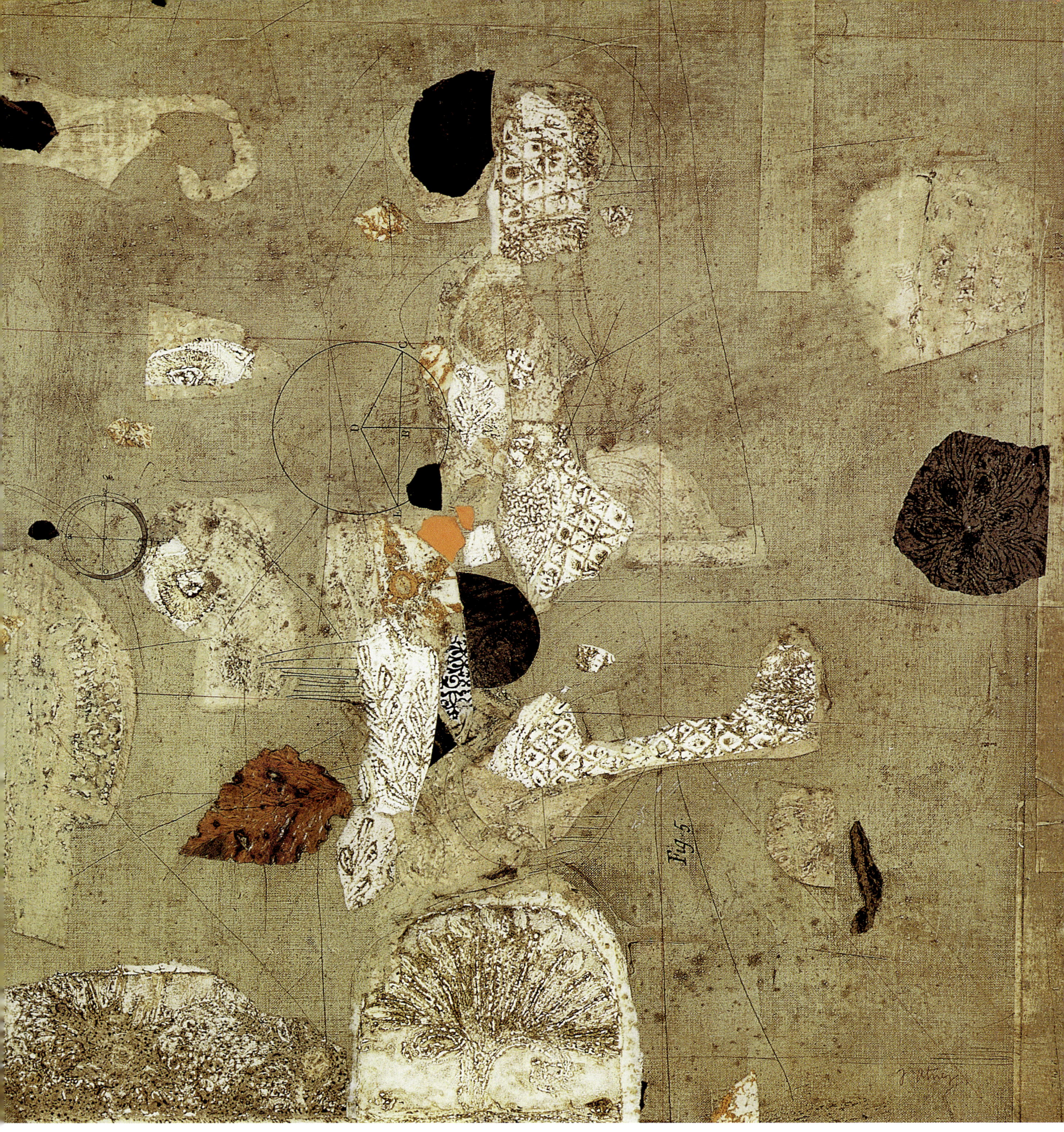
Fig. 5

27 | WINGED FIGURE 1998

Collage painting, 38" x 24 1/2"

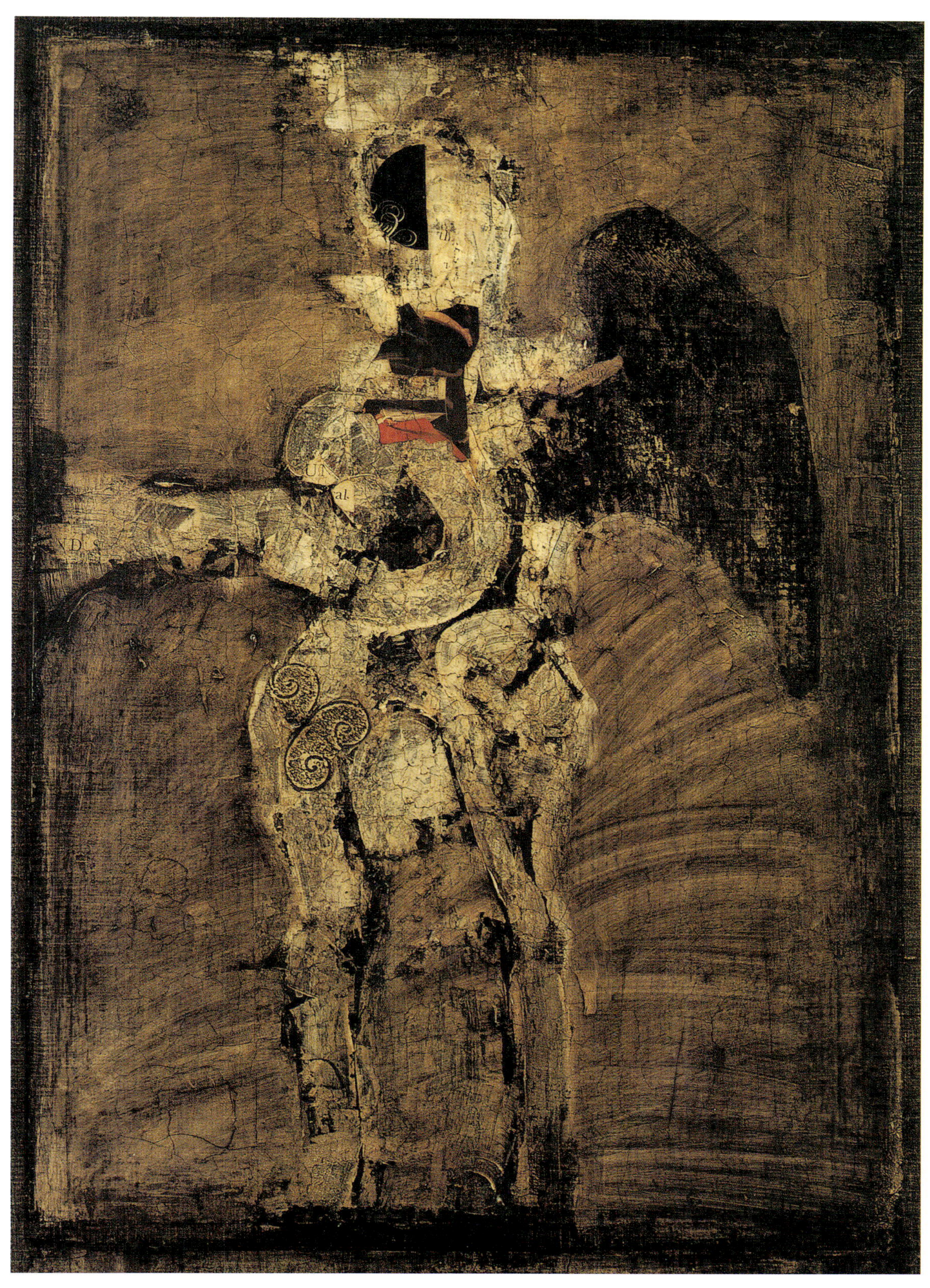

28 | FANTIN 2003

Collage painting, 21" x 18 1/2"

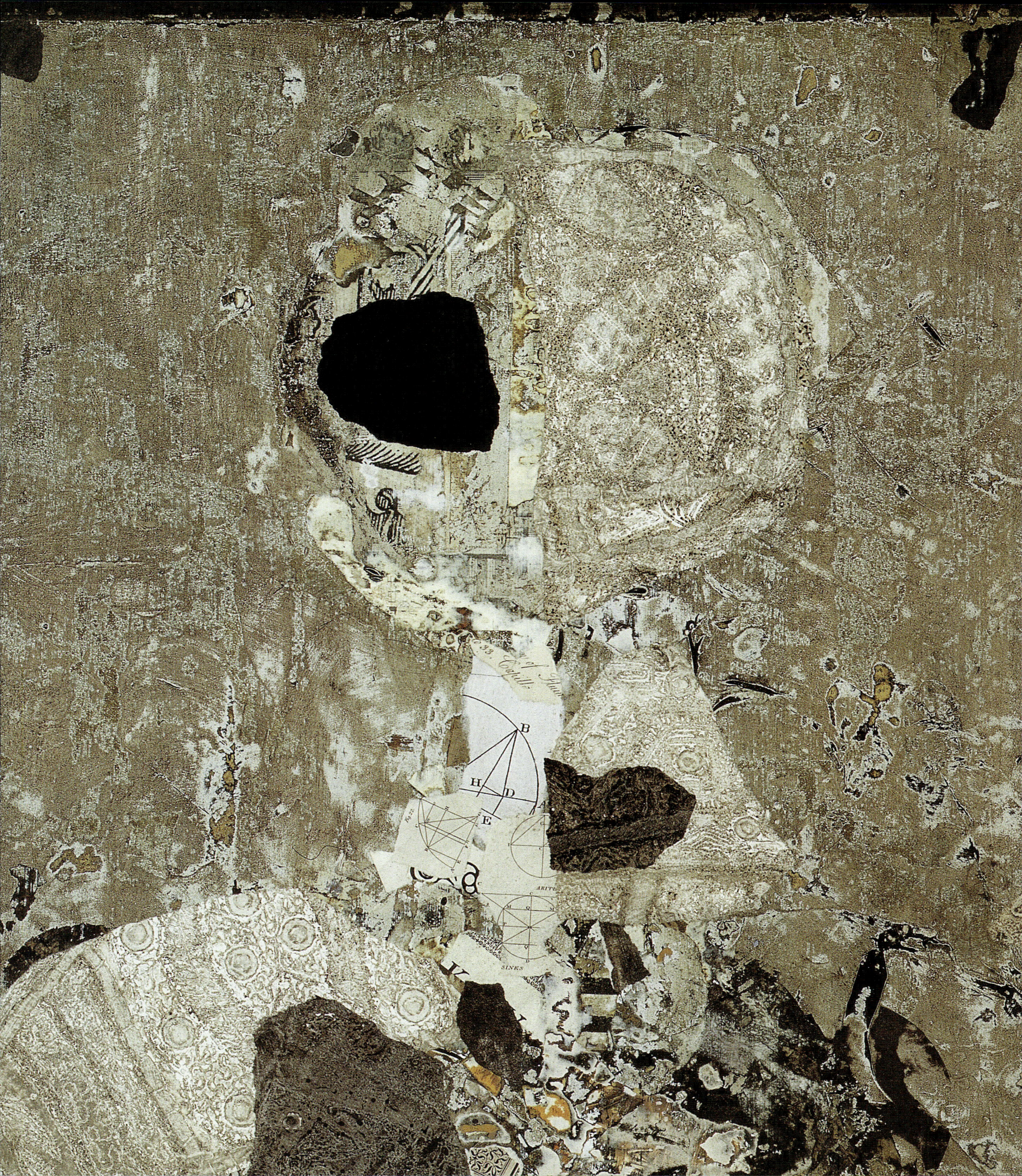
B
H
D
E
SINES

29 | BOY WITH BOAT 1998

Collage painting, photo transfer and metal boat, 48" x 48"

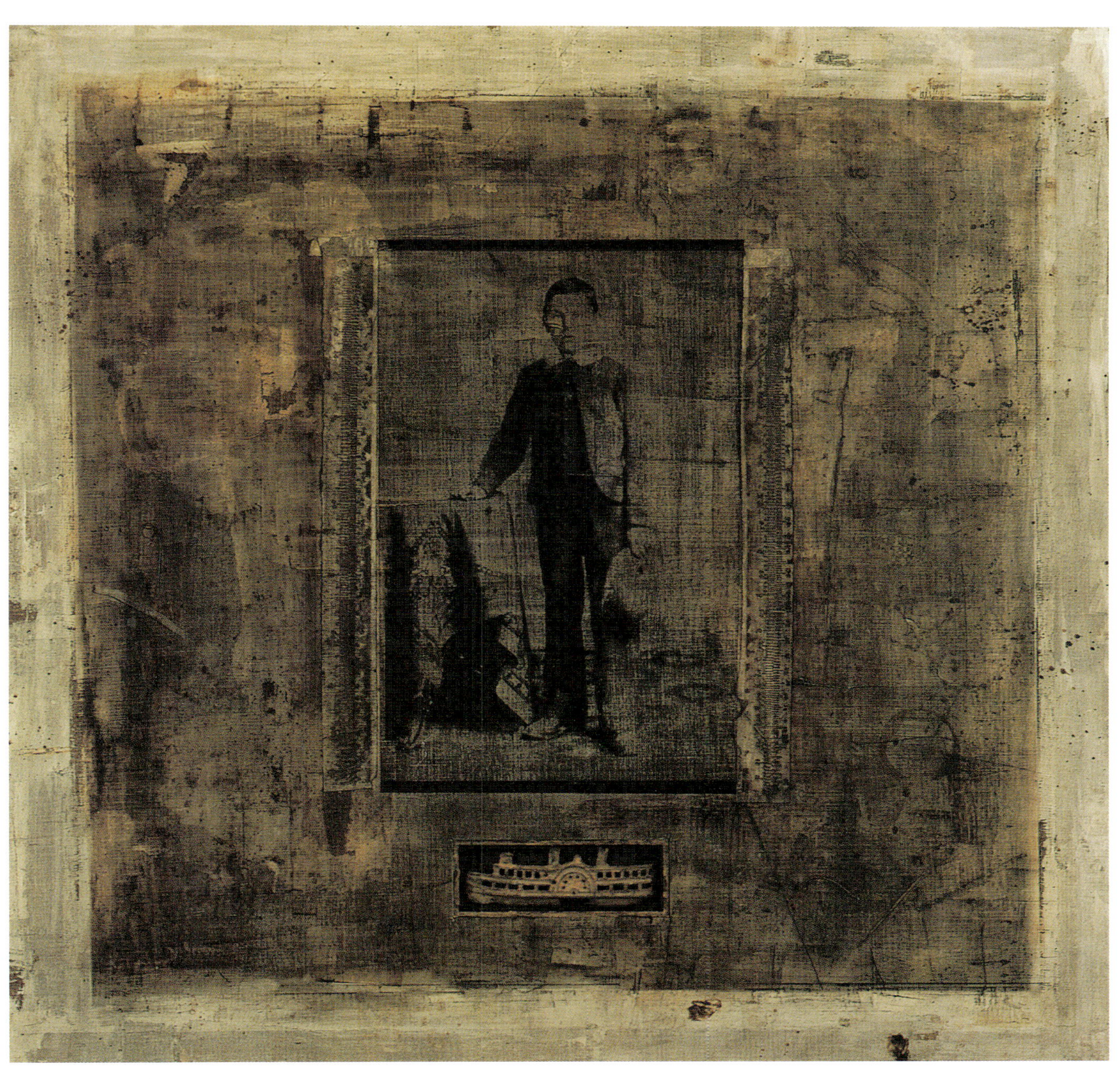

30 | TIME 1999

Mixed media collage, 24" x 20"

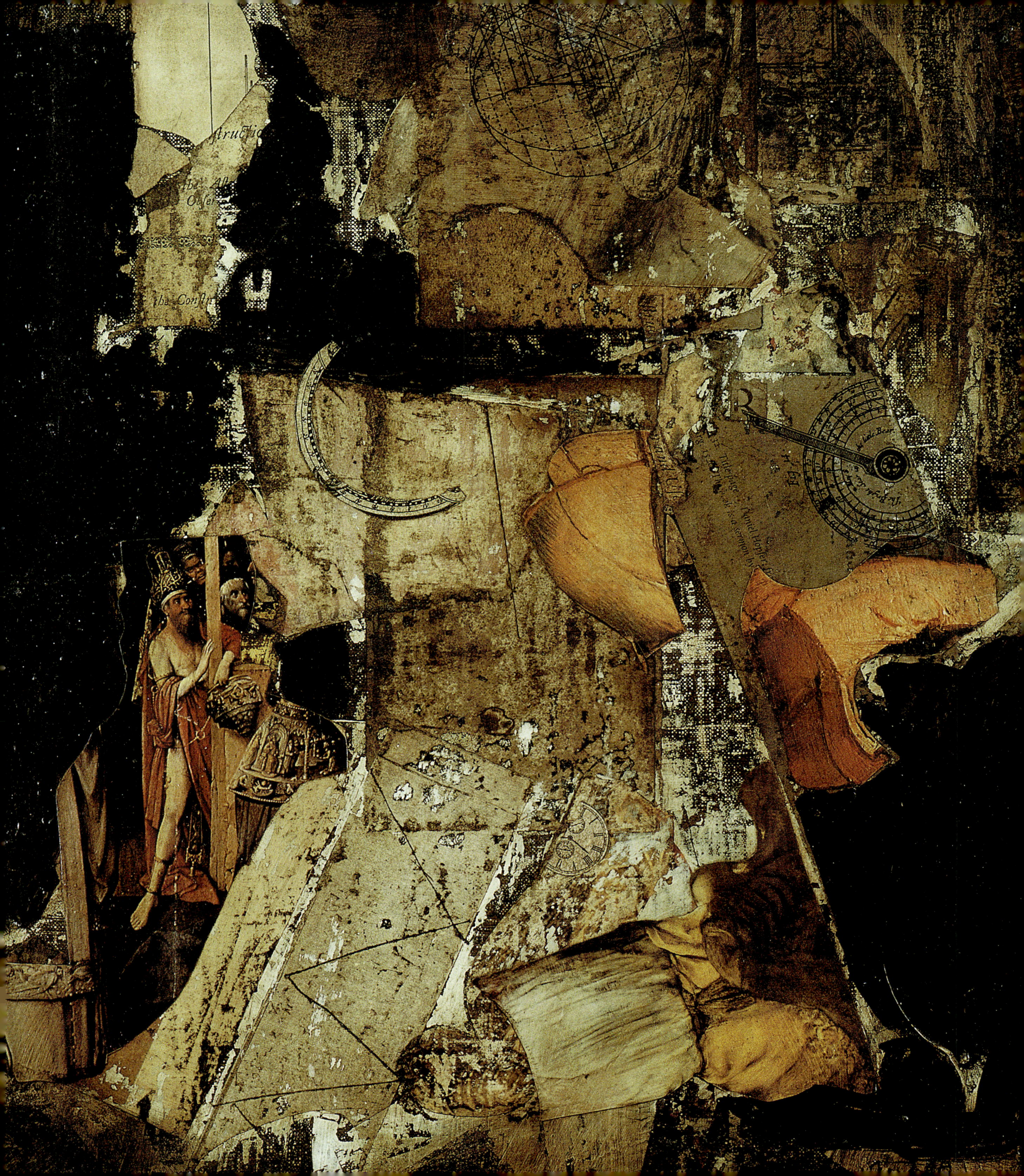

31 | VASE WITH FLOWERS | 2000

Collage and acrylic on linen, 22 1/2" x 20 3/4"

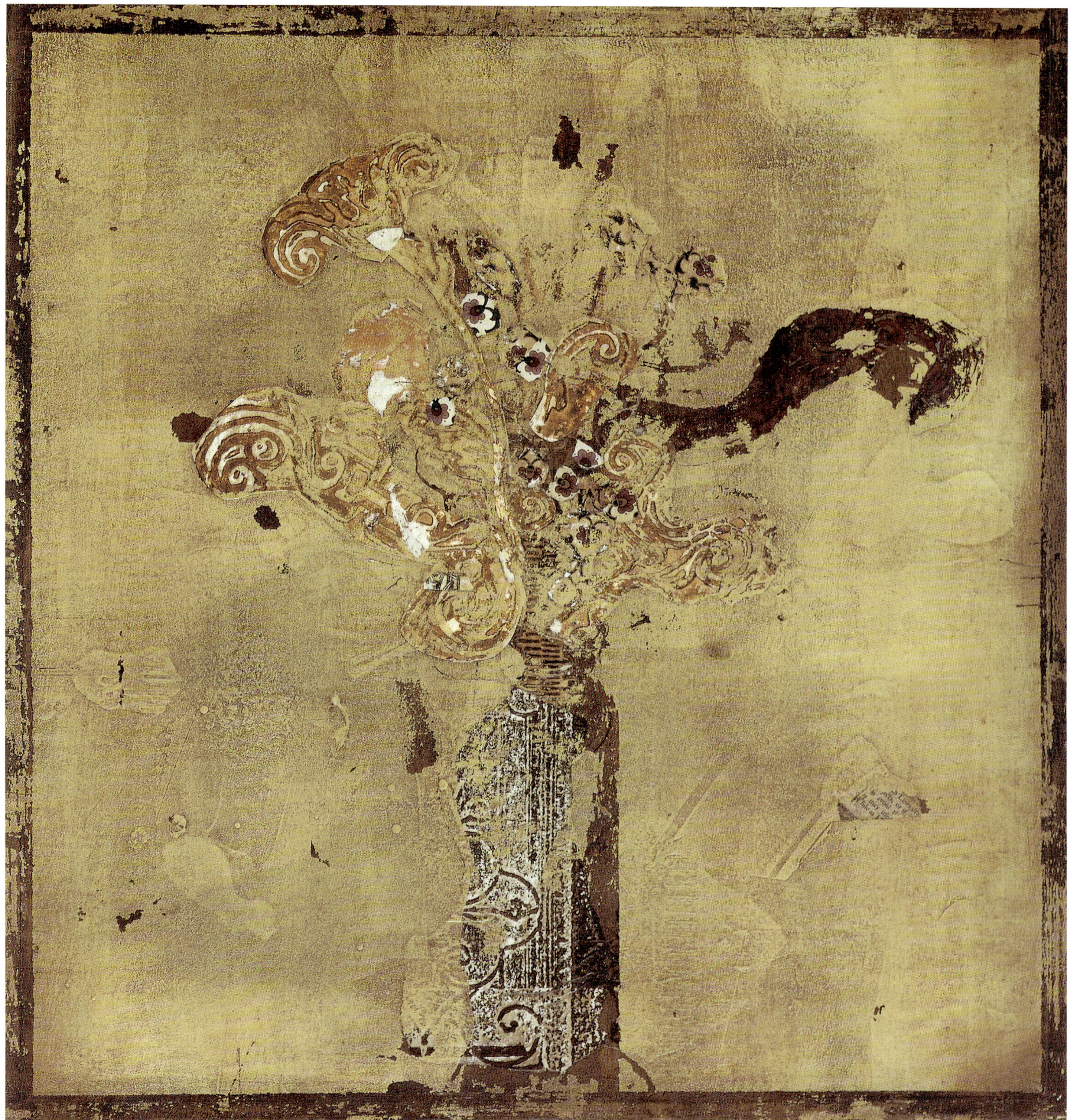

32 | MEASURING MAN 2000
Mixed media collage, 56 1/2" x 42 1/2"

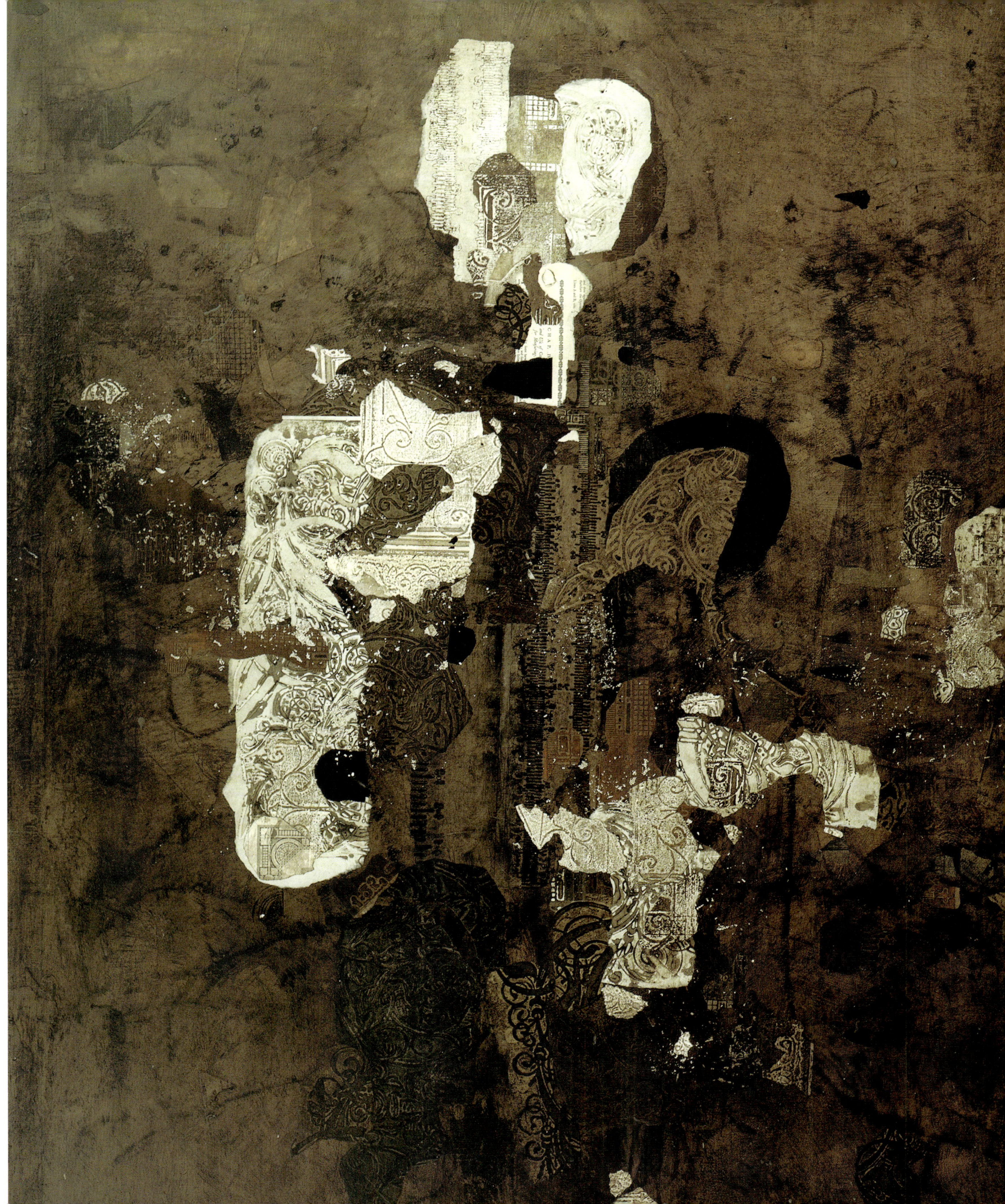

33 | UNTITLED 1998

Mixed media with photo transfer, 48" x 48"

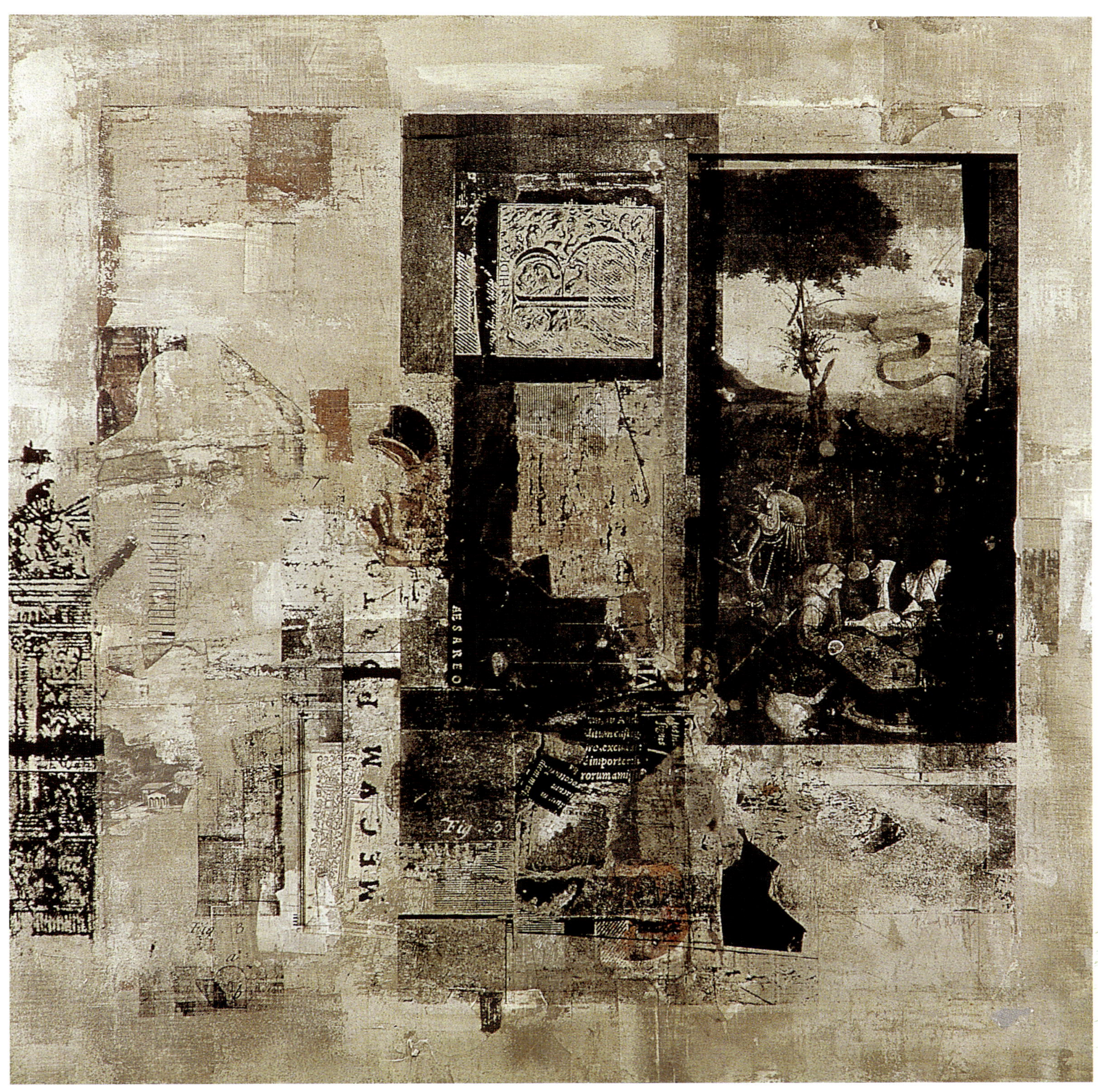

34 | SAVANNAH 2002

Mixed media collage, 39" x 30"

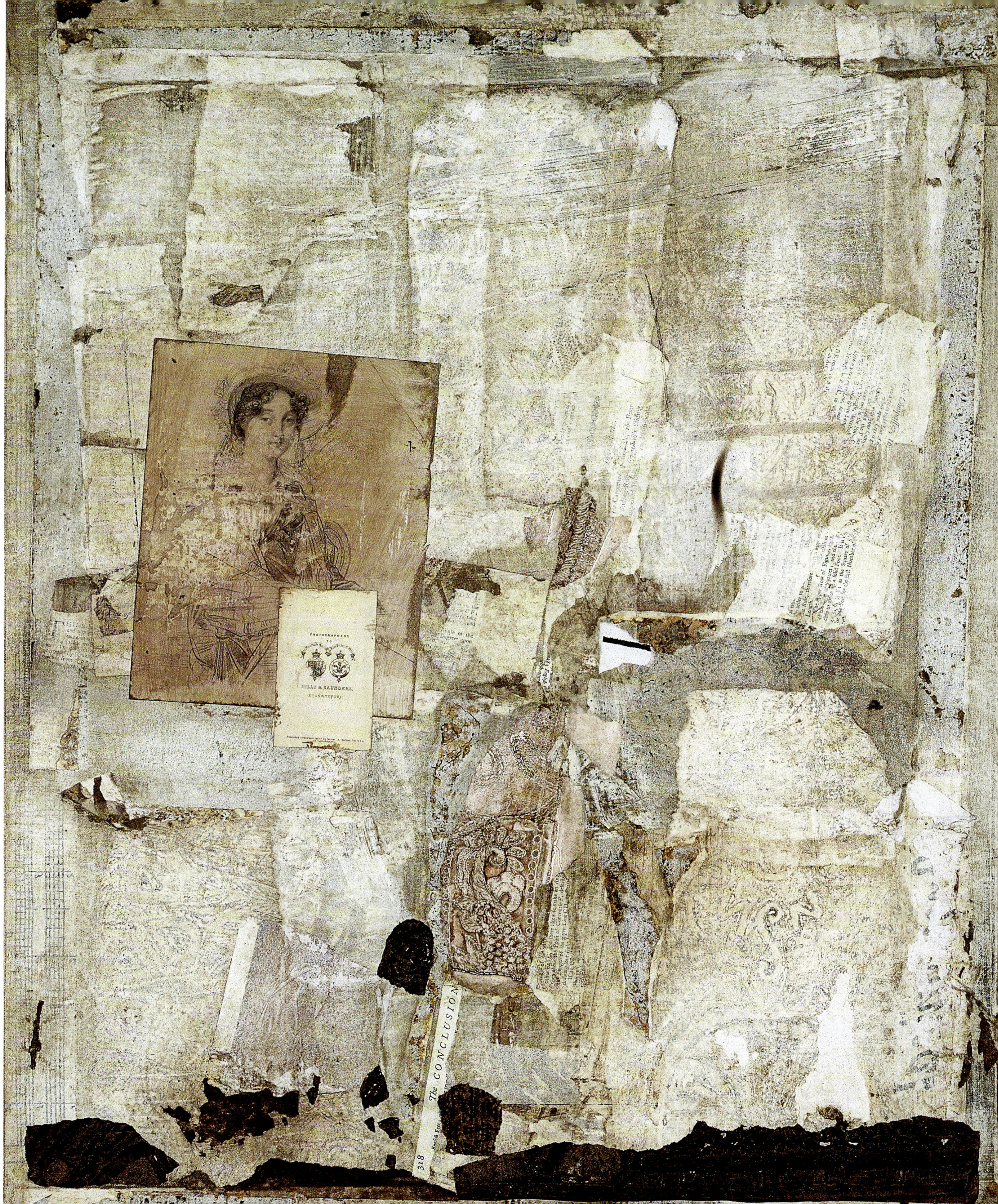

35 | UNTITLED 1996

Mixed media collage, 20" x 23"

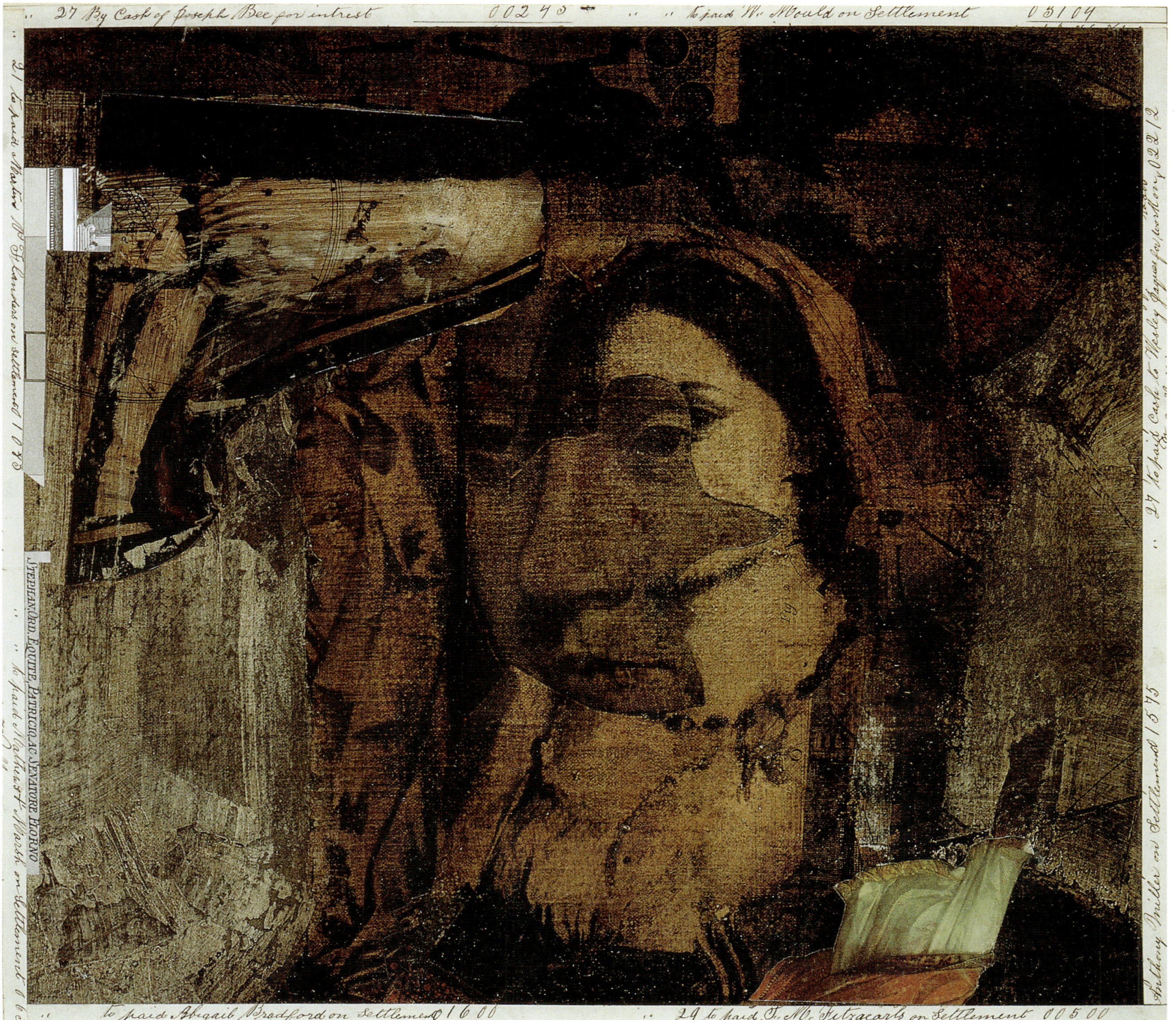
27 By Cash of Joseph Bee for intrest 0 0 2 4 5
to paid W. Mould on Settlement 0 3 1 0 4
to paid Abigail Bradford on Settlement 0 1 6 0 0
STEPHAN ORD. EQUITE, PATRICIO, AC SENATORE FLORANO

36 | ALE'NE IN THE EVENING 2003

Collage painting, 21" x 17 1/4"

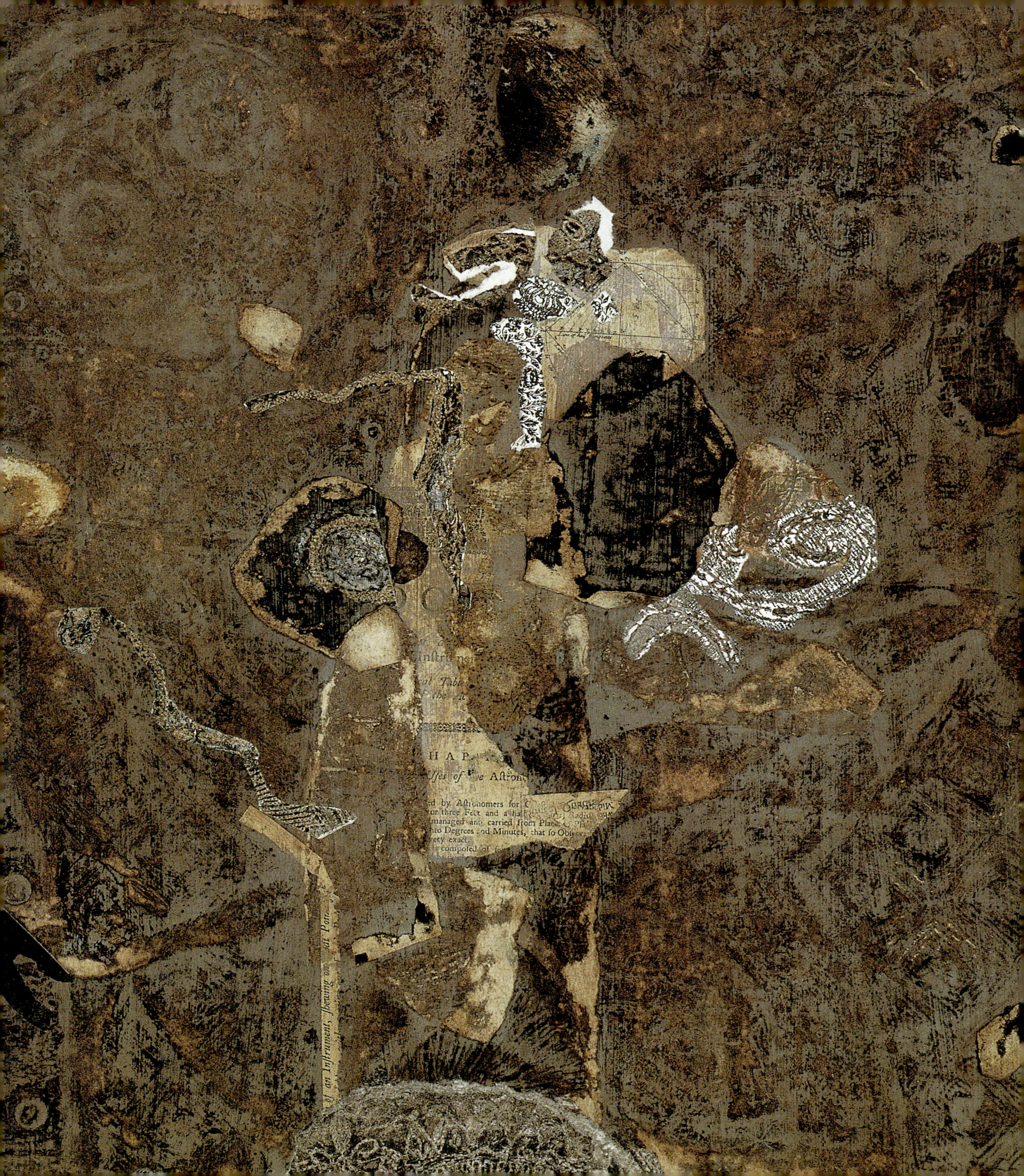
by Aftronomers for
three Feet and a
managed and carried from
Degrees and Minutes, that fo
exact
compofed of

37 | THE TREE AND I 1998

Mixed media collage and photo transfer, 43 5/8" x 39 1/4"

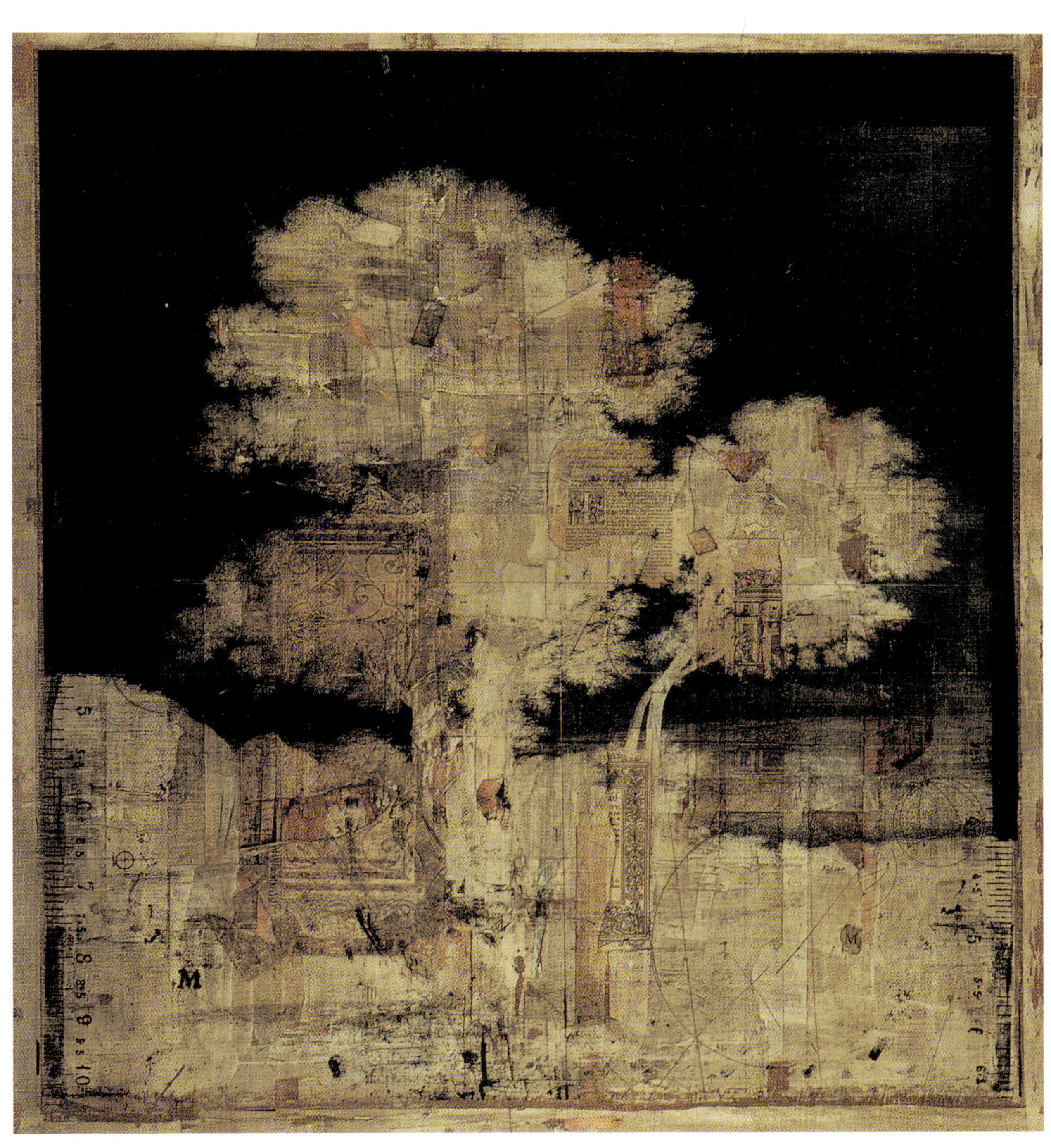

38 | MAN WITH A BLACKHEART 1998
Mixed media collage, 56 1/4" x 44 1/4"

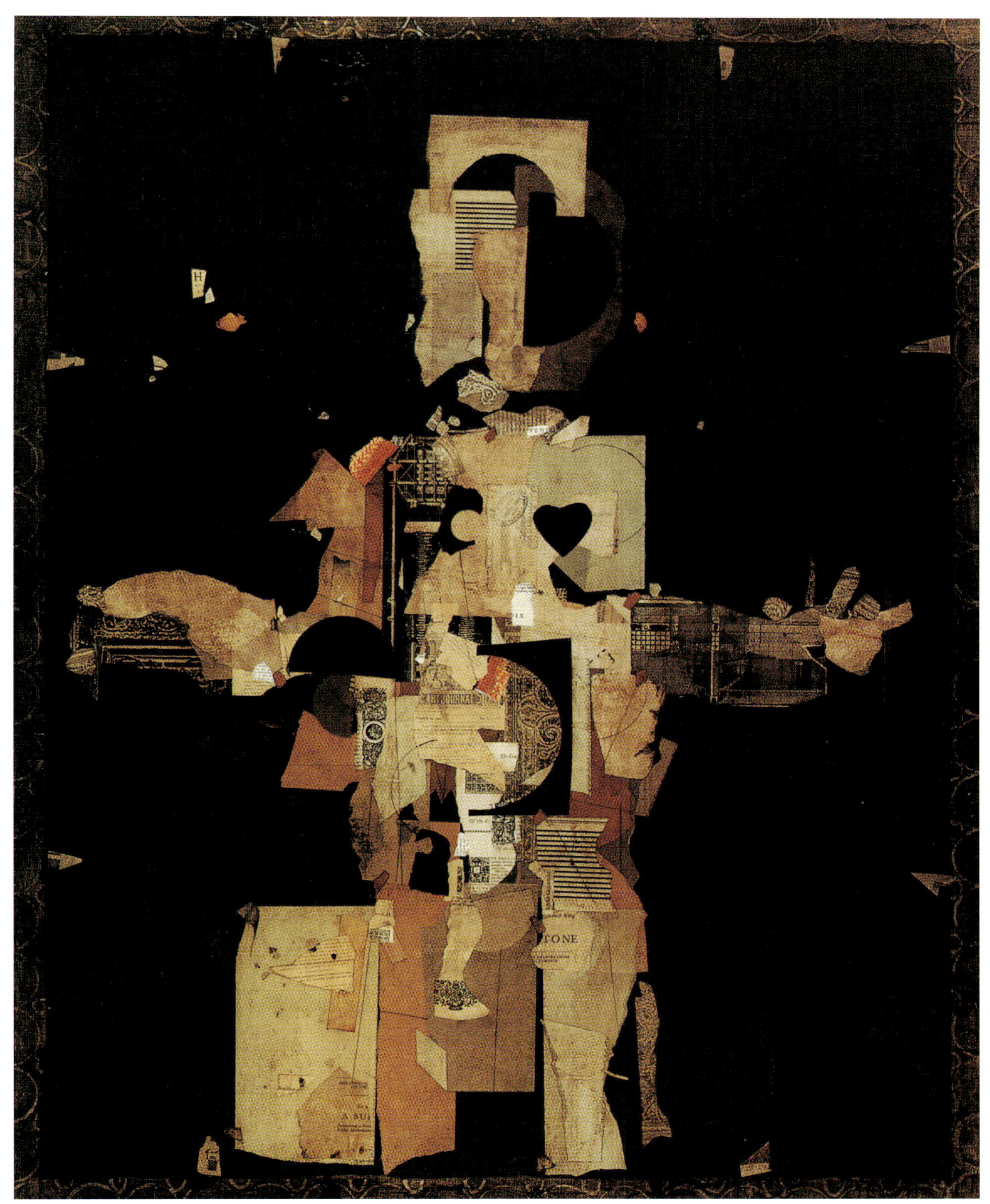

39 | SOEST 2002
Mixed media collage, 52" x 52"

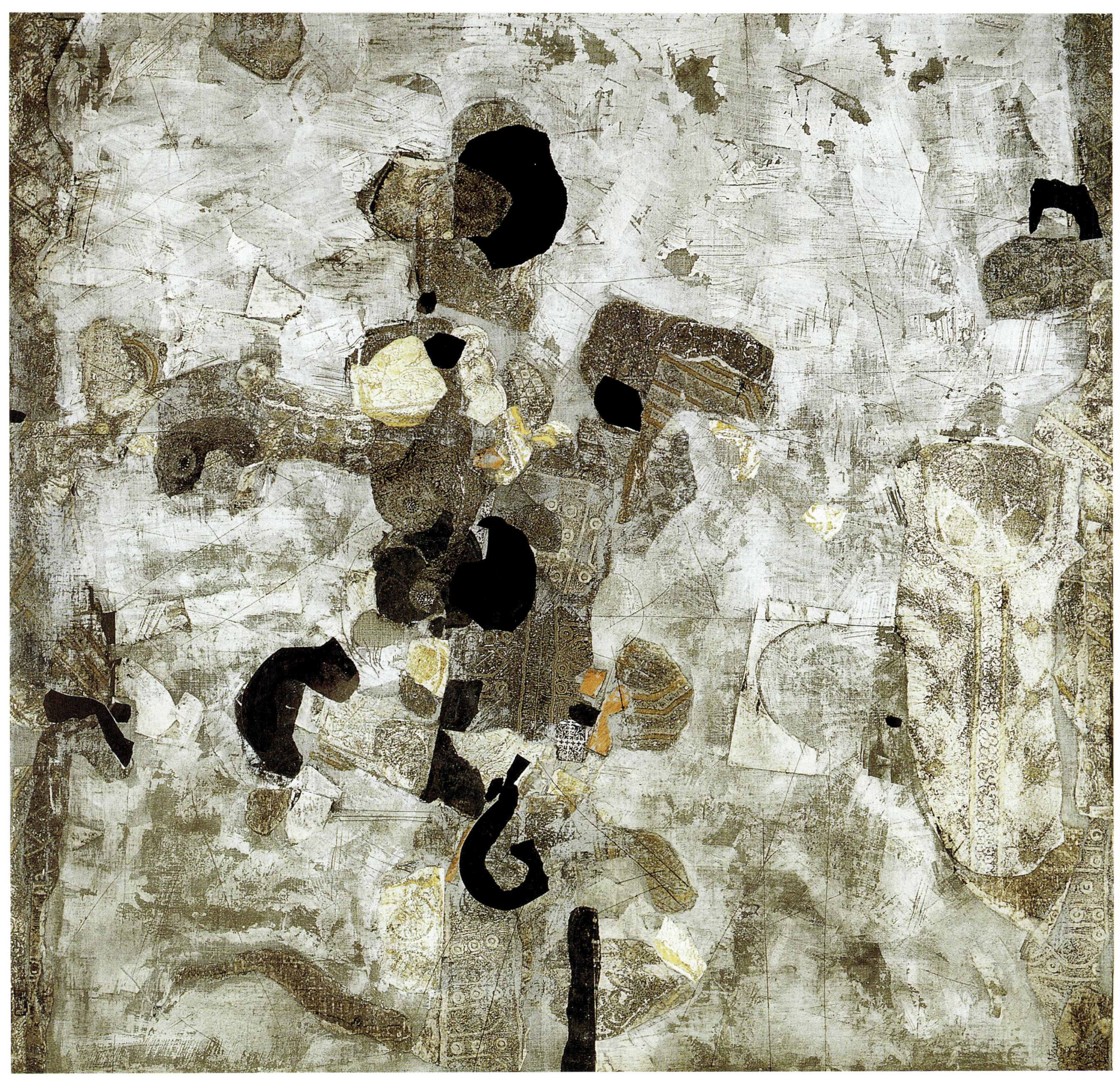

40 | UNTITLED FIGURE 2003

Collage painting, 37" x 30 1/2"

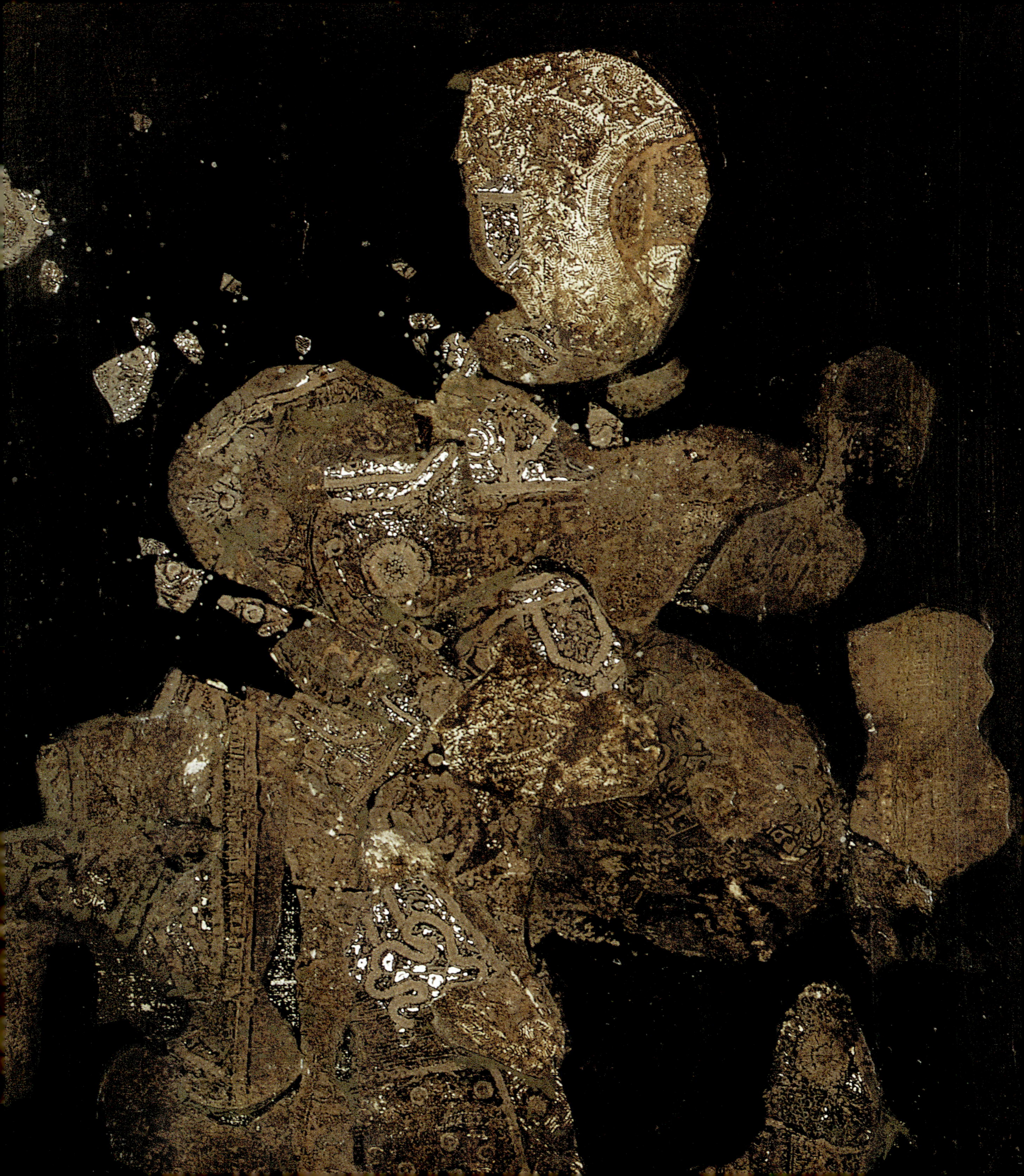

41 | SPLIT LADY 1997

Picture transfer and leaves on acrylic background, 14 1/4" x 15 3/8"

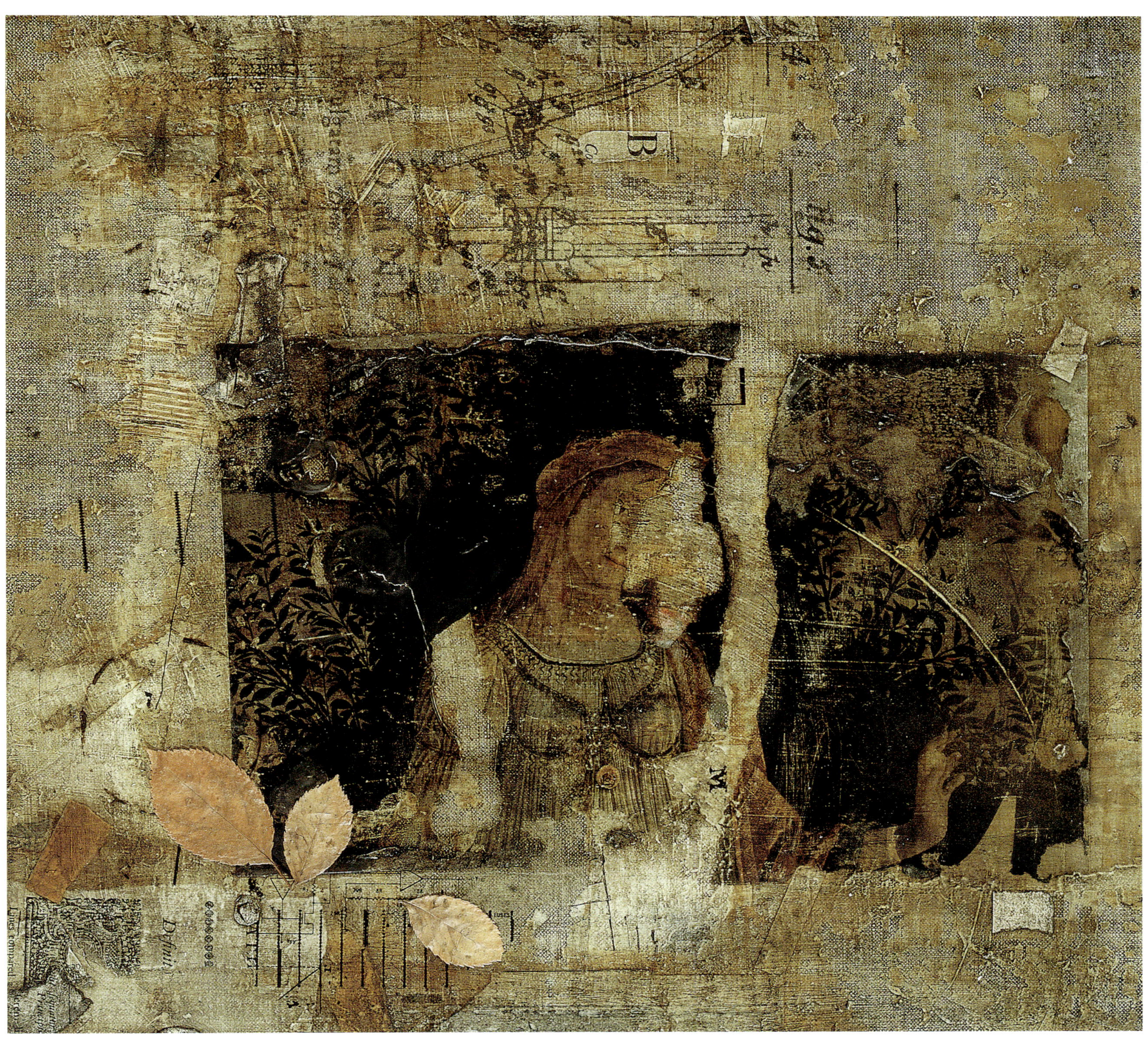

42 | ALEXEI AND MATHIS 2002

Mixed media collage, 52" x 52"

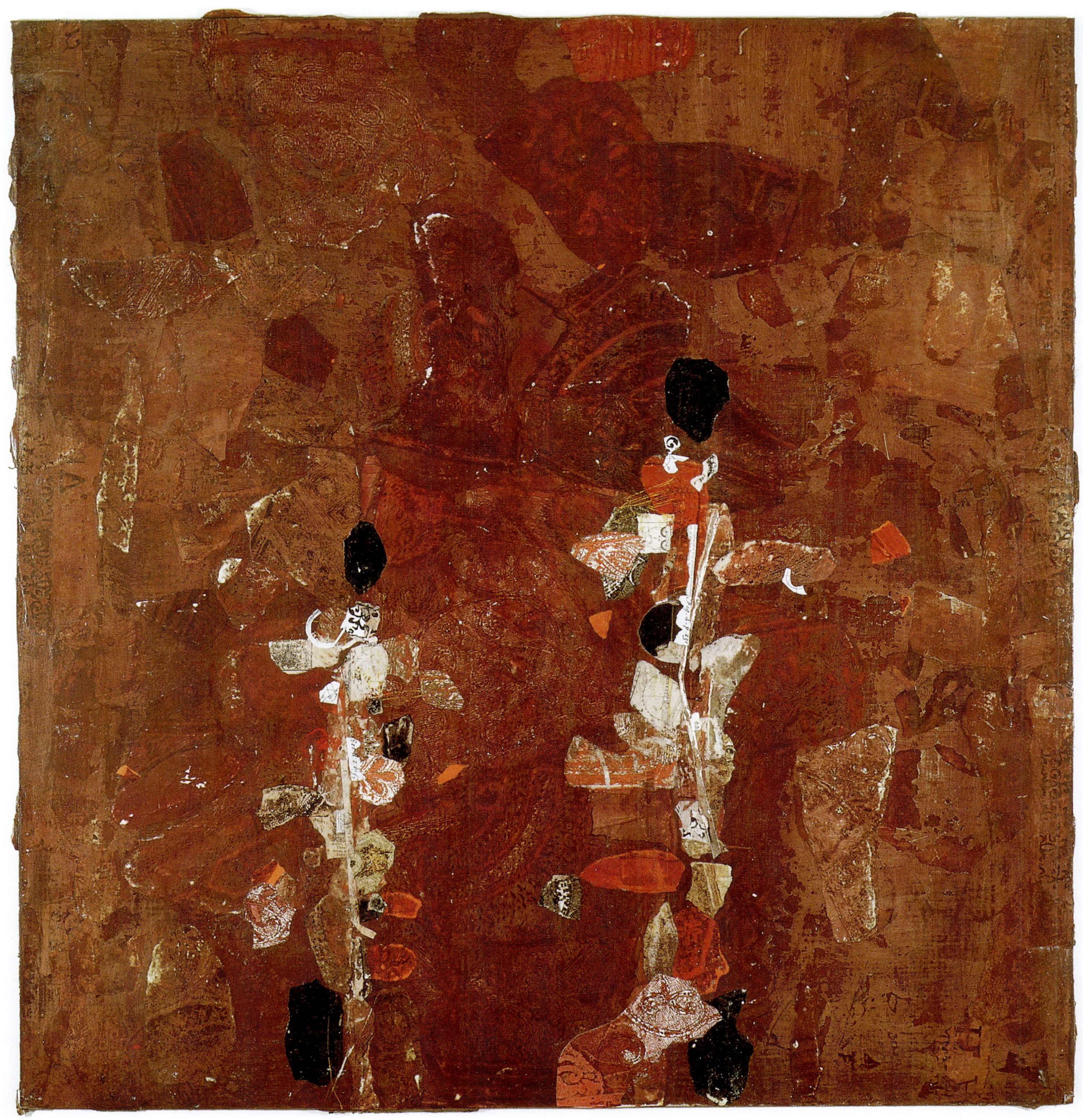

43 | WAITING FIGURE 1998

Mixed media collage painting, 48 1/2" x 33 3/4"

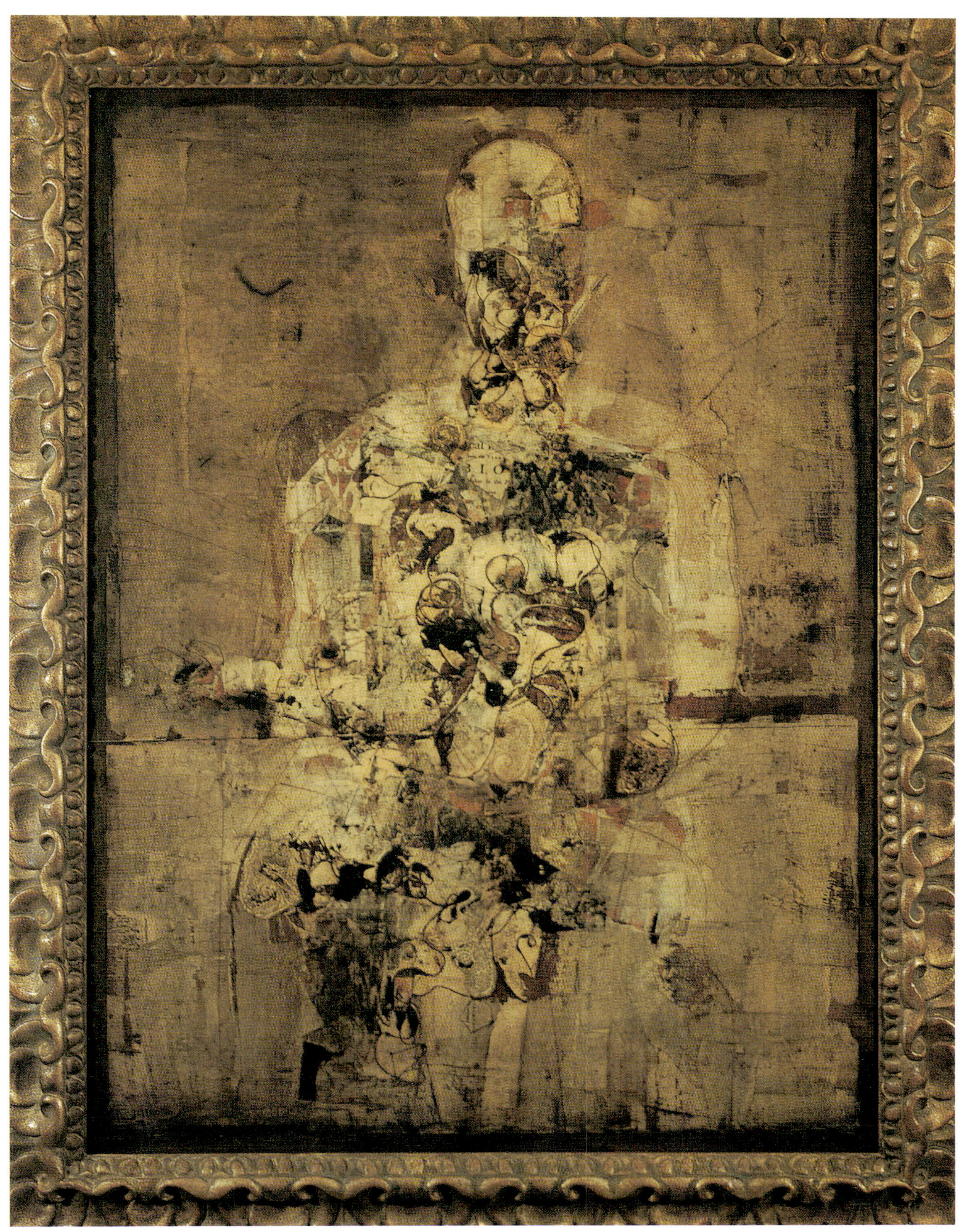

44 | POLLAI 2002
Mixed media collage, 50" x 40"

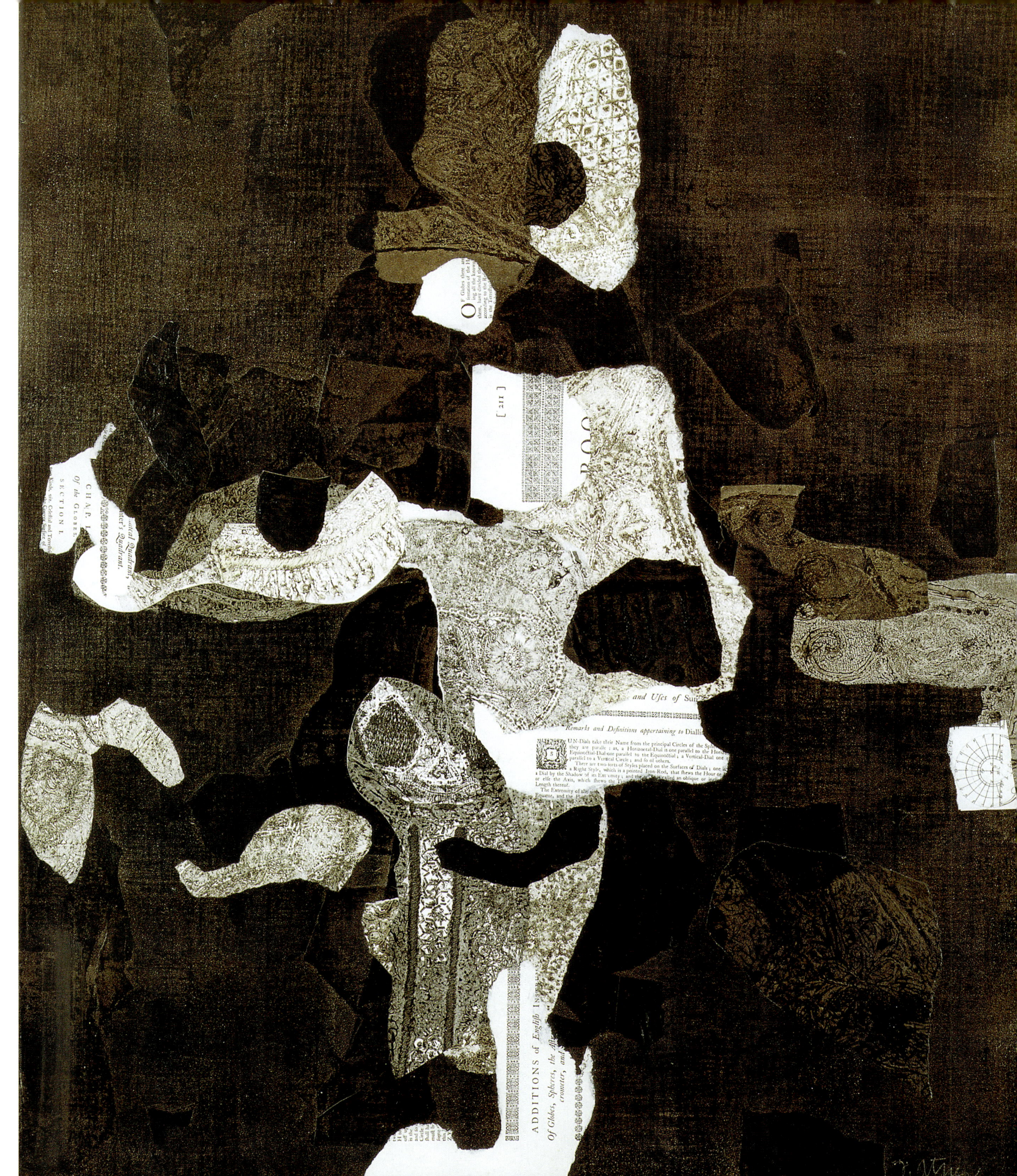

and Ufes of
Remarks and Definitions appertaining to
ADDITIONS of

45 | KUNIKO 2001

Mixed media collage, 36" x 26 1/2"

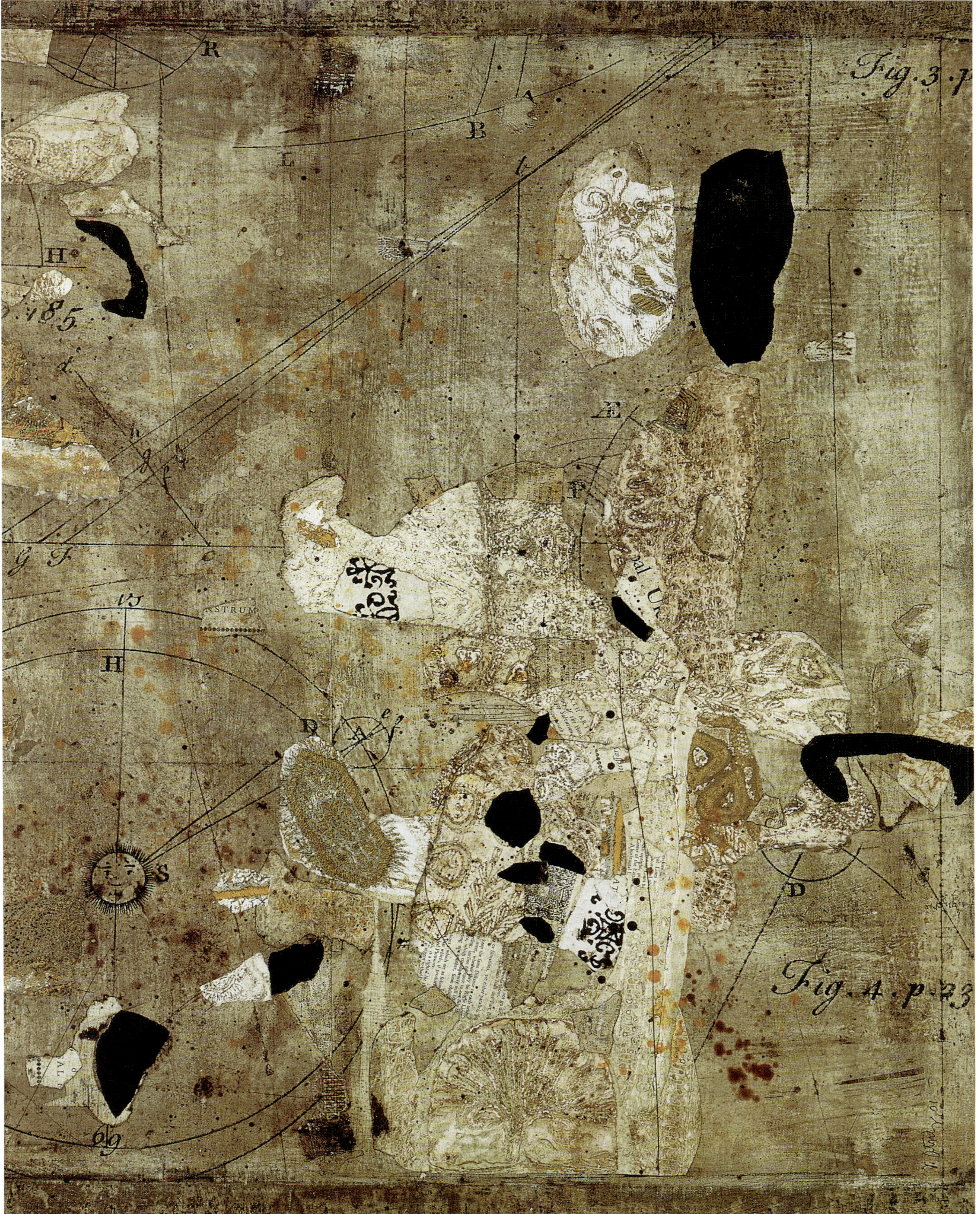
Fig. 3. p
Fig. 4. p. 23

46 | ANTICIPATION 1997

Mixed media collage, 16 3/4" x 19 1/4"

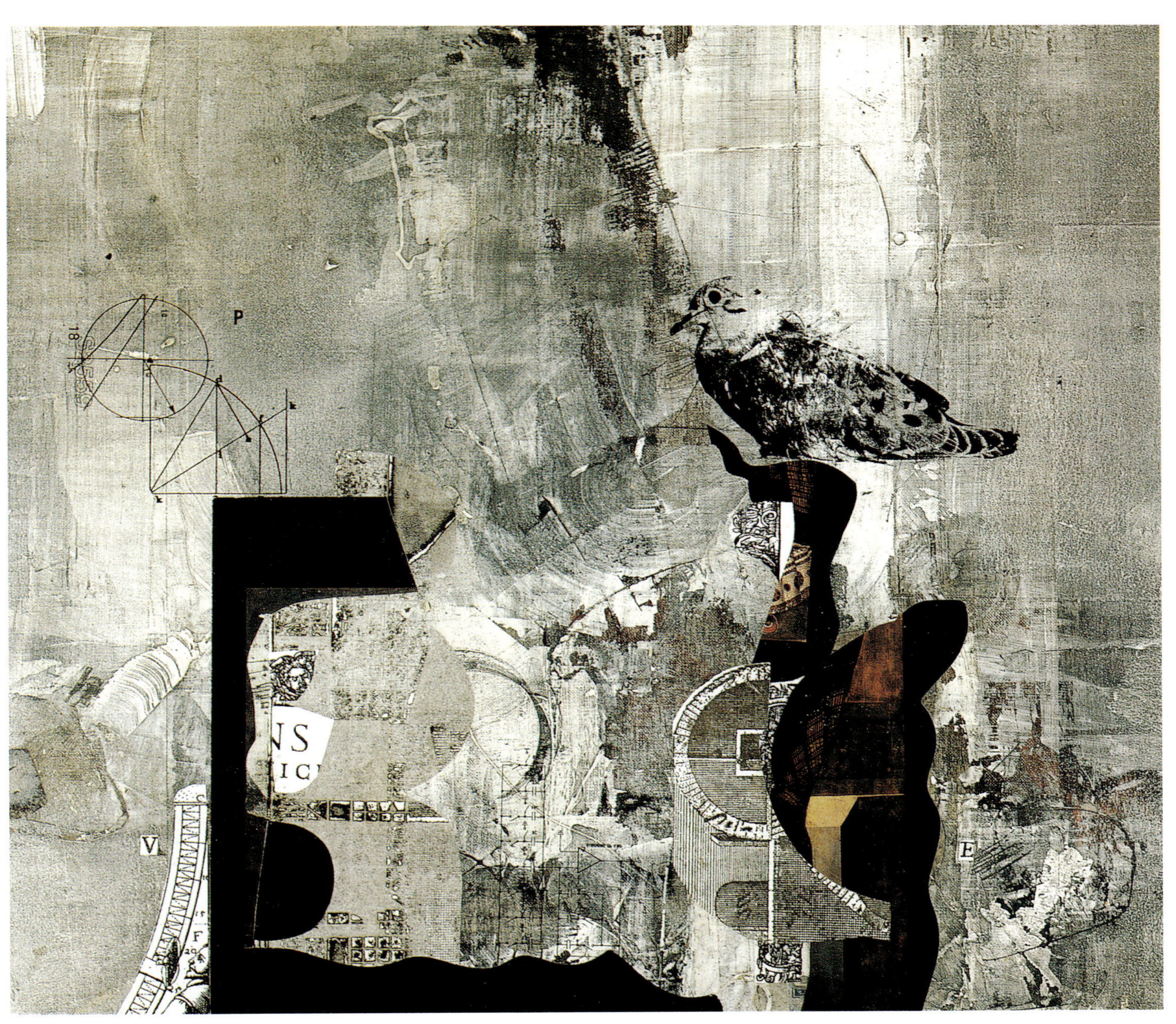

47 | PARTNERS 1999

Collage painting, 46 1/2" x 46 1/2"

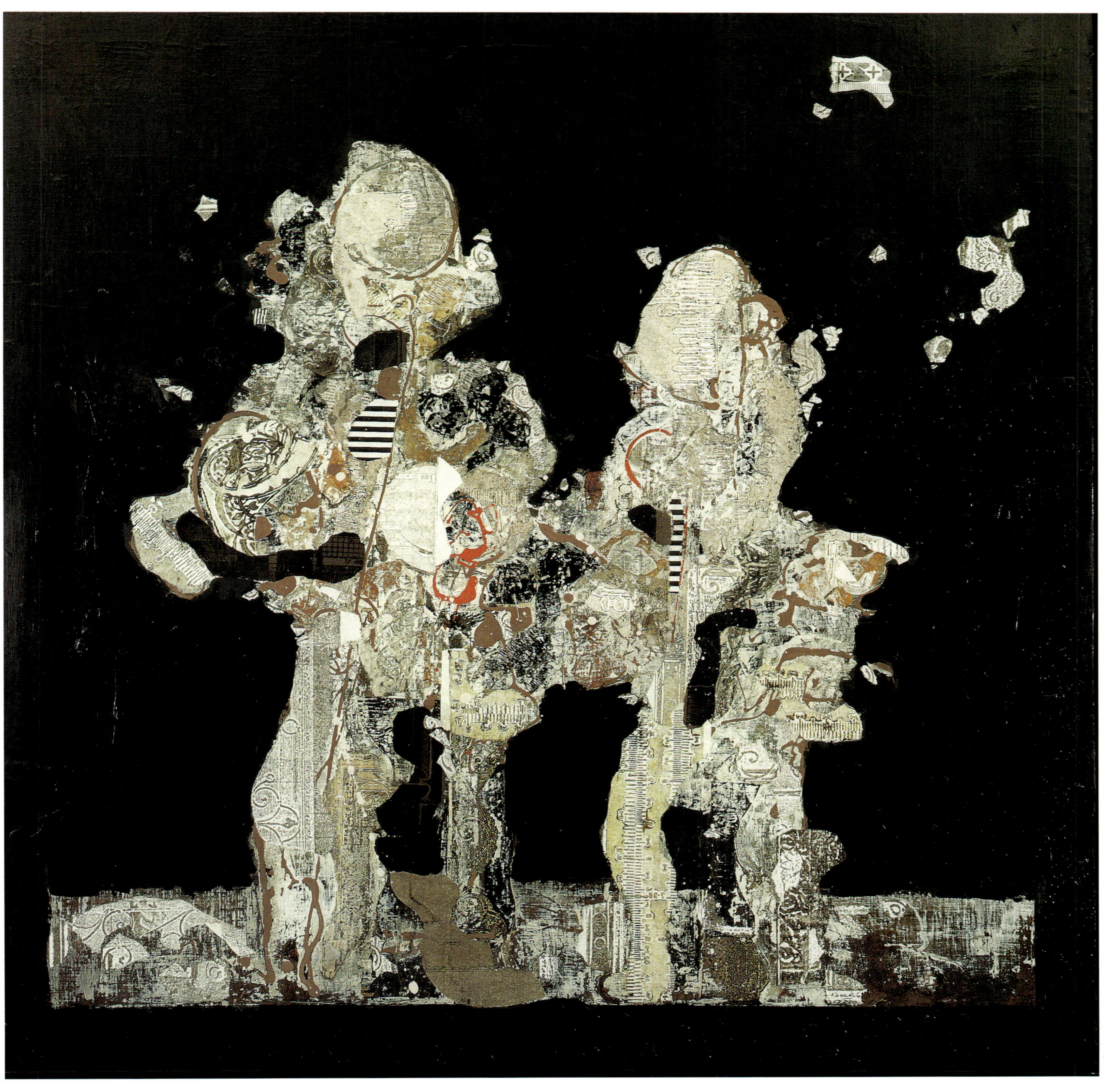

48 | ON BEING 100 2000

Mixed media assemblage, 24" x 32"

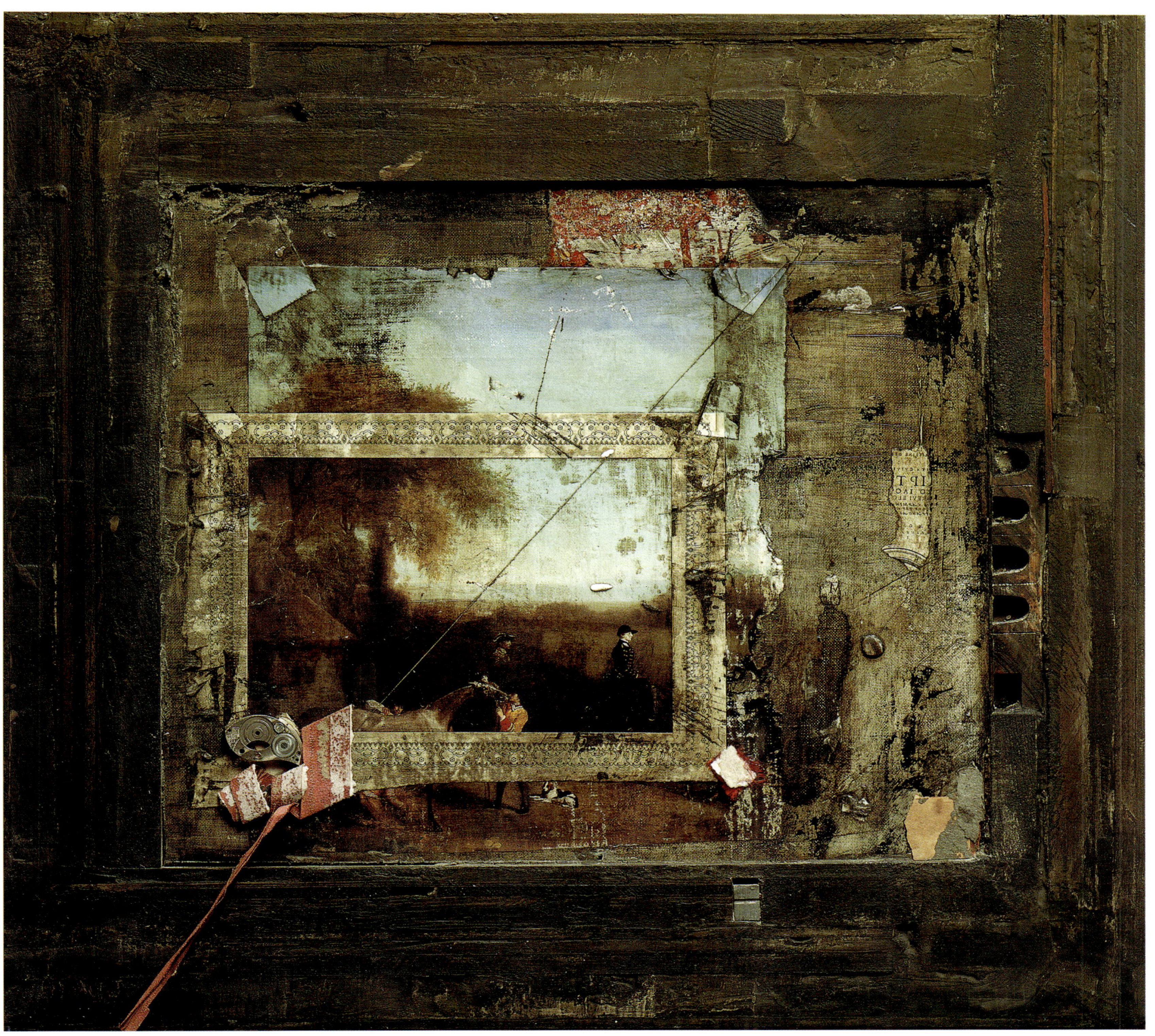

49 | KAPKA 2002

Collage painting on linen, 48" x 48"

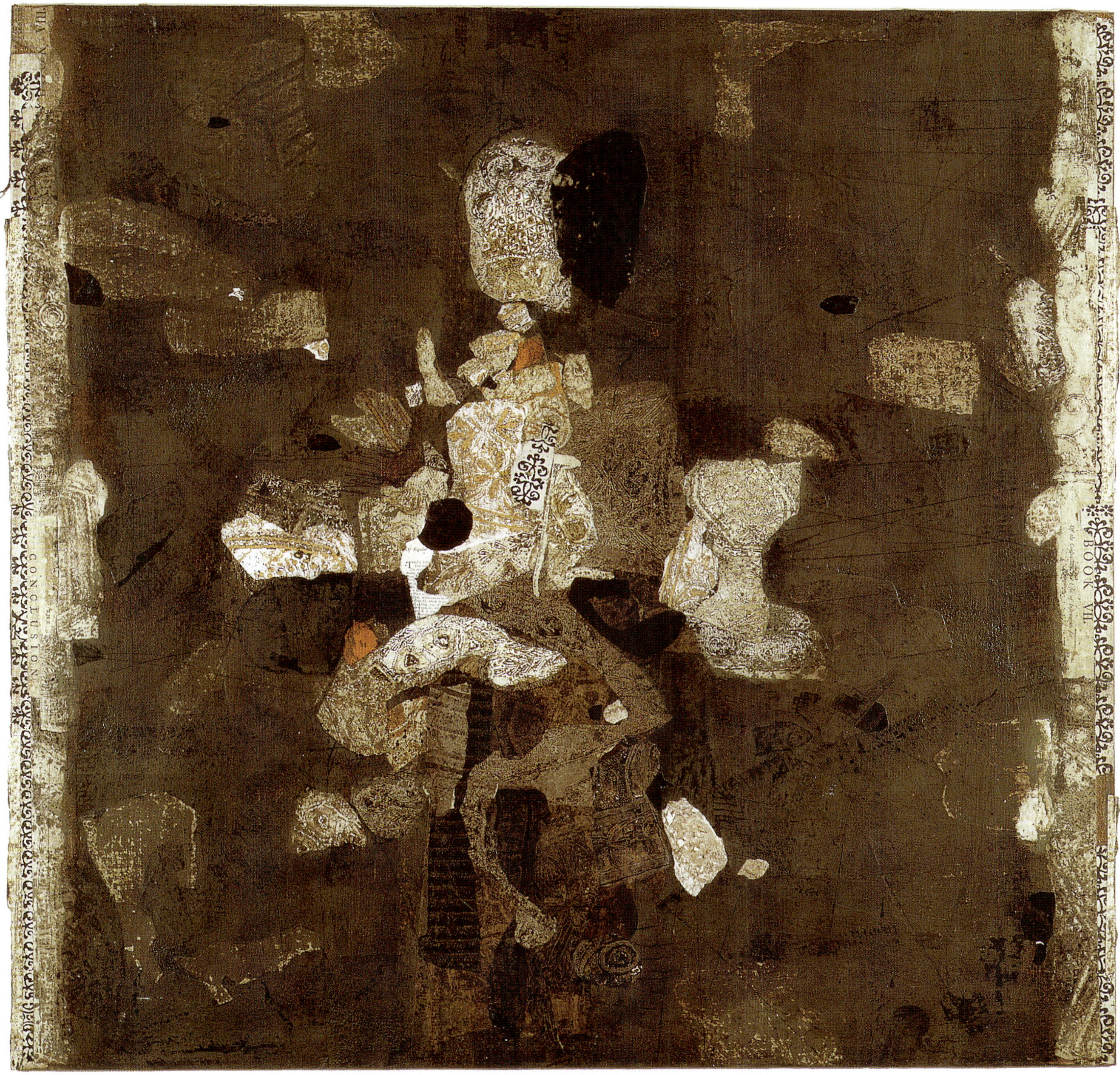

50 | SILVER BIRD 2000

Collage and etching, 15" x 16 1/4"

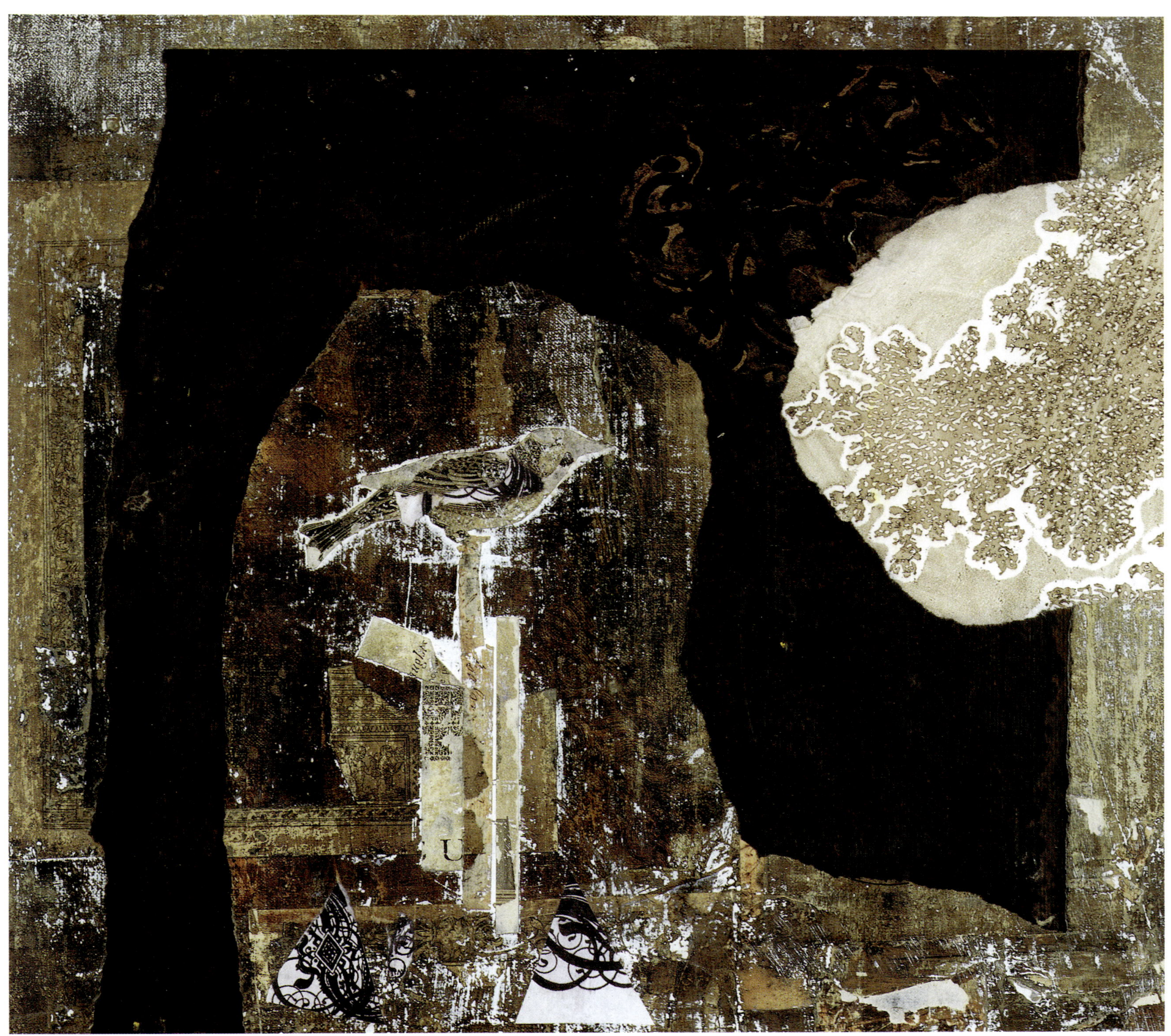

51 | RAUCH 2001

Collage painting on linen, 60" x 48"

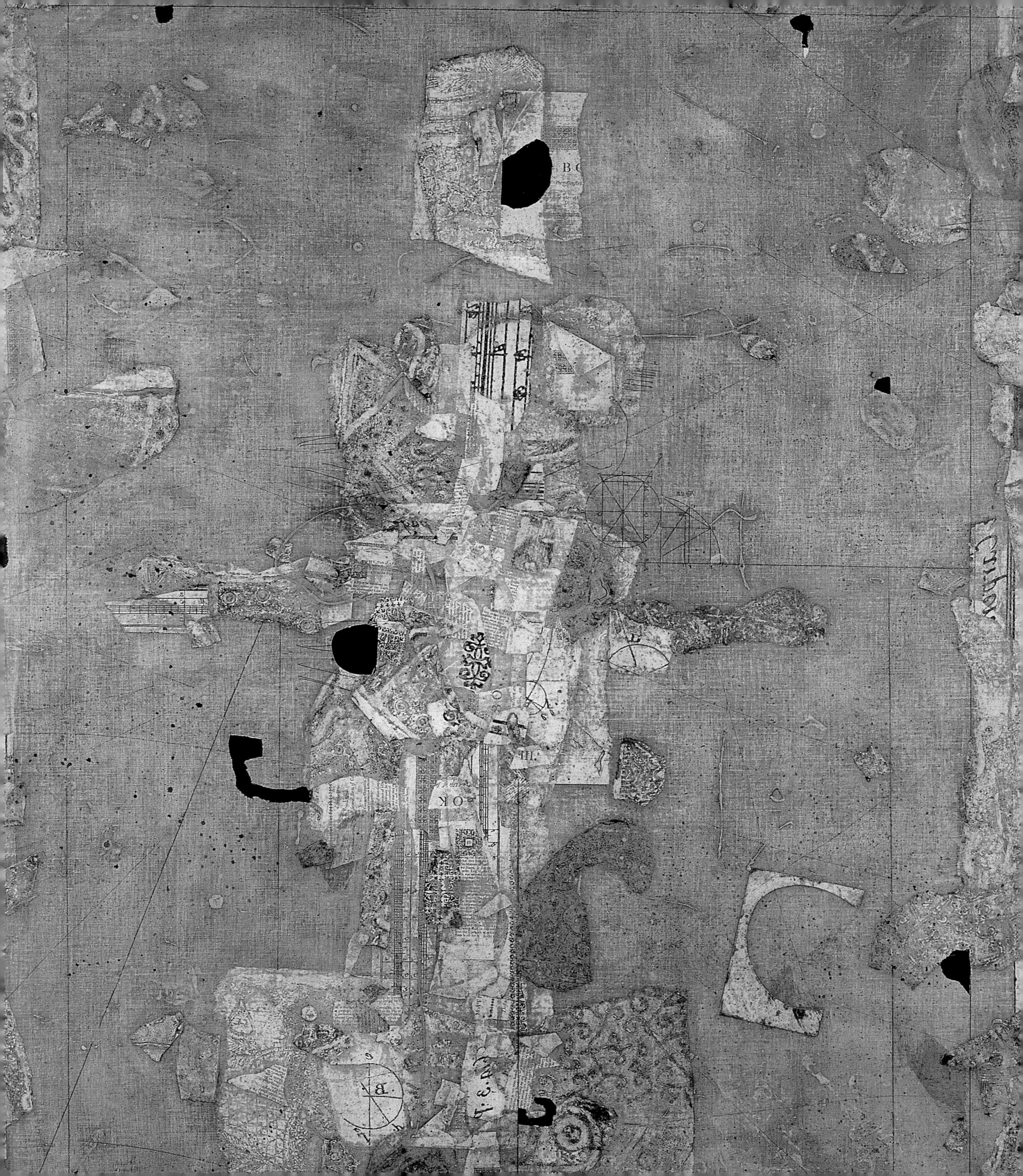

52 | UNTITLED 1976

Mixed media collage, 20" x 20"

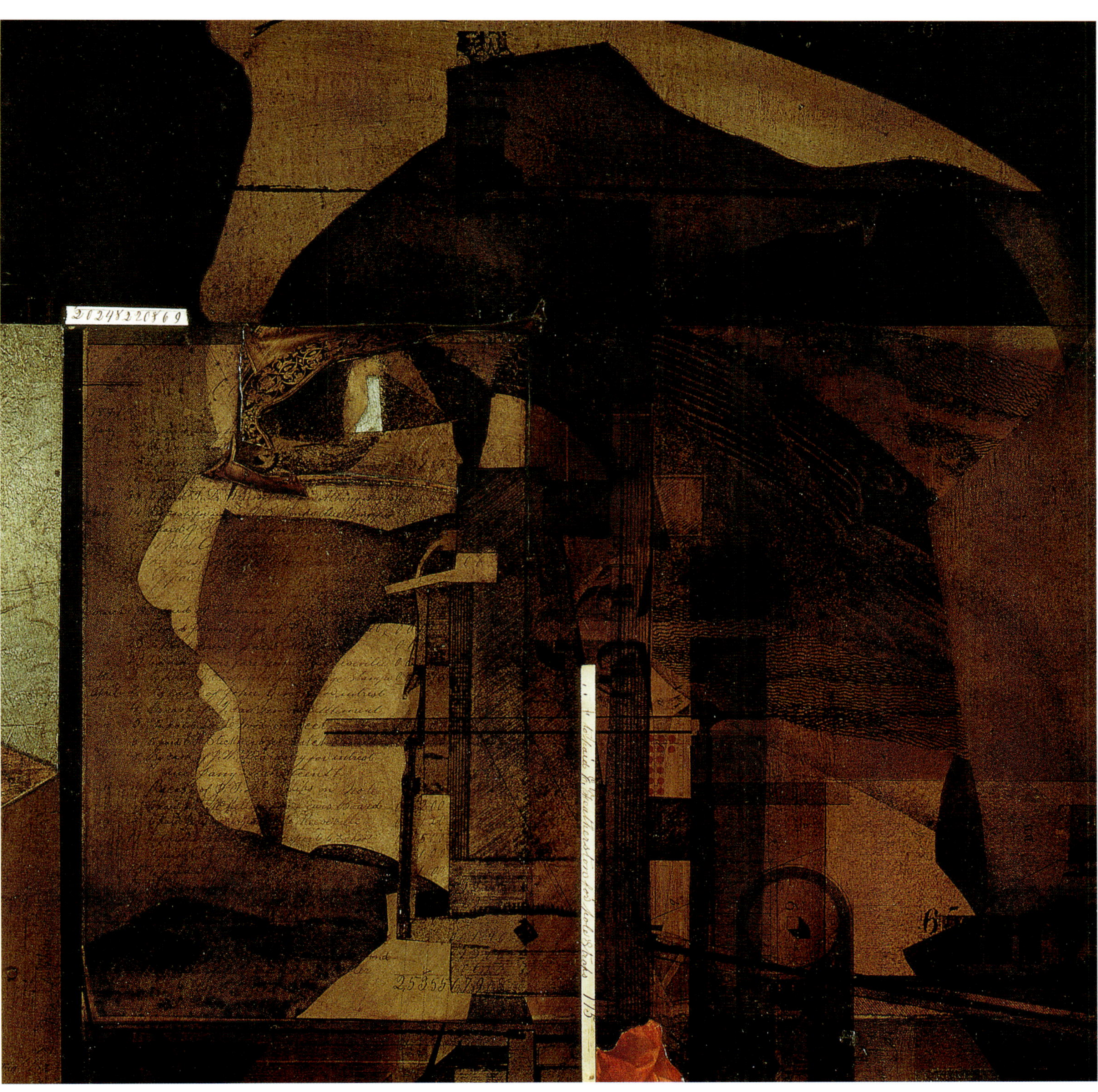

53 | CHATEAU DeBENOUVILLE 1992
Collage painting, 12 1/4" x 16 1/2"

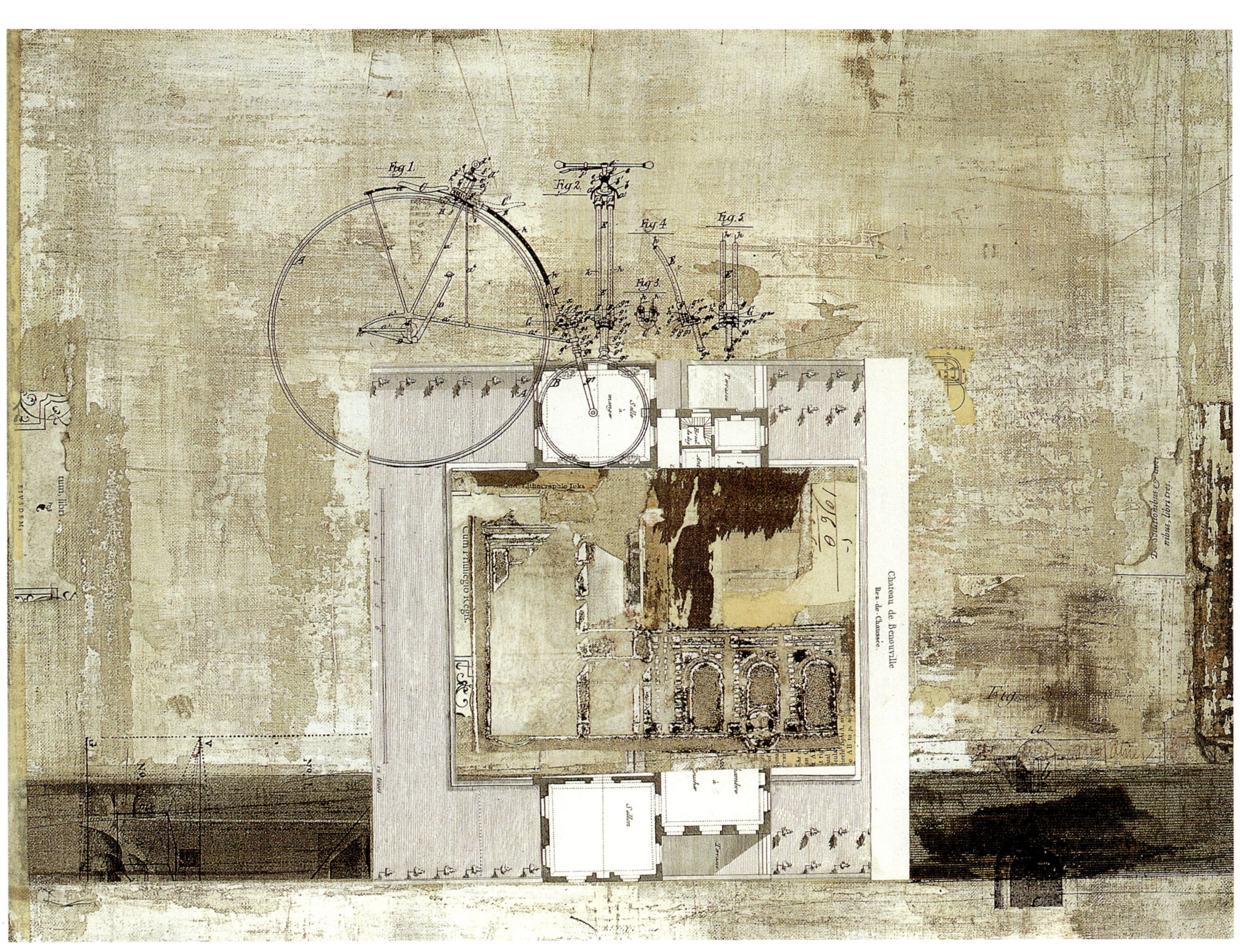

54 | THE RED HEAD 2002
Mixed media collage, 24" x 20"

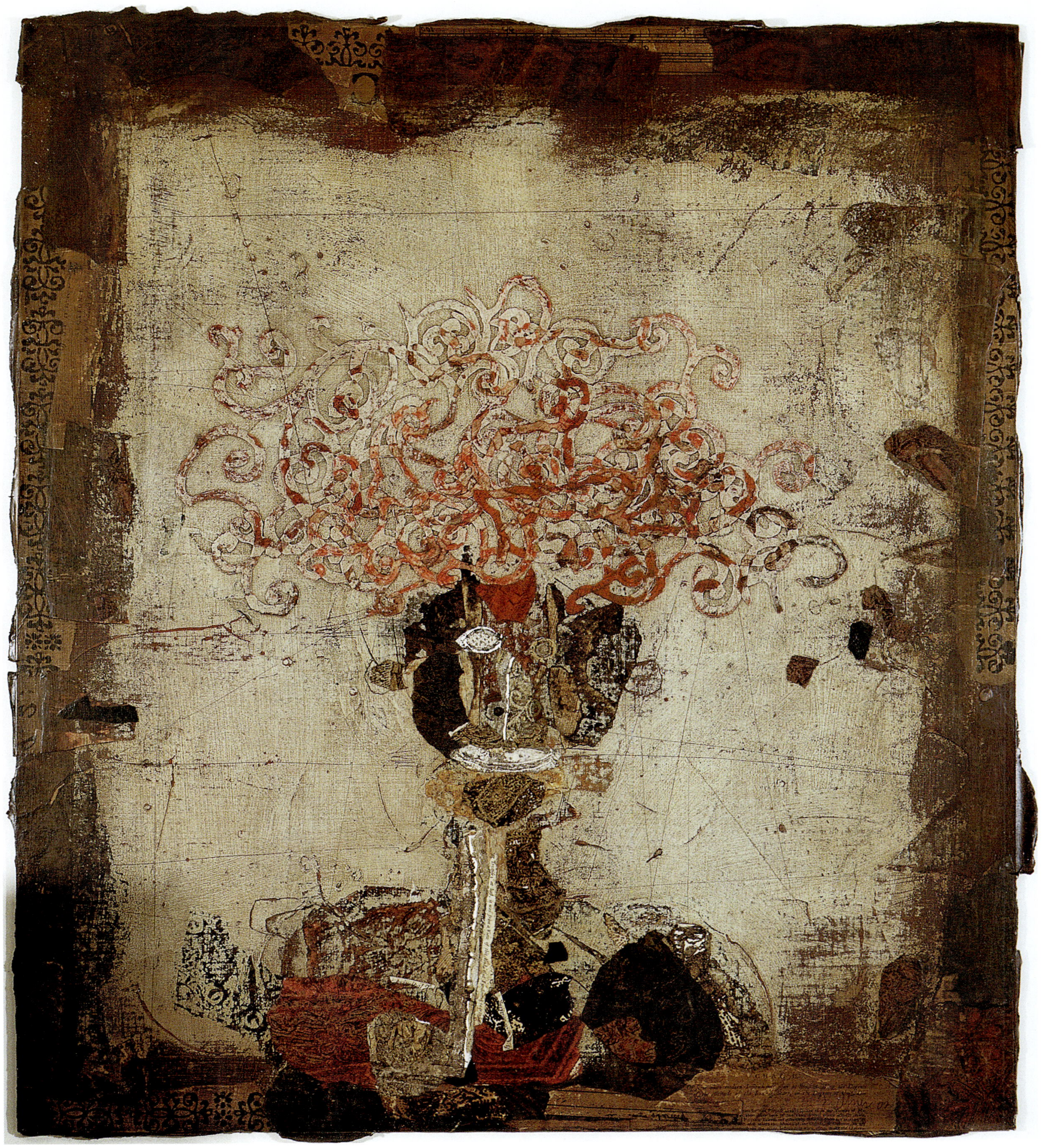

55 | CASTIGLIONE 1999

Mixed media collage, 23 1/4" x 23 1/4"

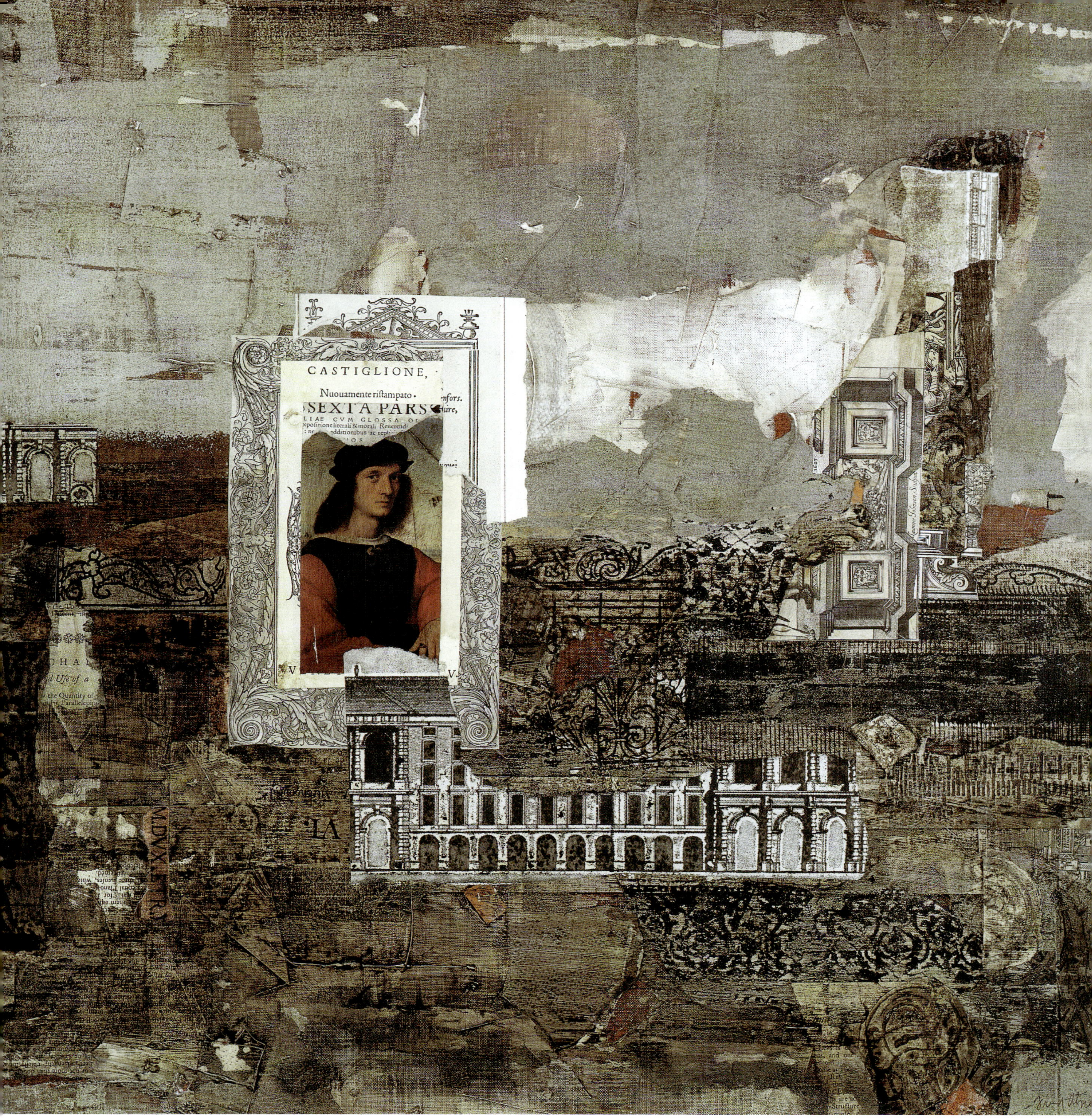
CASTIGLIONE,
Nuouamente ristampato.
SEXTA PARS

56 | THE SEEDS CHIEFLY 1992

Collage painting, 14" x 18"

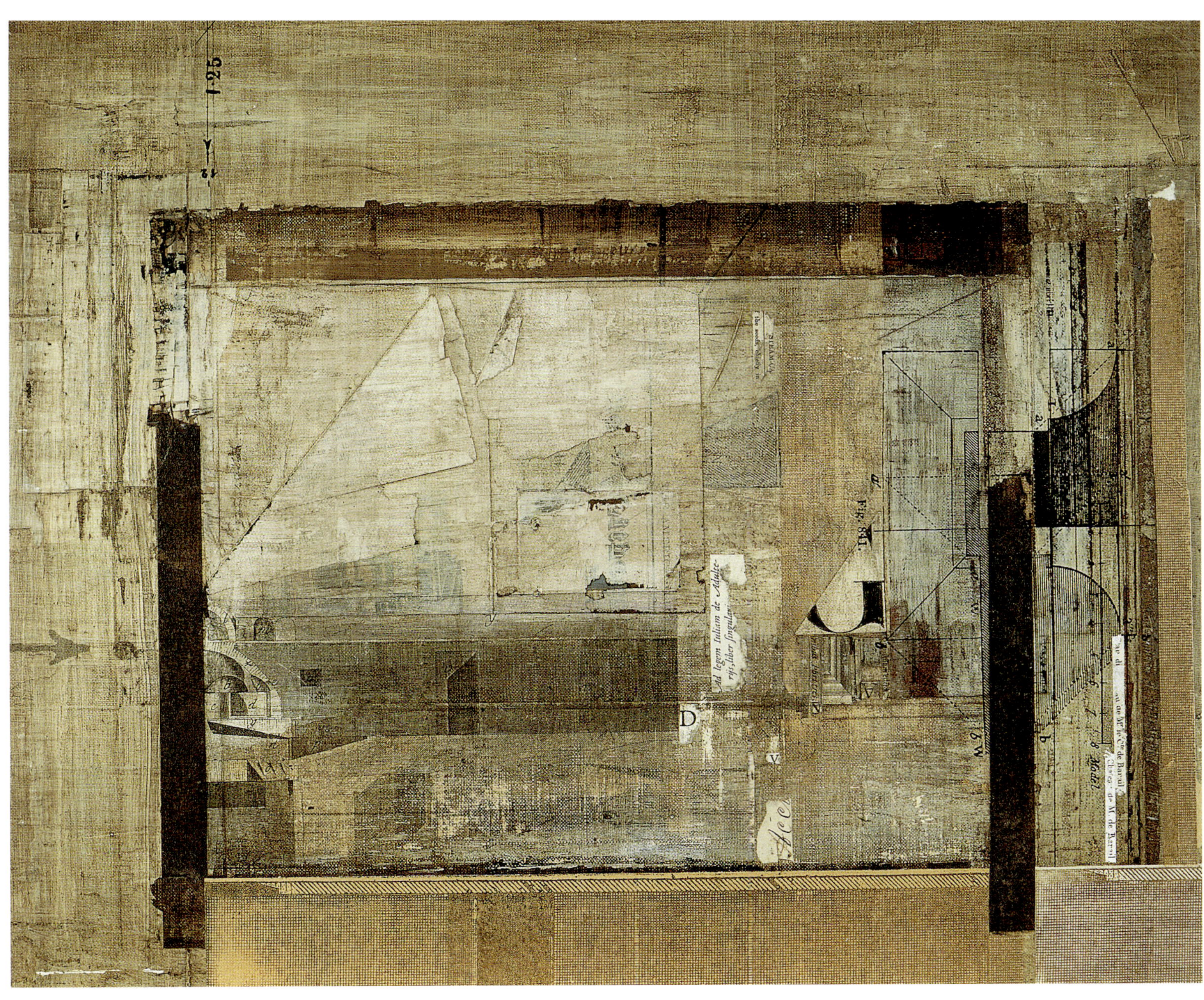

57 | NIGHT FEAR 1998

Mixed media assemblage, 20" x 23"

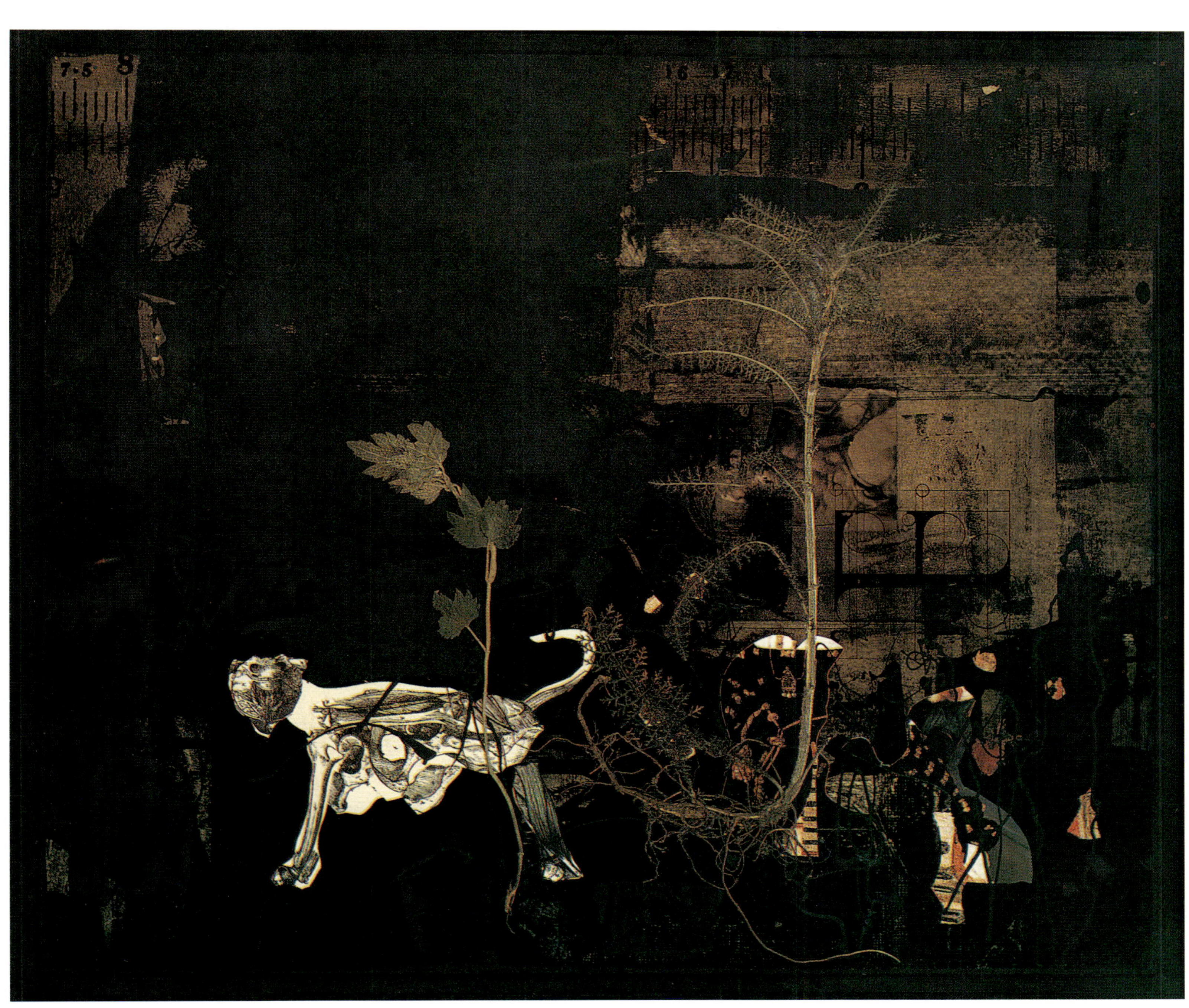

58 | LITTLE KIMBAL 1998

Mixed media collage, 23 1/2" x 22"

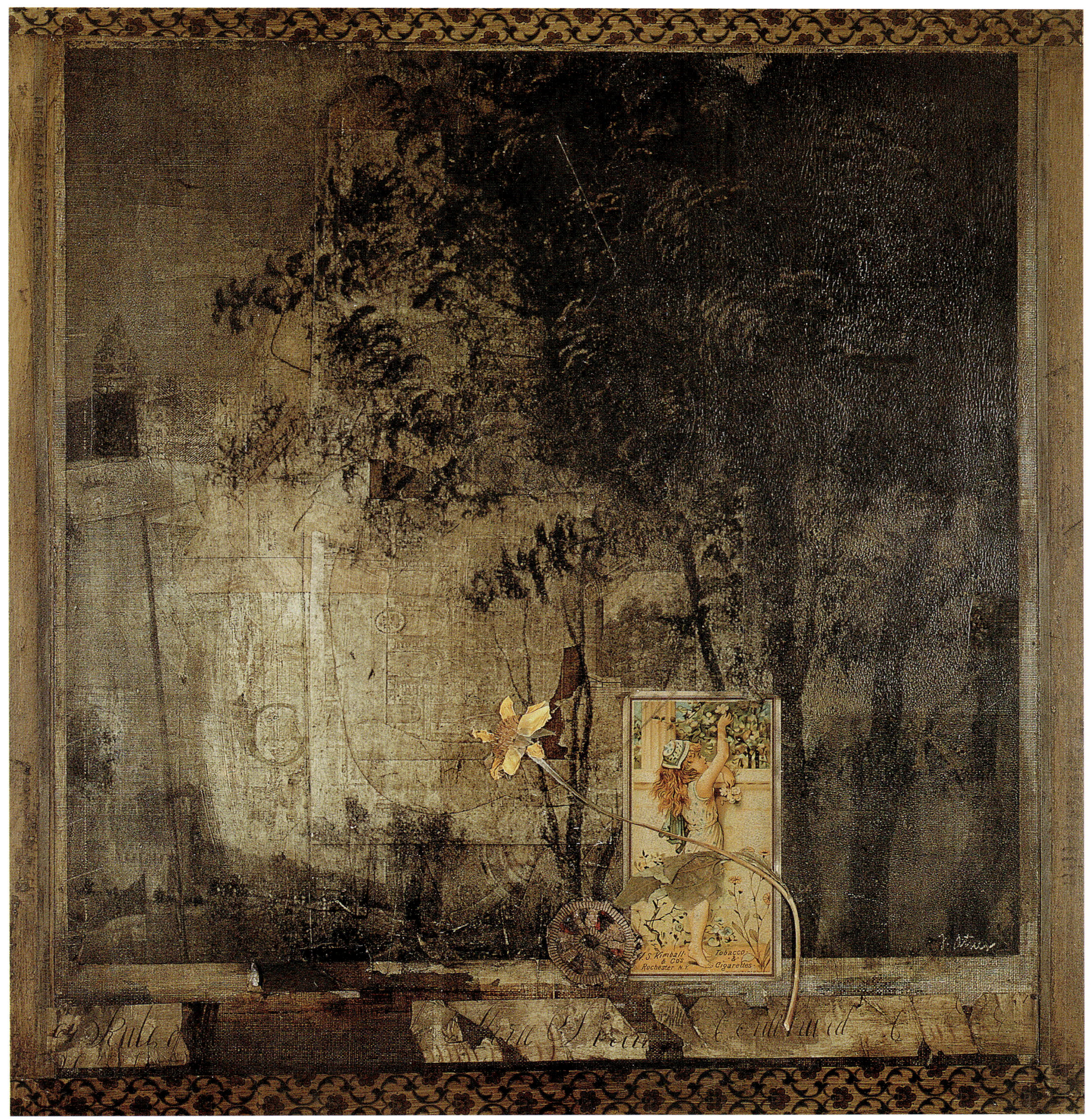
S. Kimball & Co's
Rochester N.Y.
Tobacco & Cigarettes

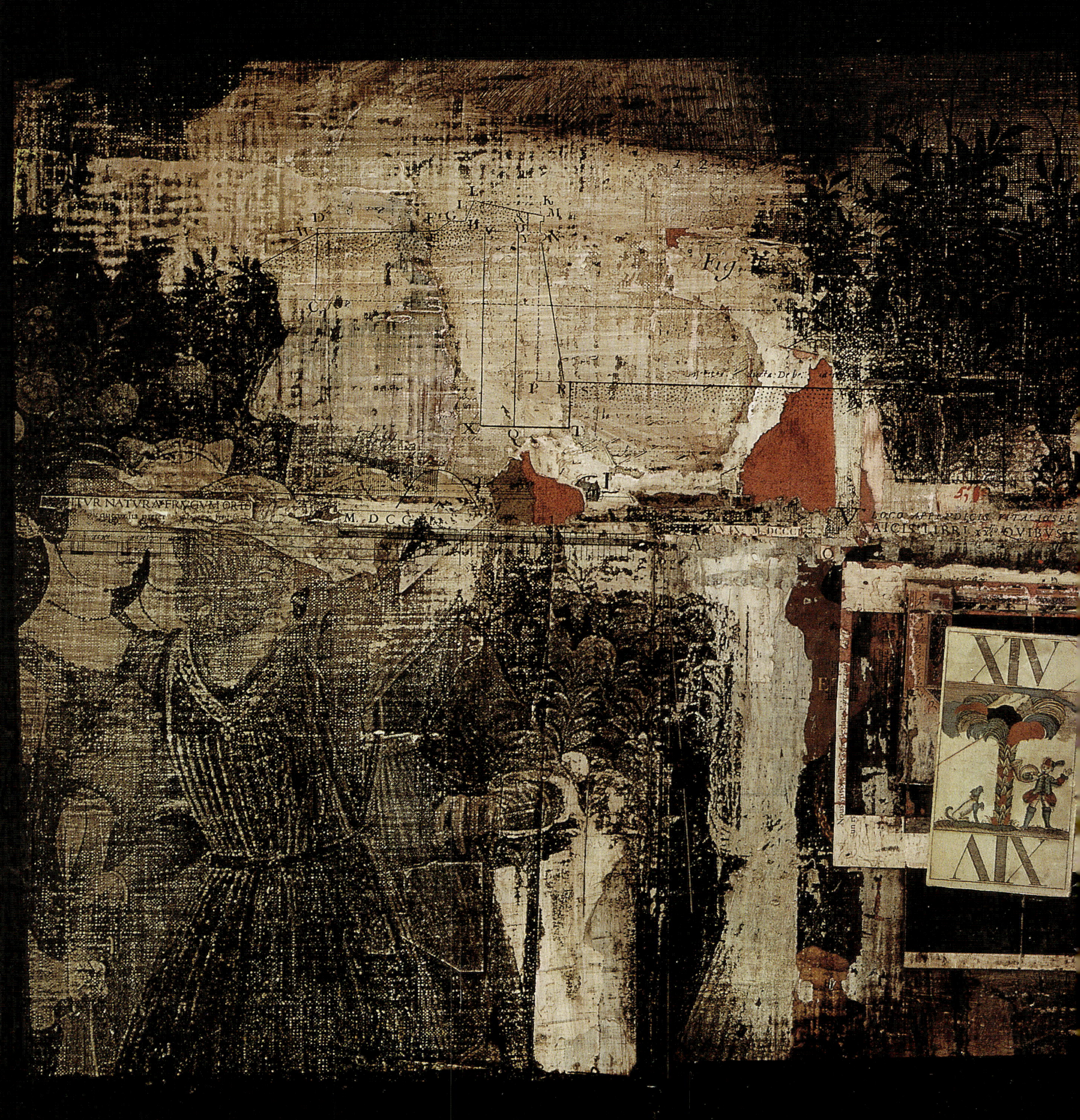

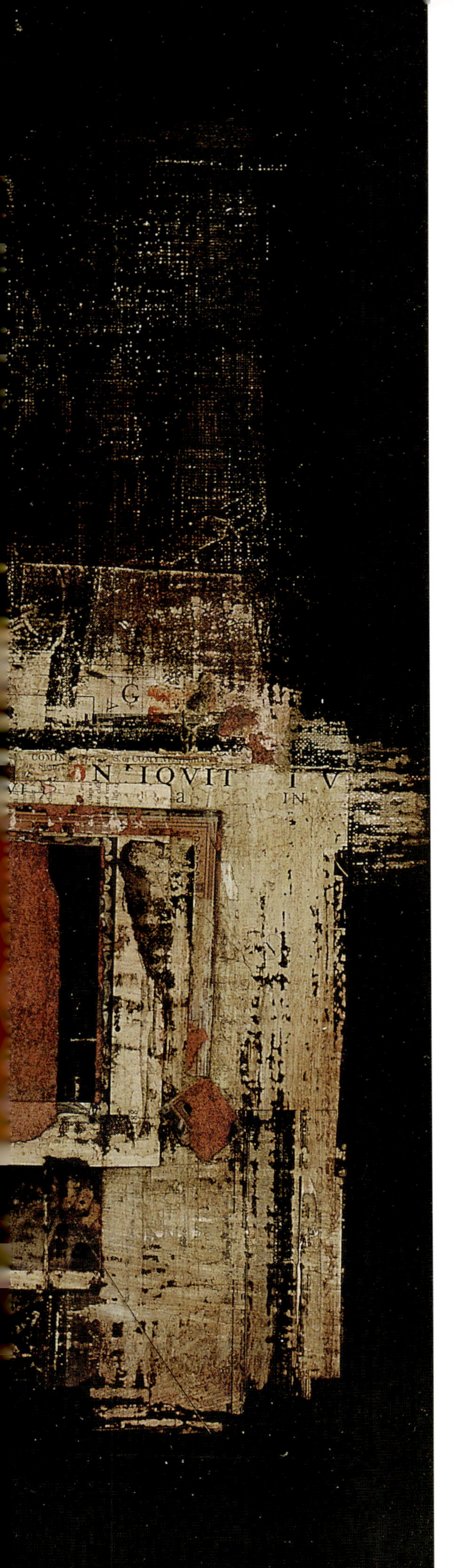

59 | THE DAY OF THE FOURTEENTH 1998
Mixed media collage, 18" x 23 1/2"

60 | A LITTLE LADY 1998

Mixed media collage, 15" x 14 1/2"

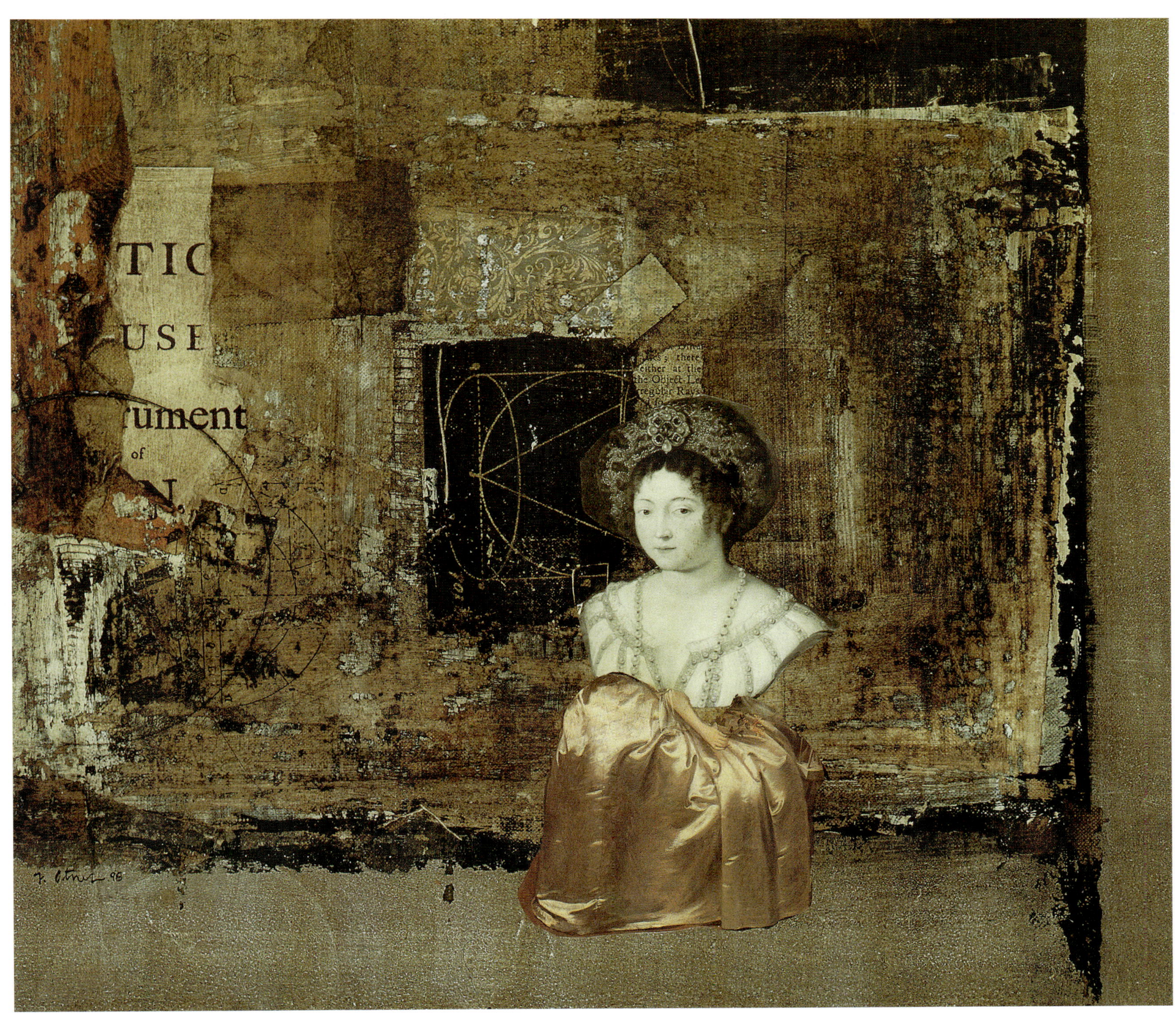
TIC
USE
ument
of

61 | BIRD IN CAGE 1997

Acrylic and collage on linen, 26 3/4" x 26 3/4"

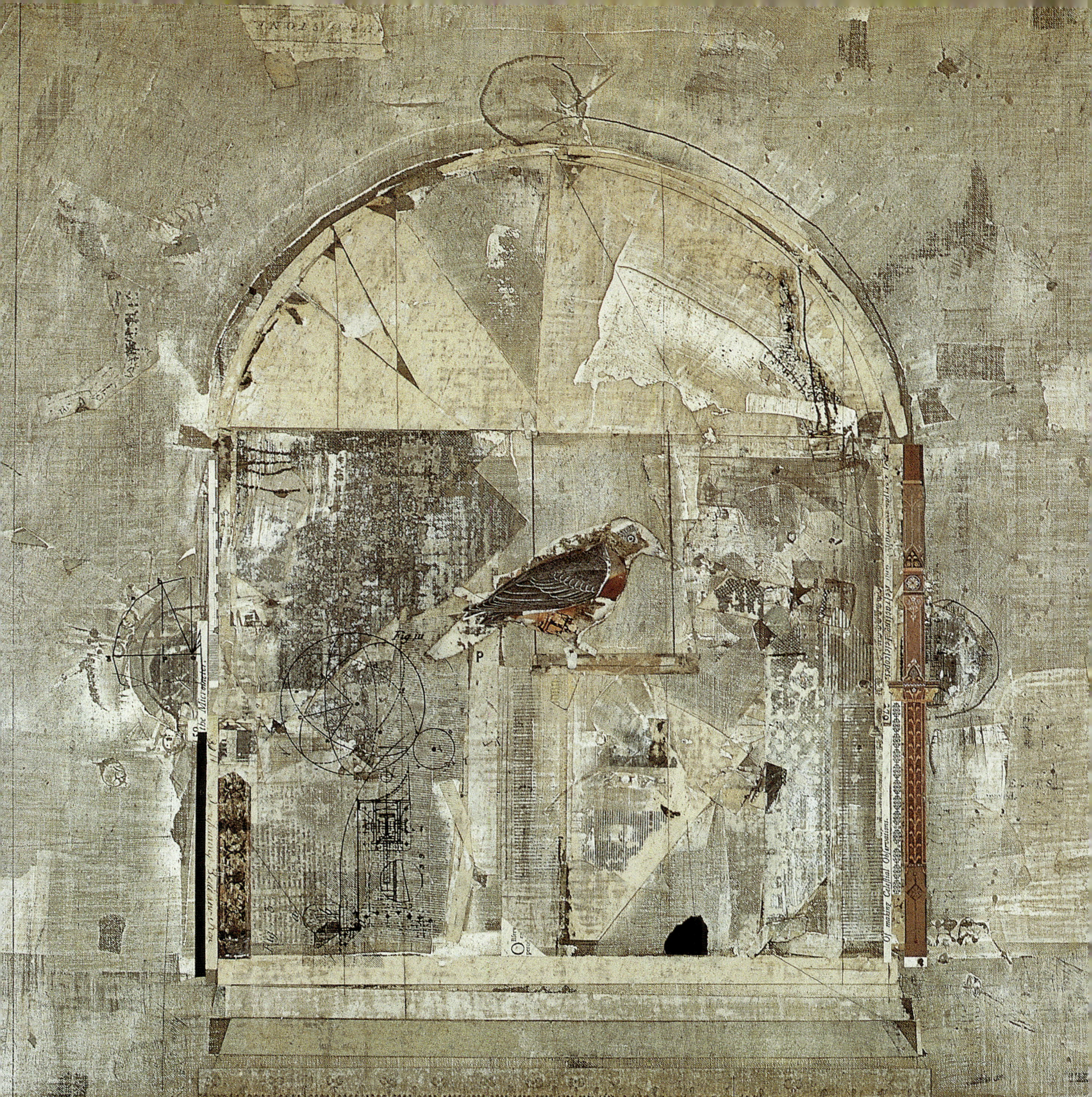
Refracting Telescopes.
270
Of making Celestial Observations.

62 | TAKEN 1997

Mixed media collage with flower, 14" x 13 7/8"

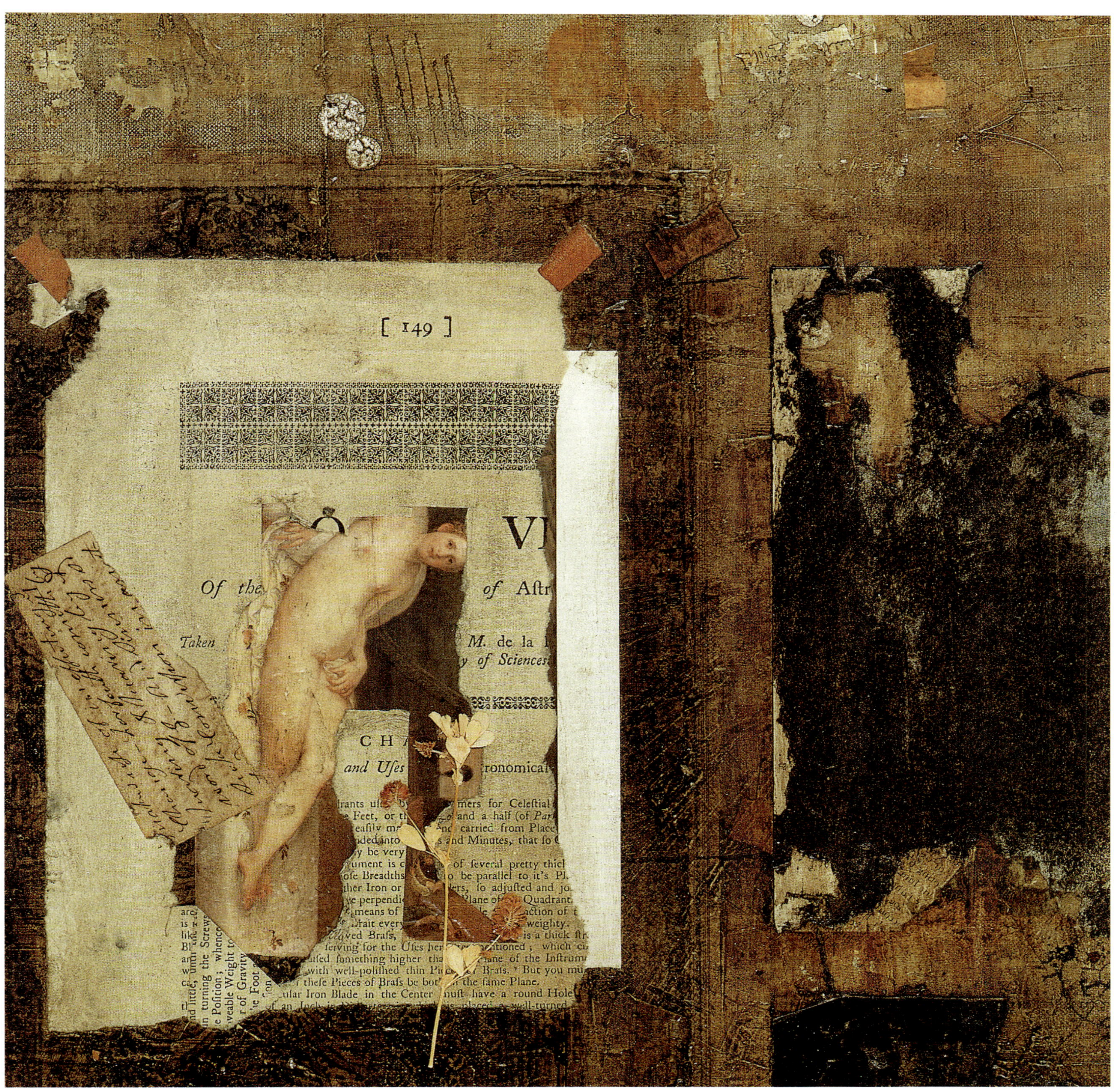

63 | NATIS 1998

Mixed media collage, 48" x 36"

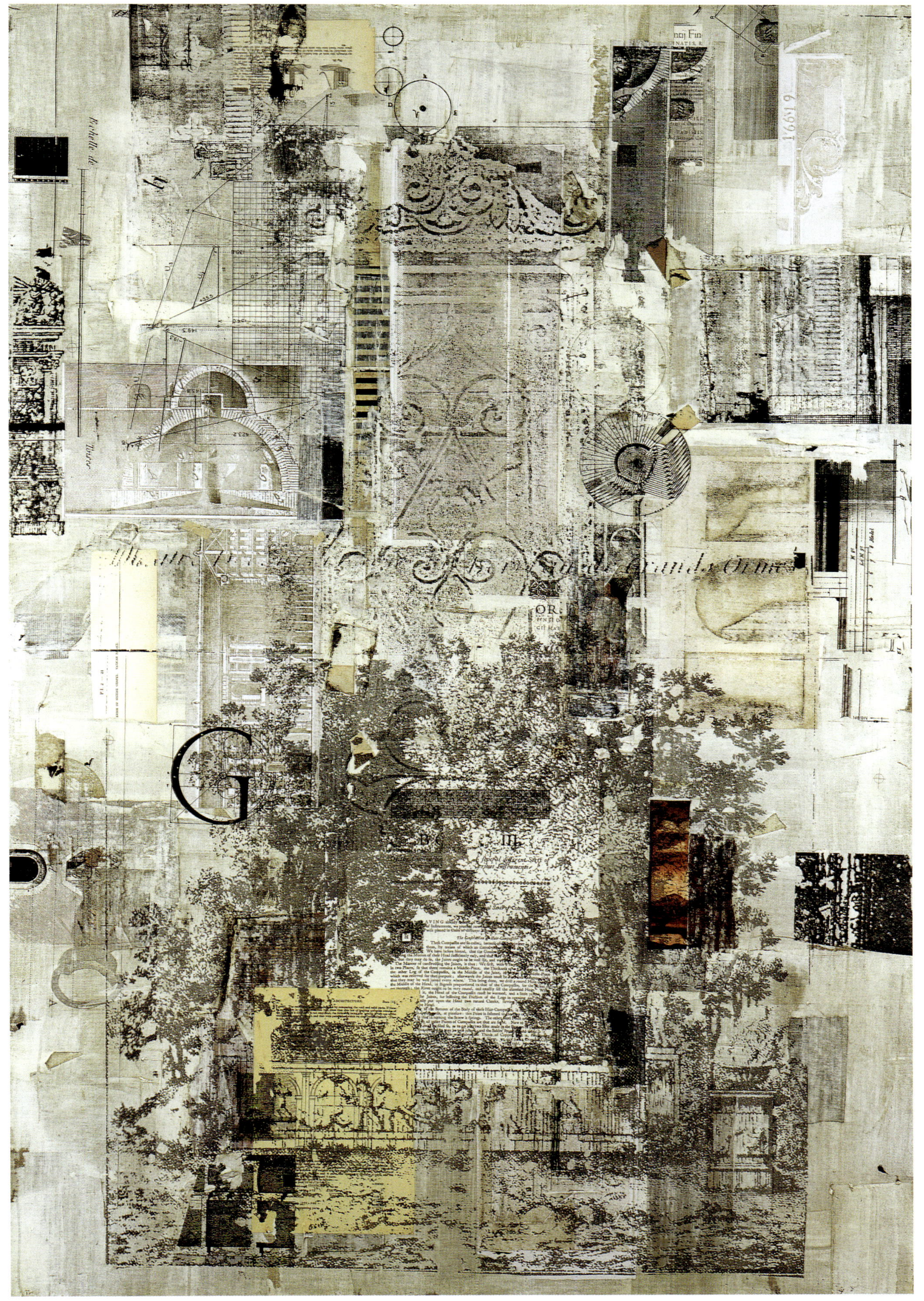

64 | CHAPEN 1998

Mixed media collage painting, 60" x 48"

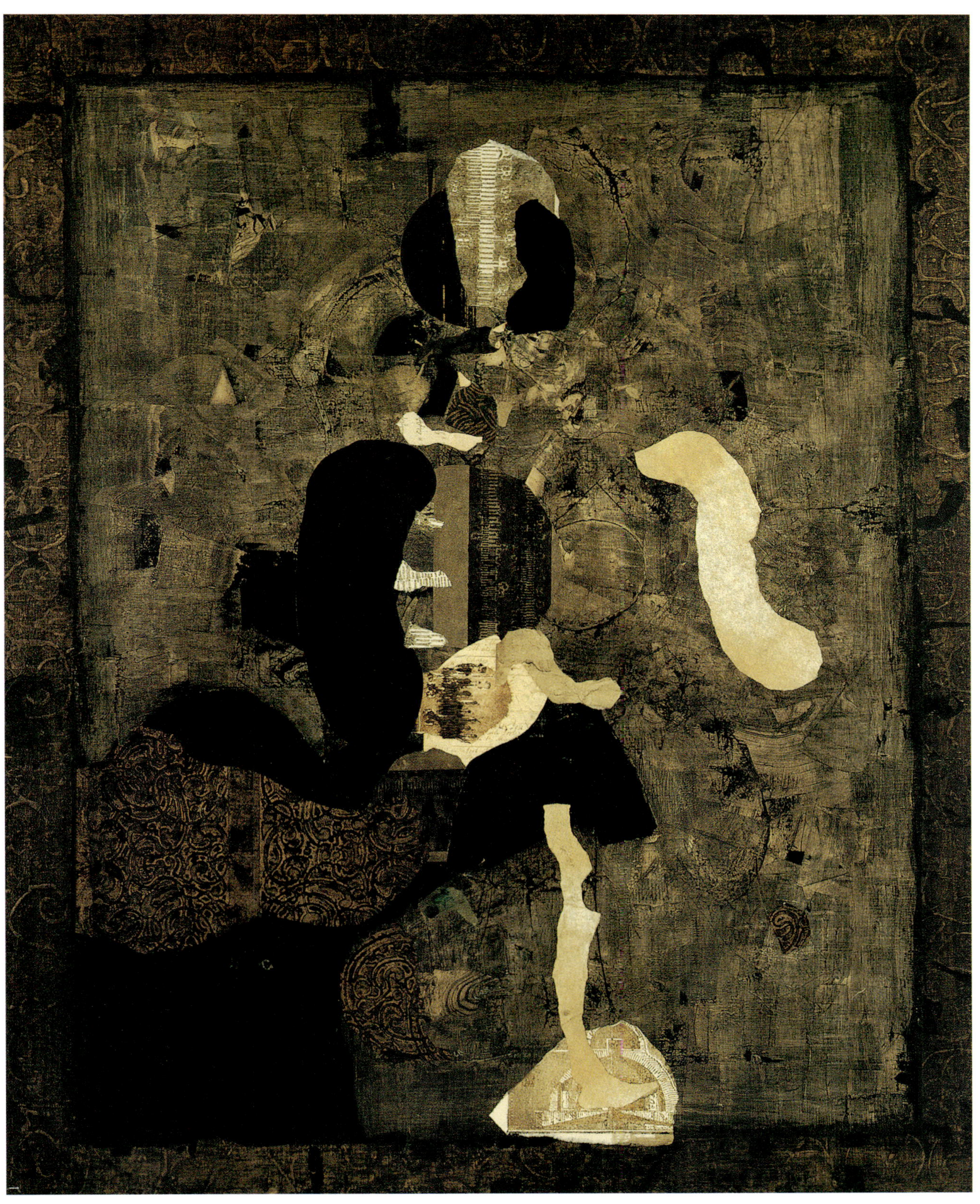

65 | QUEEN OF HEARTS 1994

Mixed media collage, 26 3/8" x 20 1/2"

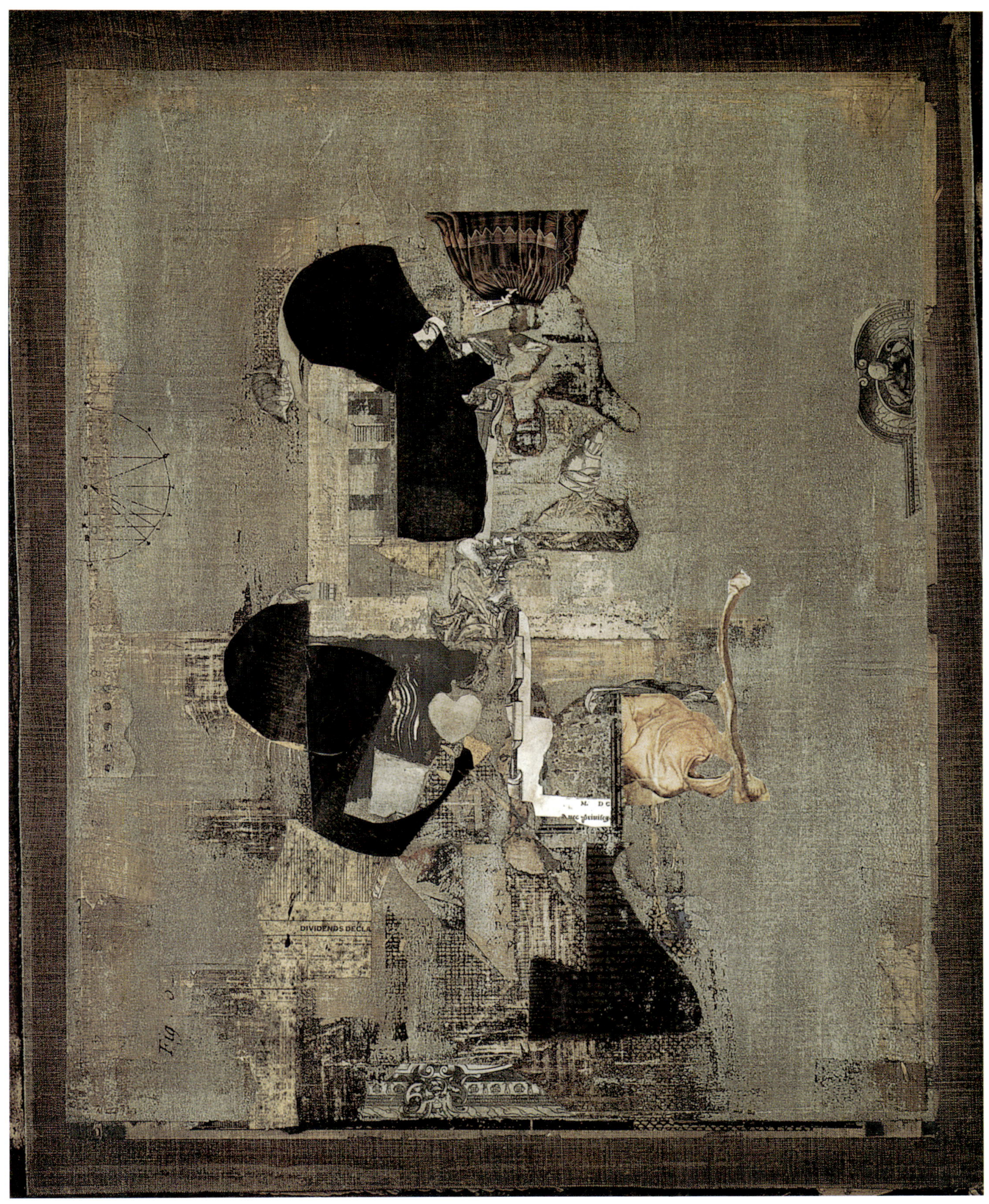

66 | MIRIFICI 2001

Collage painting on linen, 20 3/4" x 22 1/2"

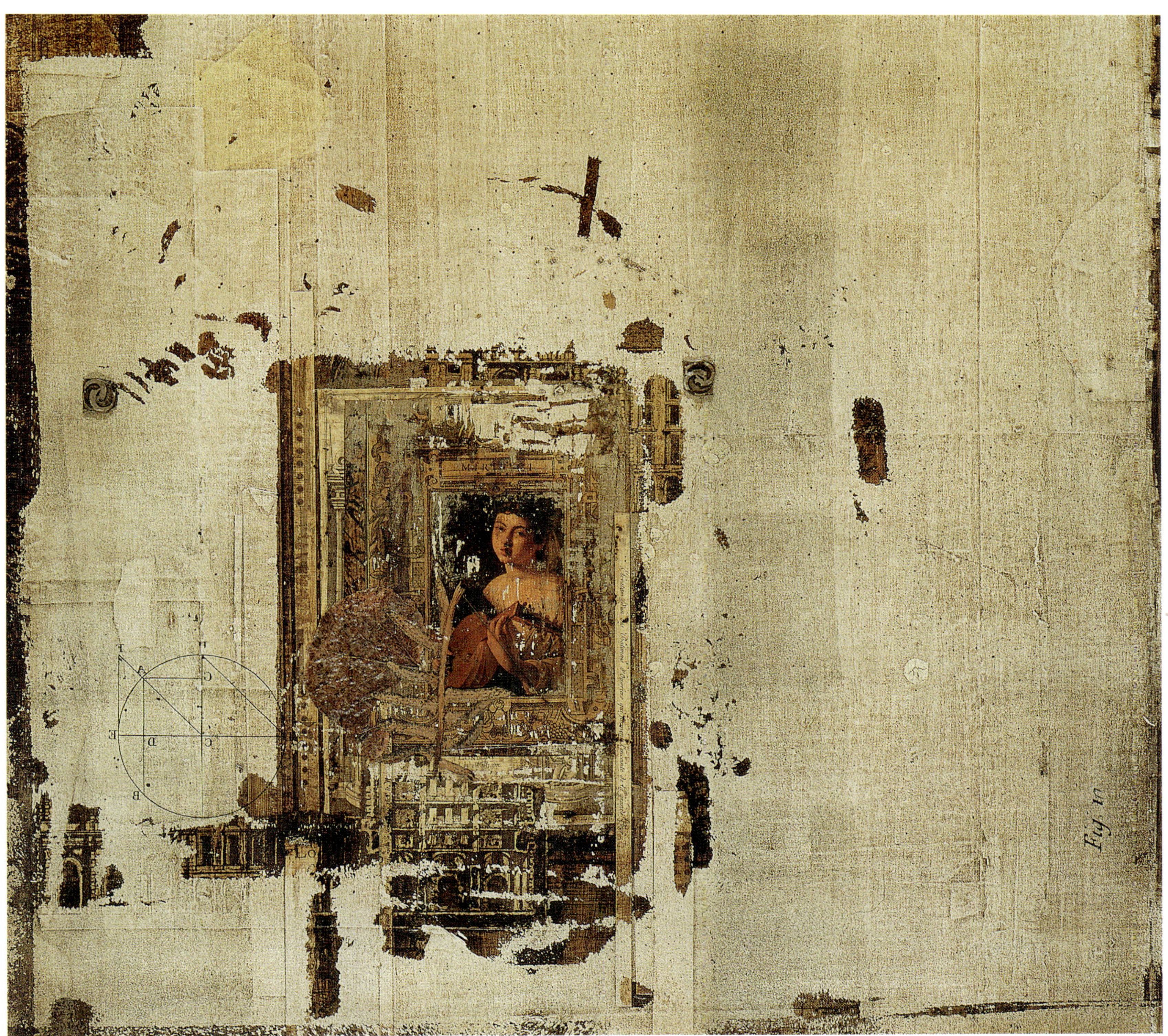

67 | A DARK FIGURE 1997

Mixed media collage, 50" x 50"

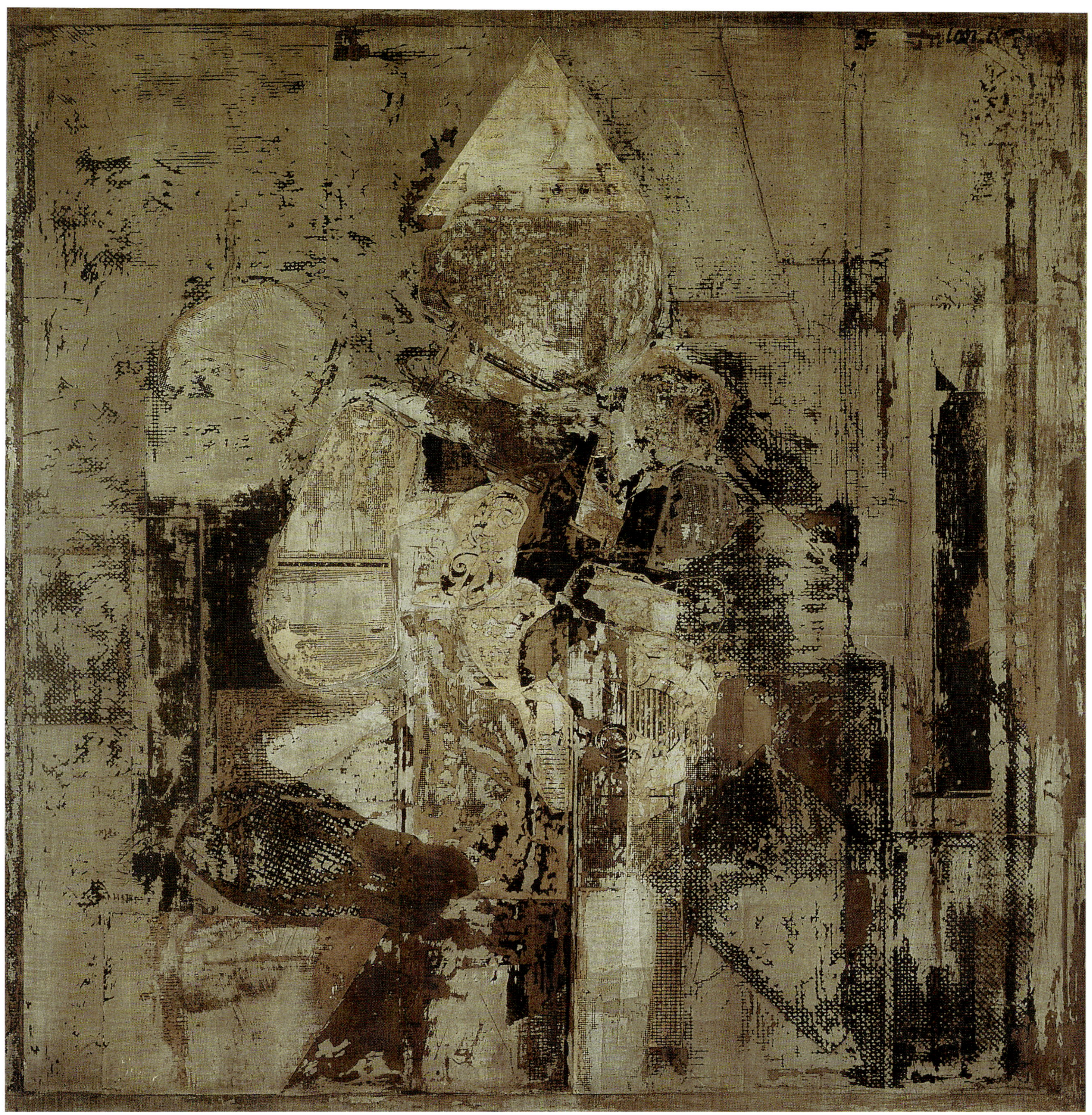

68 | LIAGRE 2002

Collage painting on linen, 60" x 48"

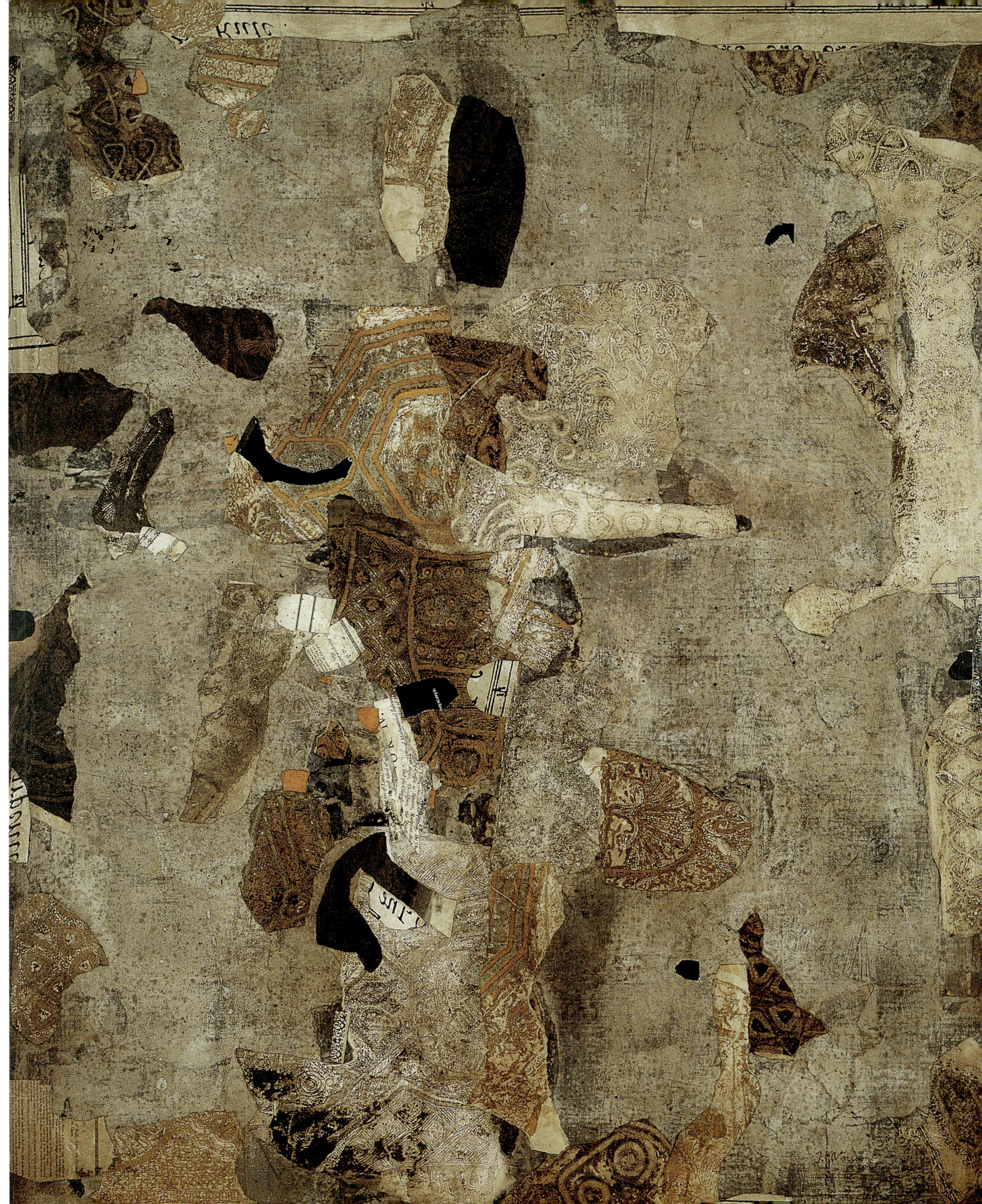

69 | THE G TREE 2000

Mixed media and photo transfer, 60" x 48"

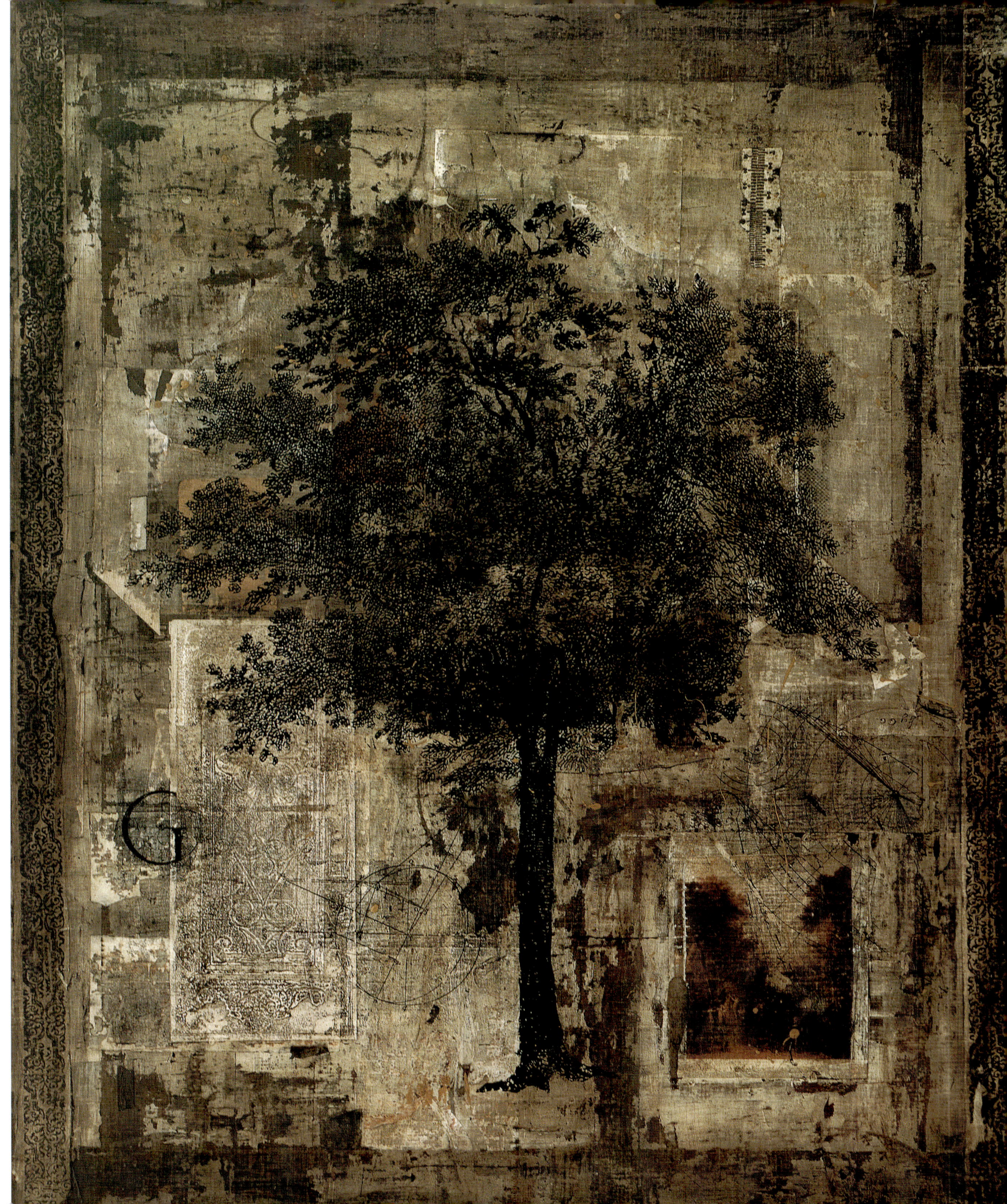

70 | MAYBE LISA 2001

Collage painting on linen, 31 1/2" x 24"

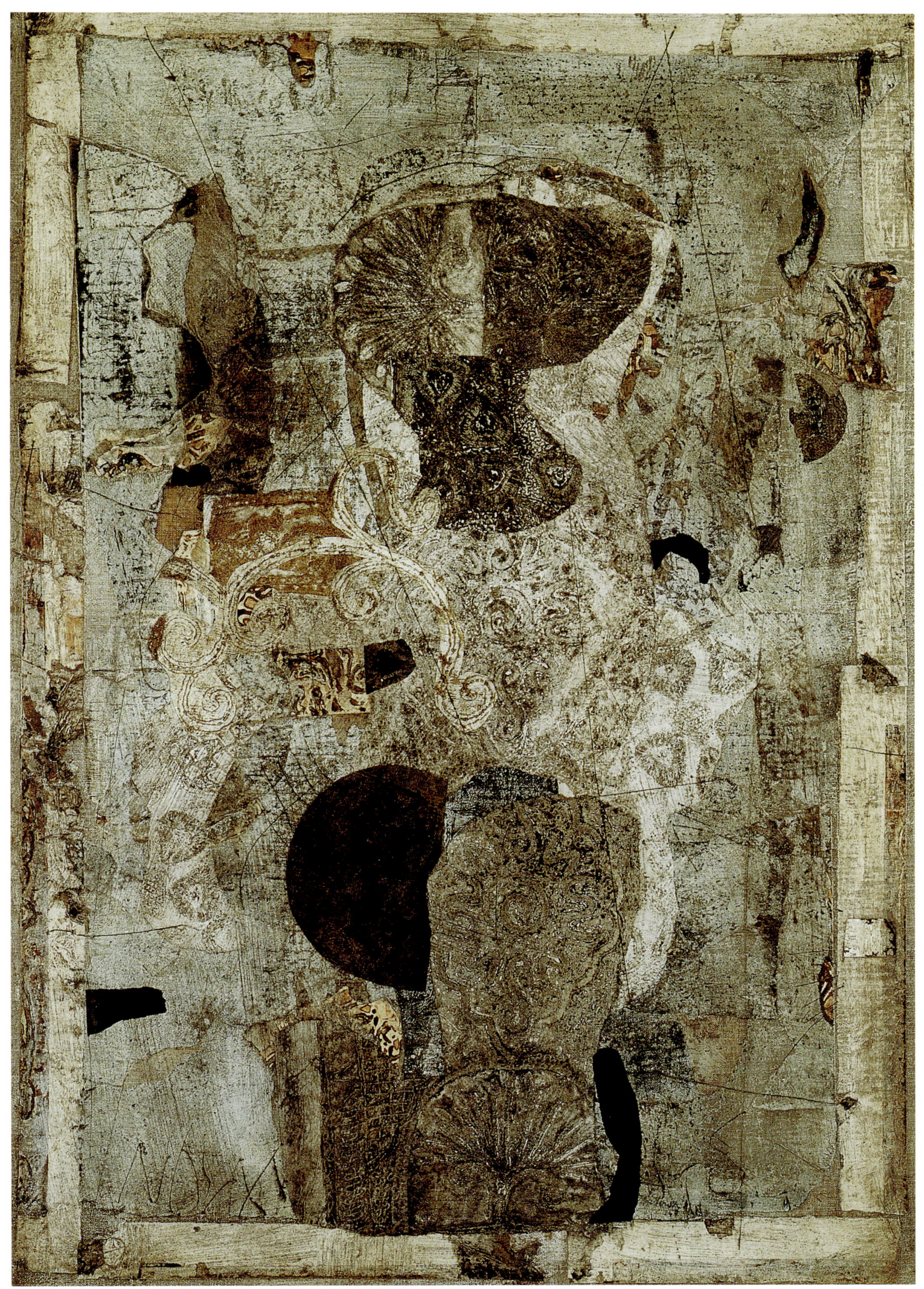

71 | 314 AND W 1997

Collage on board, 19" x 18 3/4"

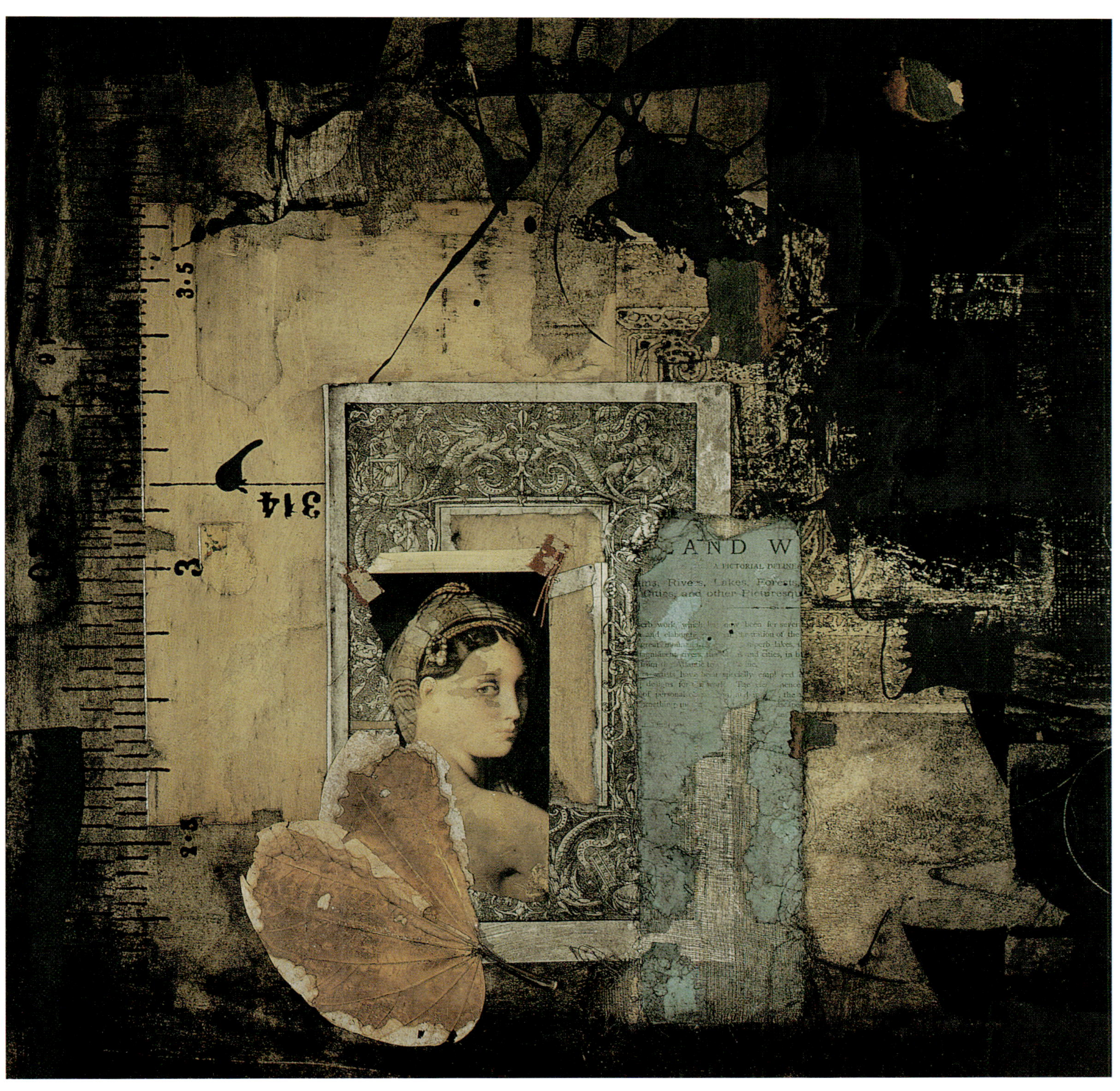
3.5
3
AND W
A PICTORIAL DELINE

72 | AESAREO 1993

Collage painting with metal type, 14" x 18"

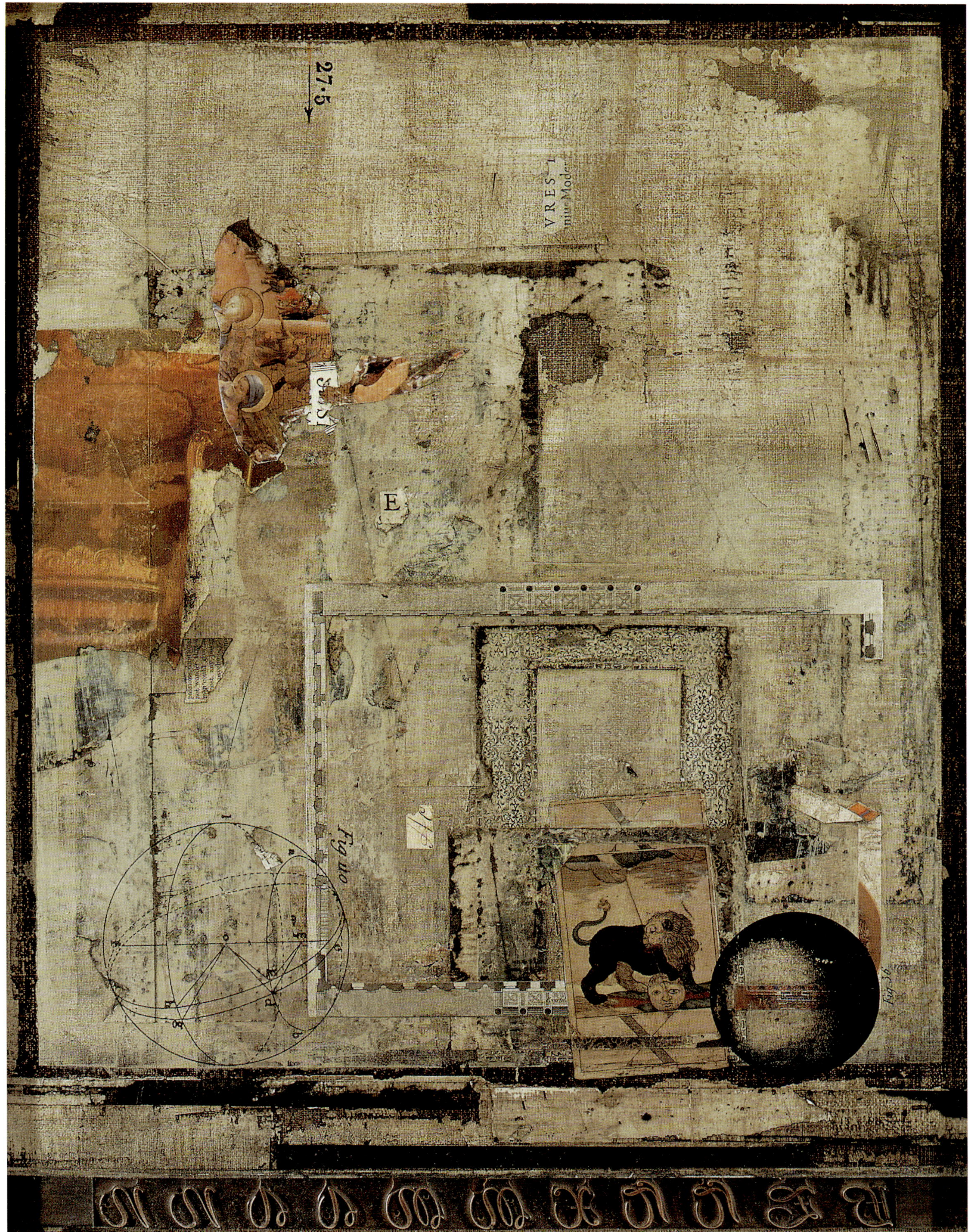

73 | MORETTOS REFLECTION 2001

Collage, photo transfer and flower, 19 1/2" x 17 /14"

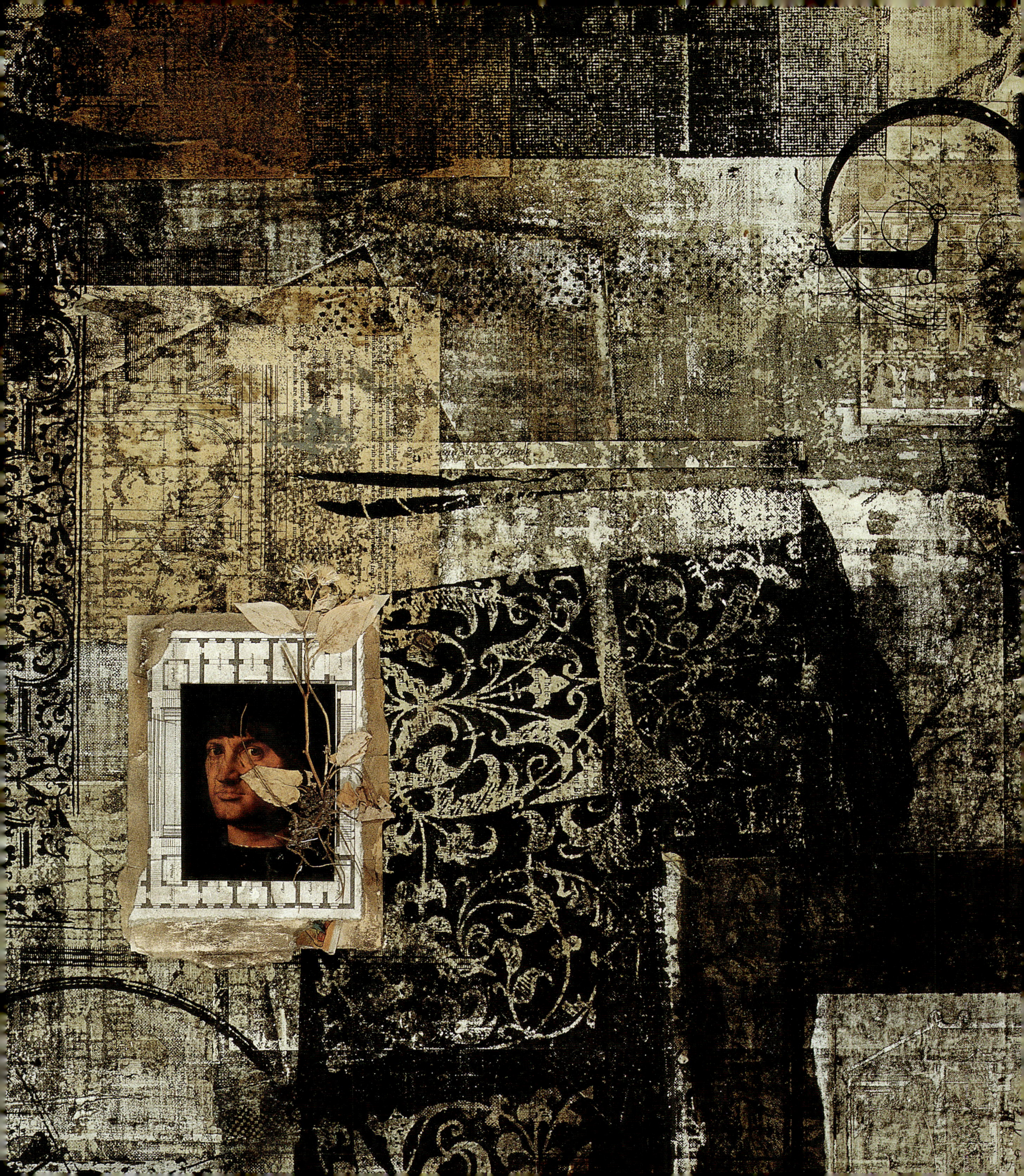

74 | UNTITLED 1992

Collage on paper, 18" x 14"

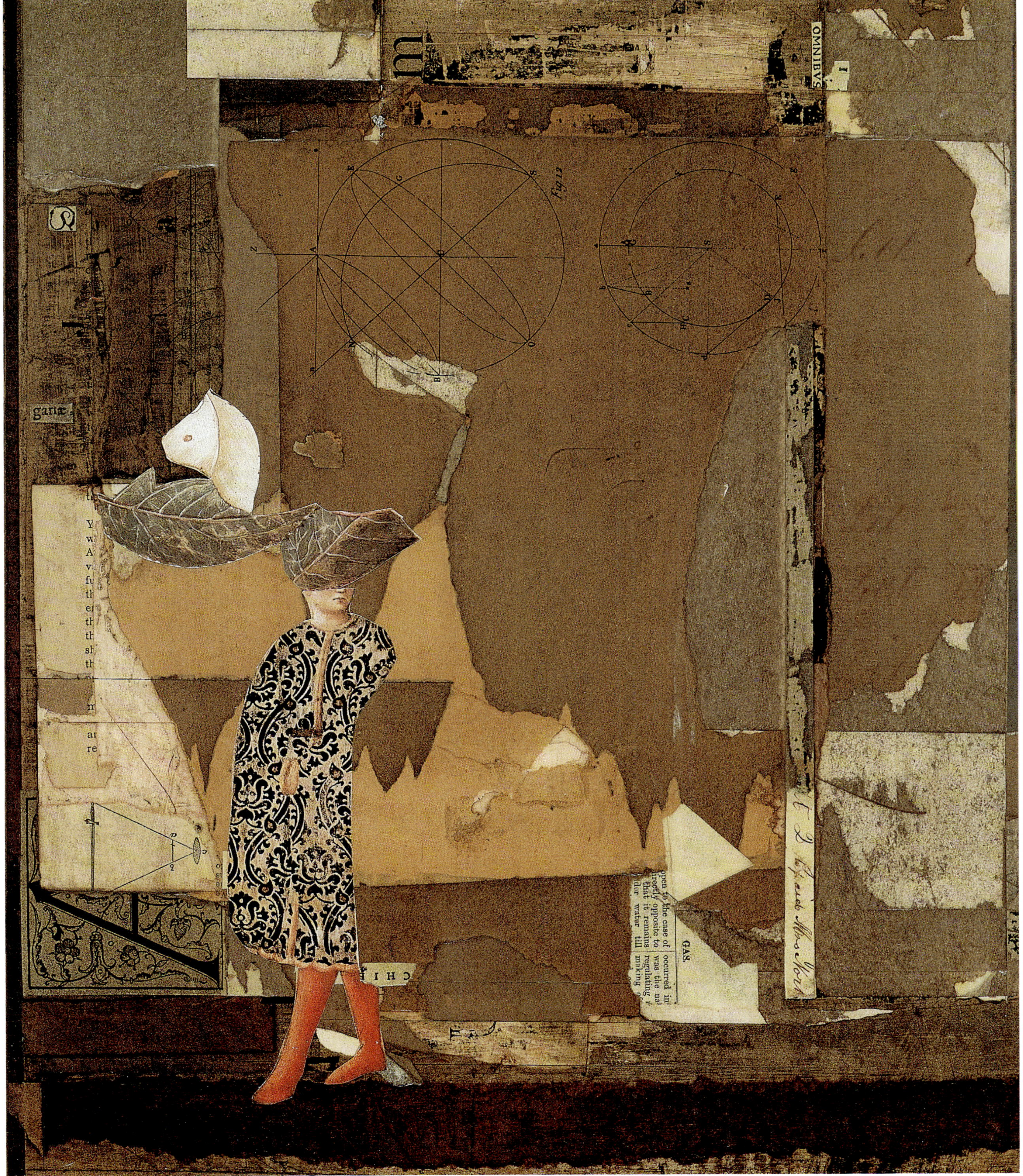

75 | IN THE GARDEN 1992

Collage painting, 24" x 21"

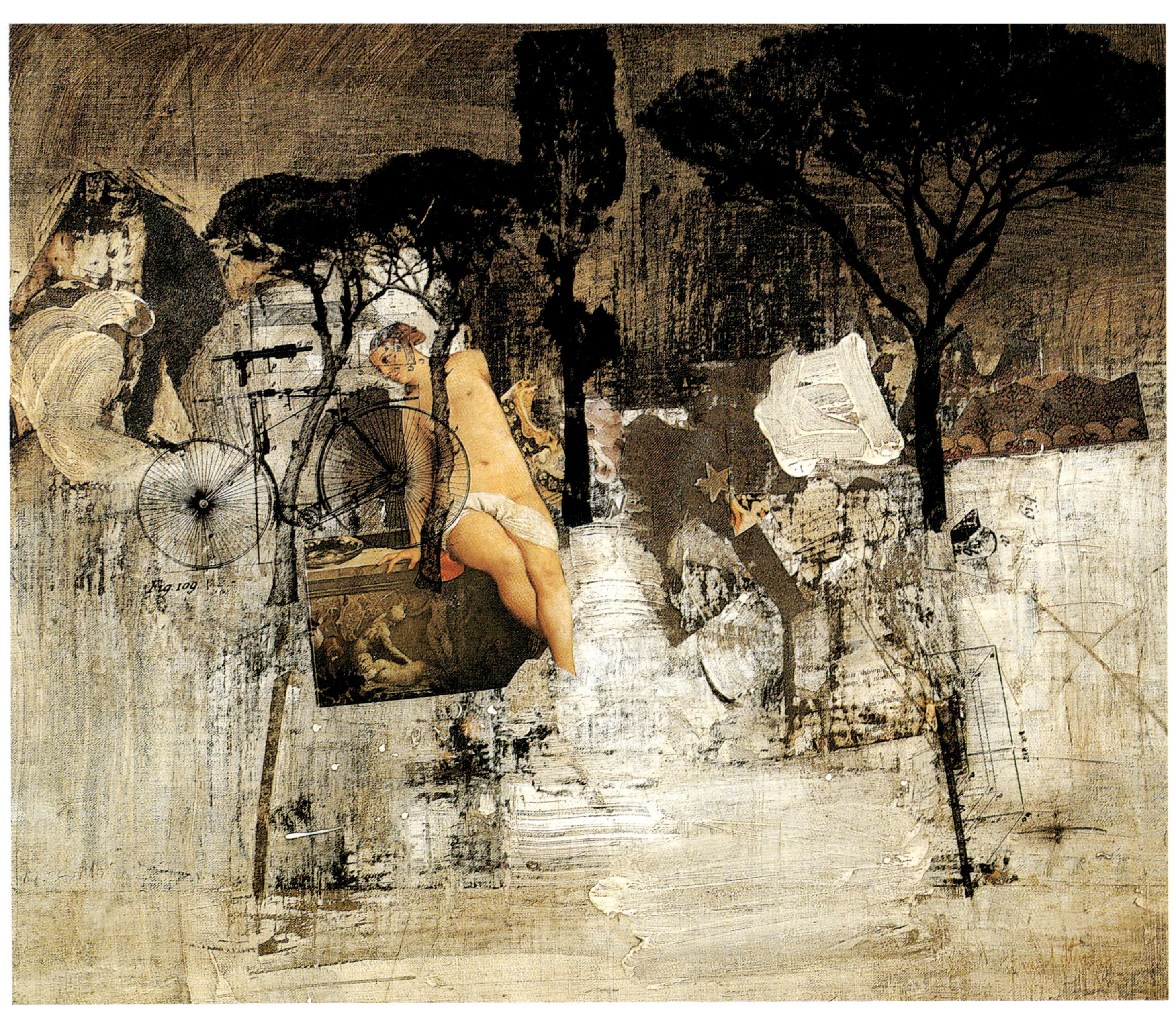
Fig. 109

76 | UNTITLED 1998

Collage on linen, 60" x 48"

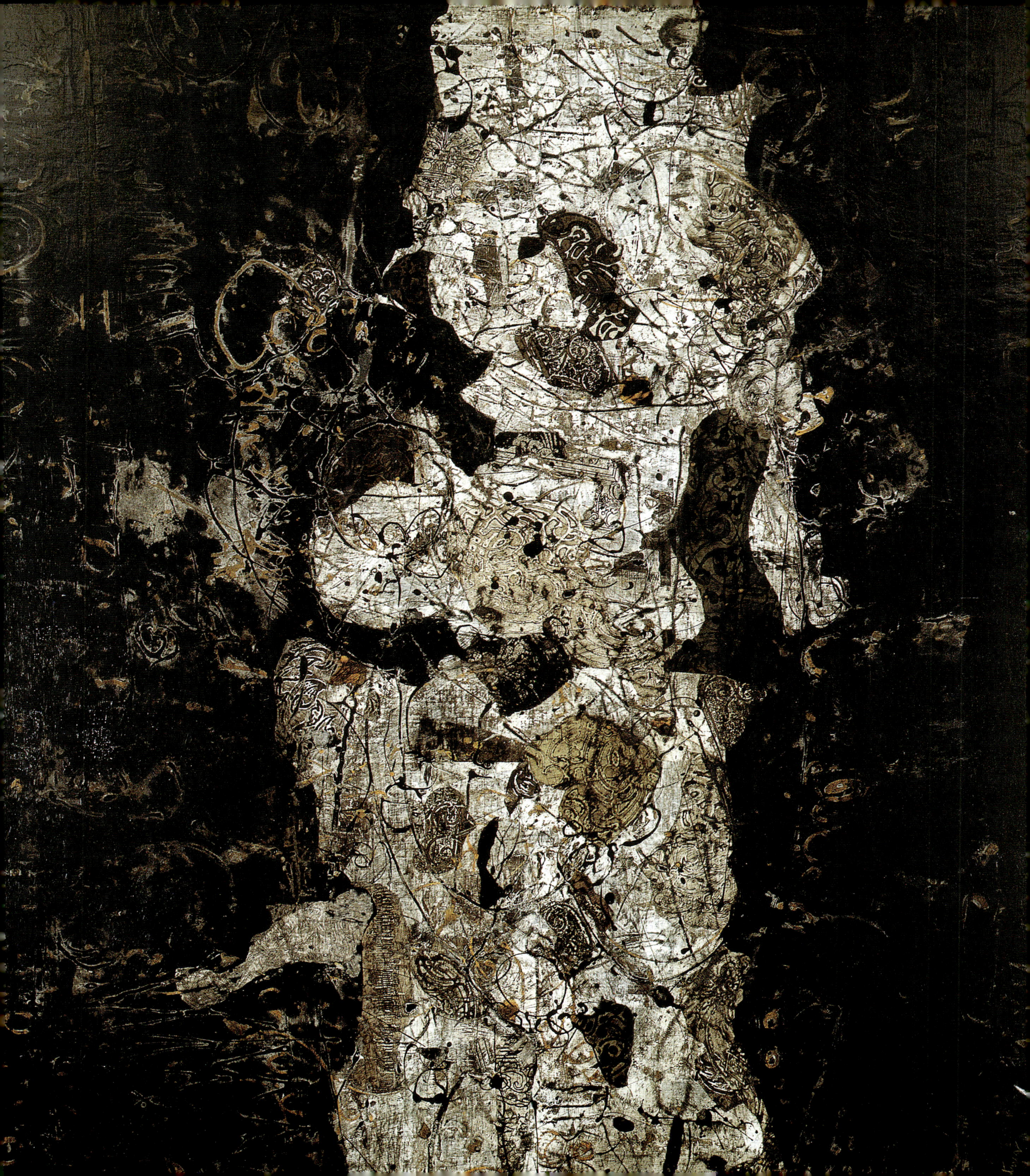

77 | INTERVAL 2000

Mixed media collage on linen, 29 1/2" x 28 3/4"

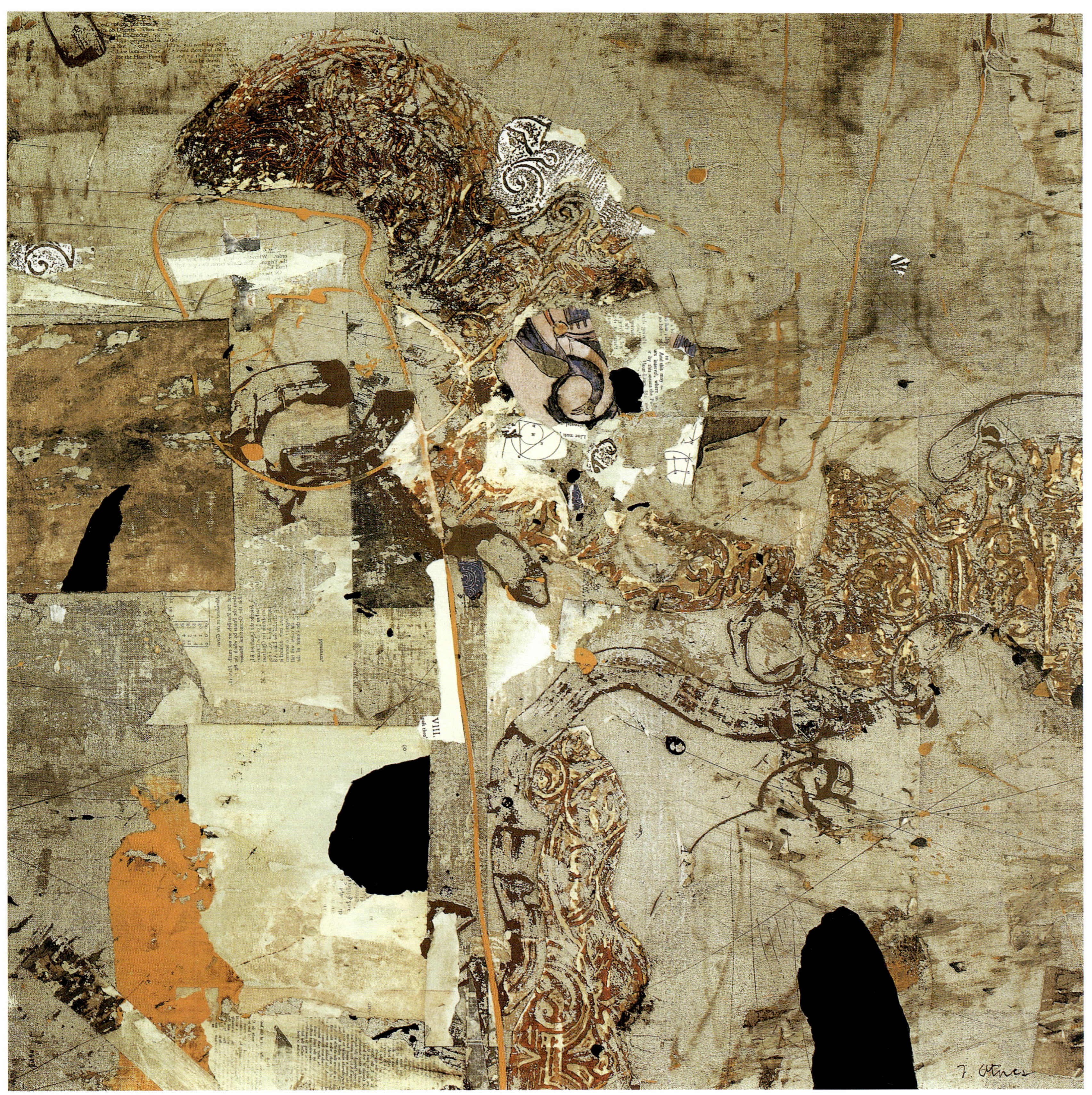

78 | SILENT FIGURE 1999

Collage painting, 34 1/2" x 29 1/2"

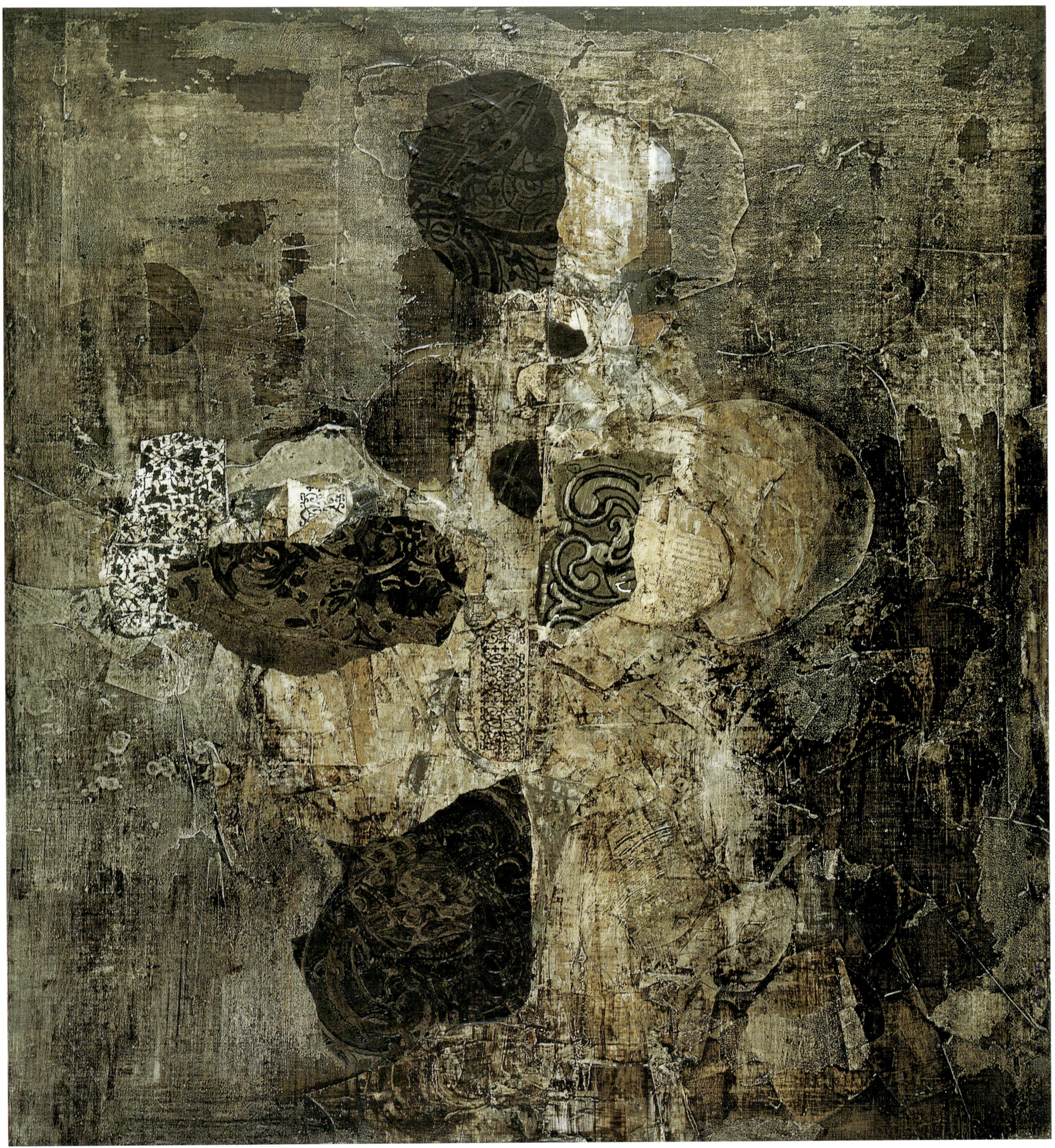

79 | MATHEMA 1998

Mixed media collage, 41 1/2" x 33 1/2"

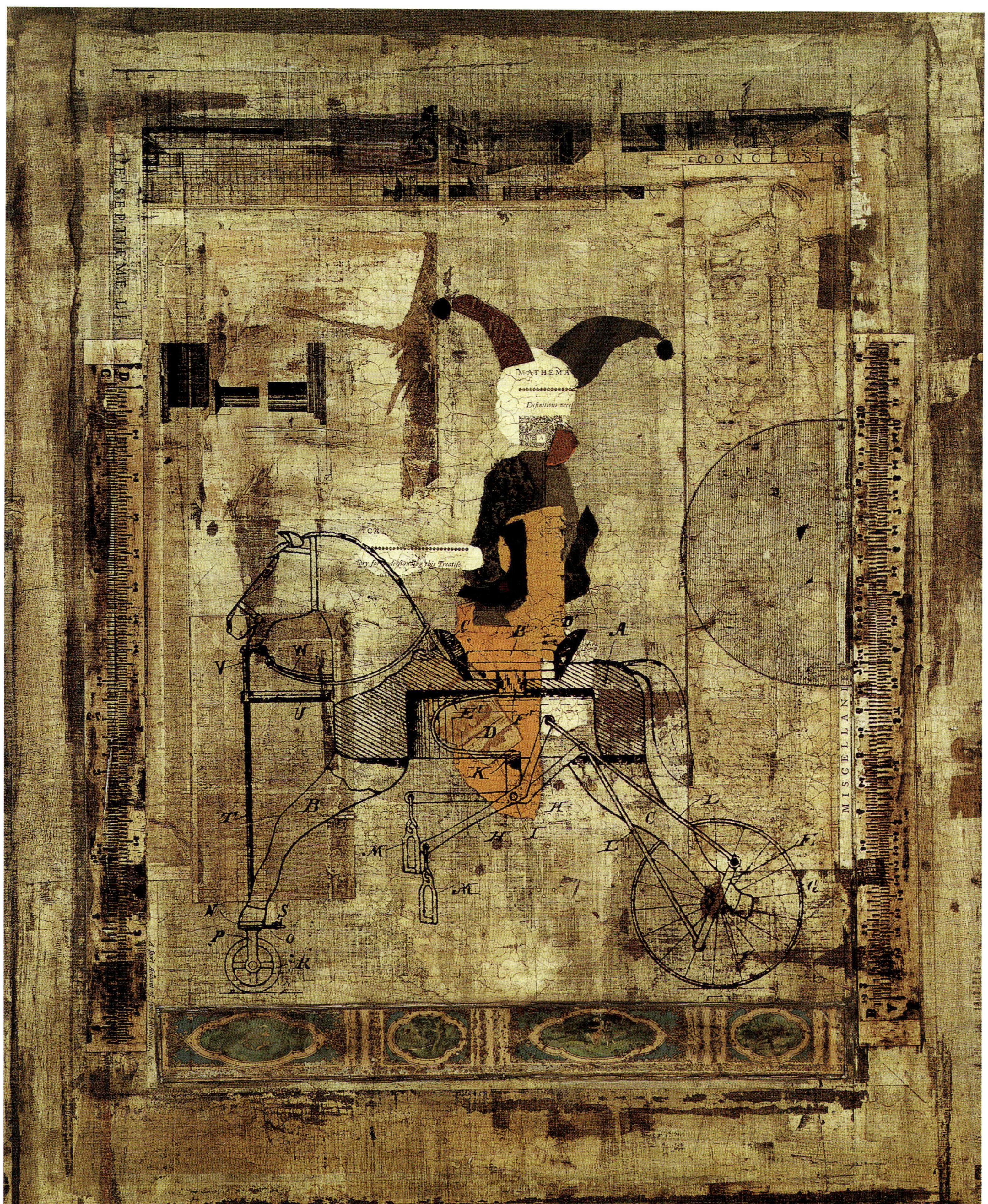
CONCLUSIO
MATHEMA
MISCELLANI

80 | UNTITLED 1998

Collage and photo transfer, 22" x 32"

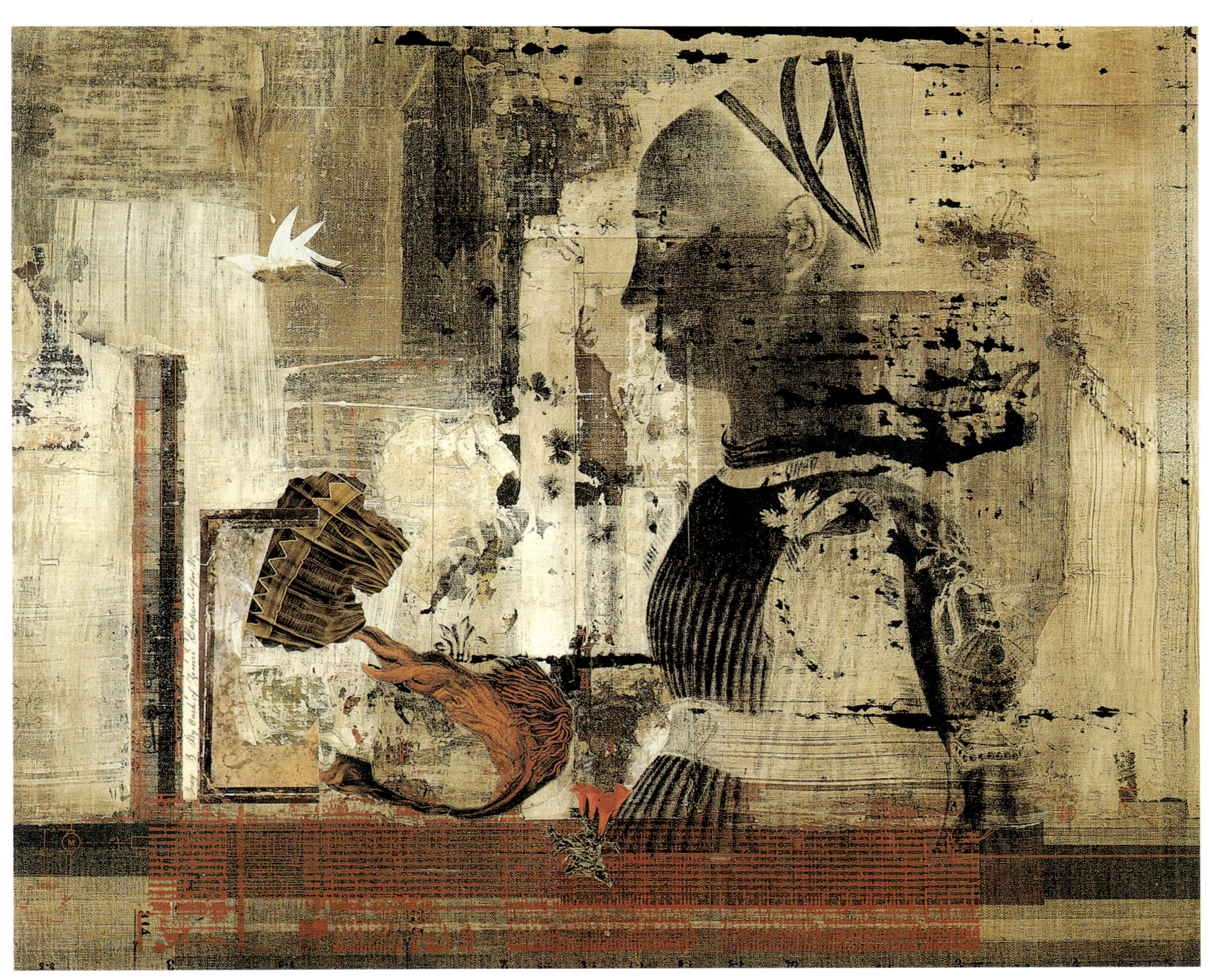

81 | POLLAI 2001

Collage painting on linen, 33 3/4" x 27 1/2"

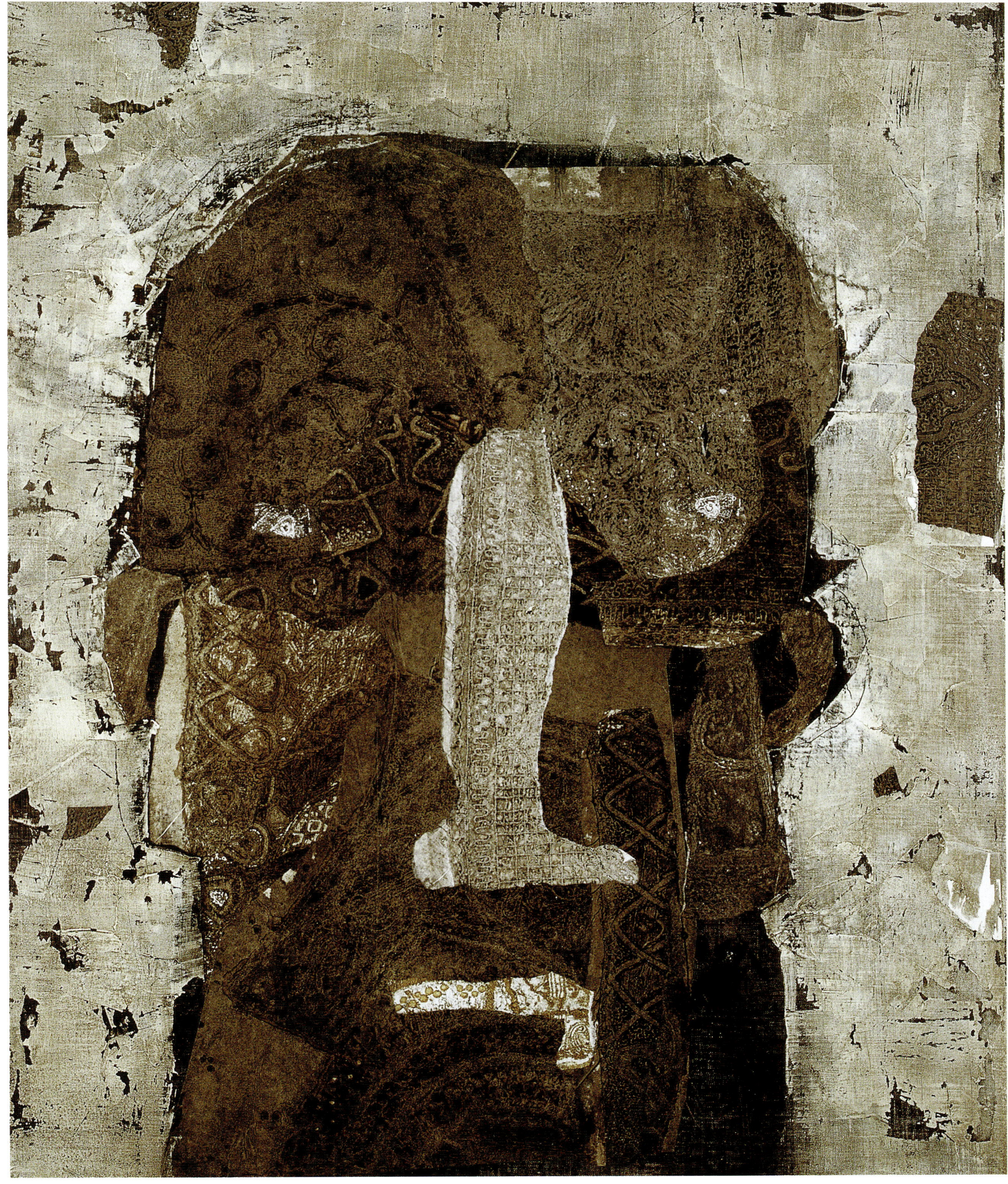

82 | THE JESTER 2000

Mixed media collage painting, 38" x 38"

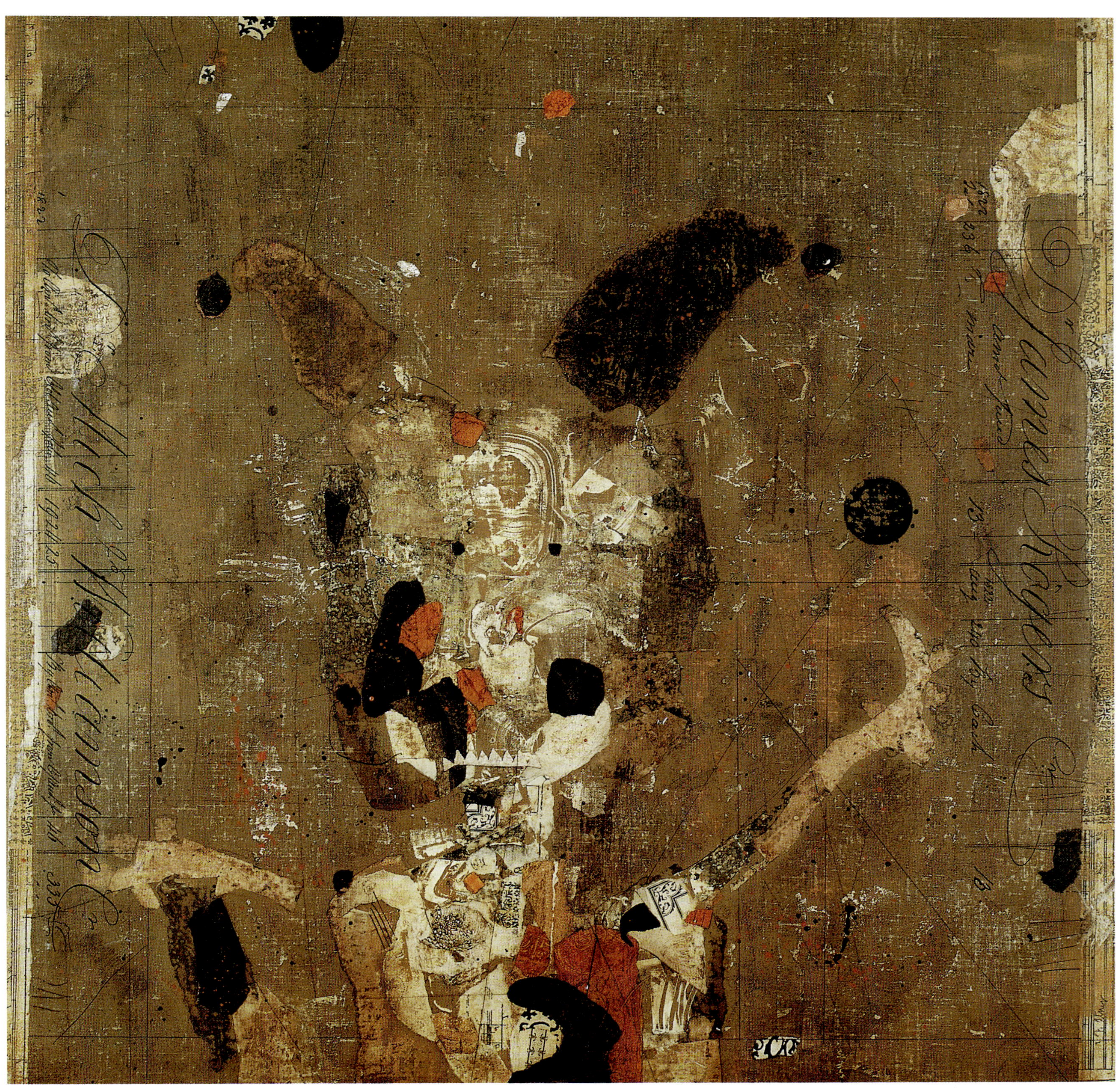

83 | FLAYED 2000

Mixed media collage painting, 22 1/4" x 19 3/8"

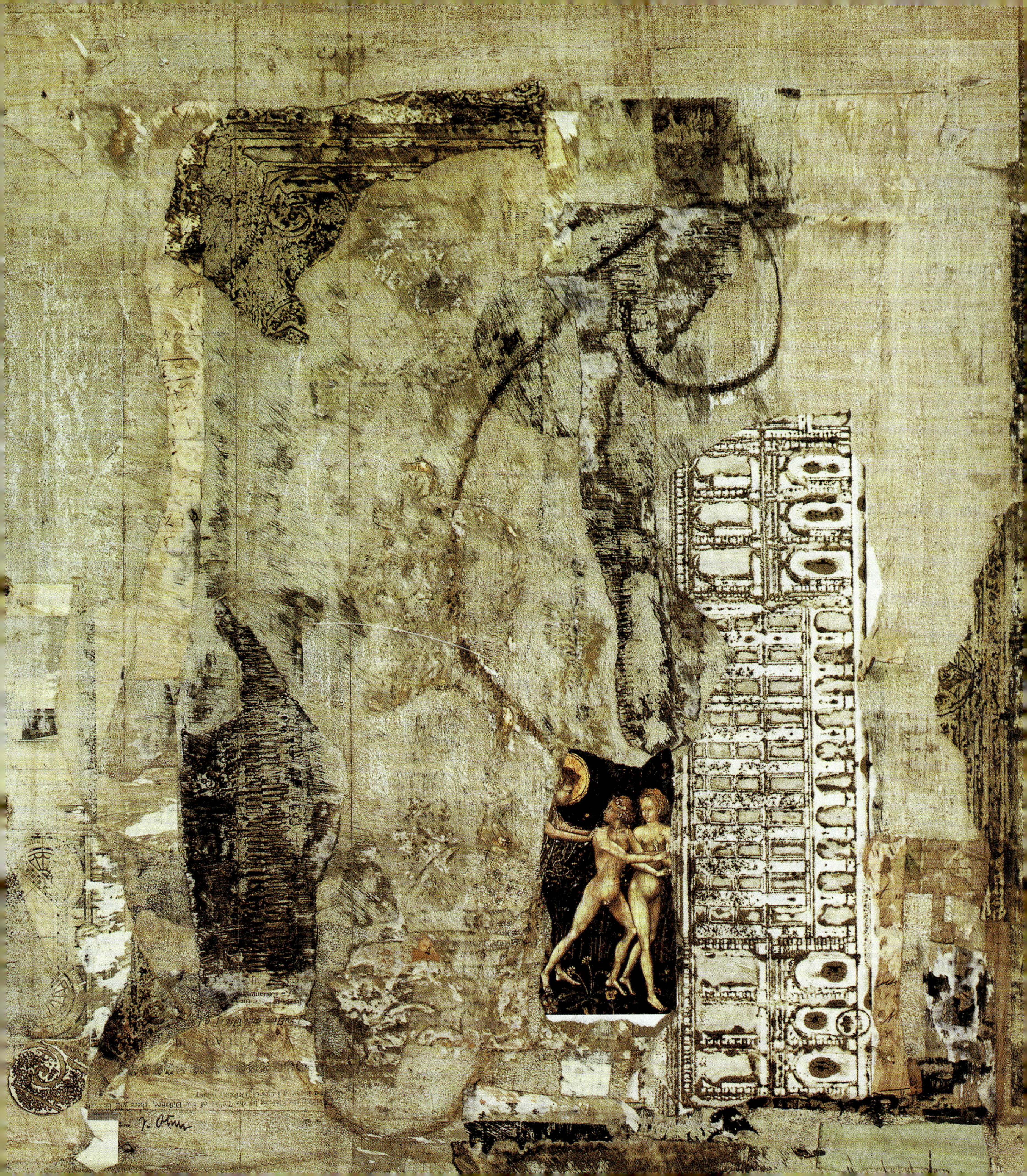

84 | COLINES 1998

Mixed media assemblage, 39 3/8" x 31 /14"

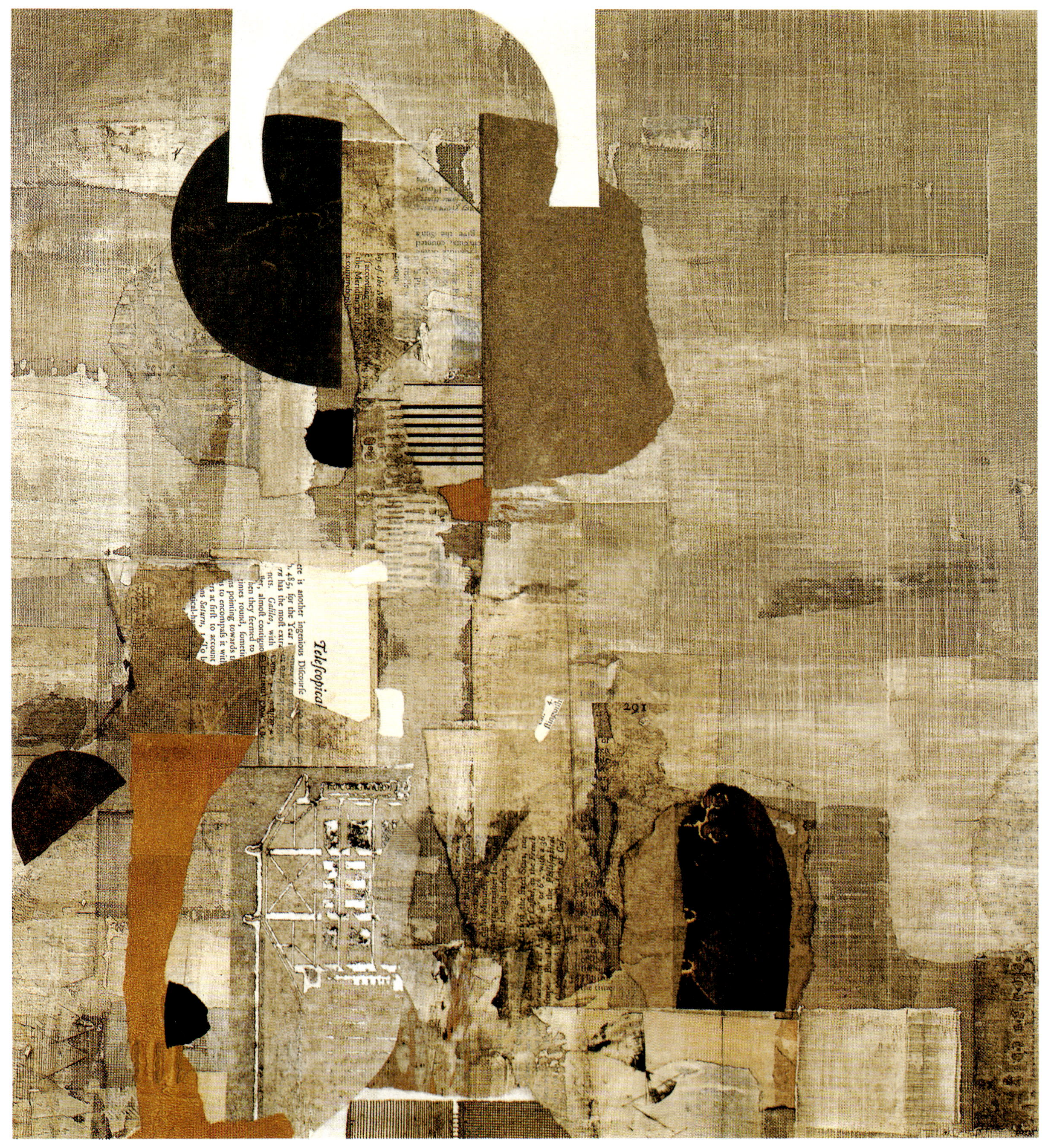
Teleſcopical

85 | JOACHIM 2001

Collage painting on linen, 21" x 19 1/2"

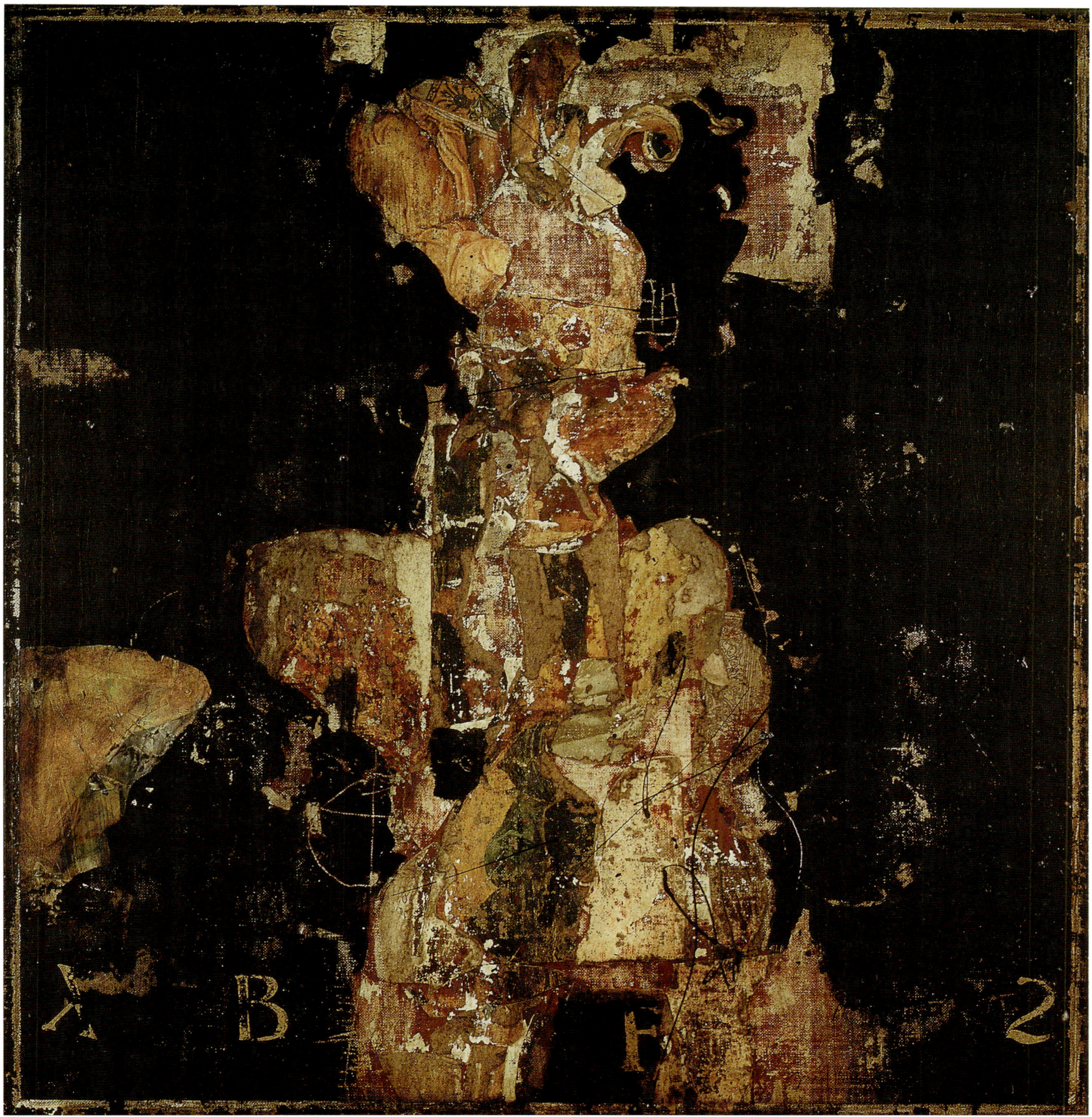
B
F
2

86 | HOMAGE TO BRONZINO 1997

Mixed media collage painting with photo transfer, 48 1/4" x 44 1/2"

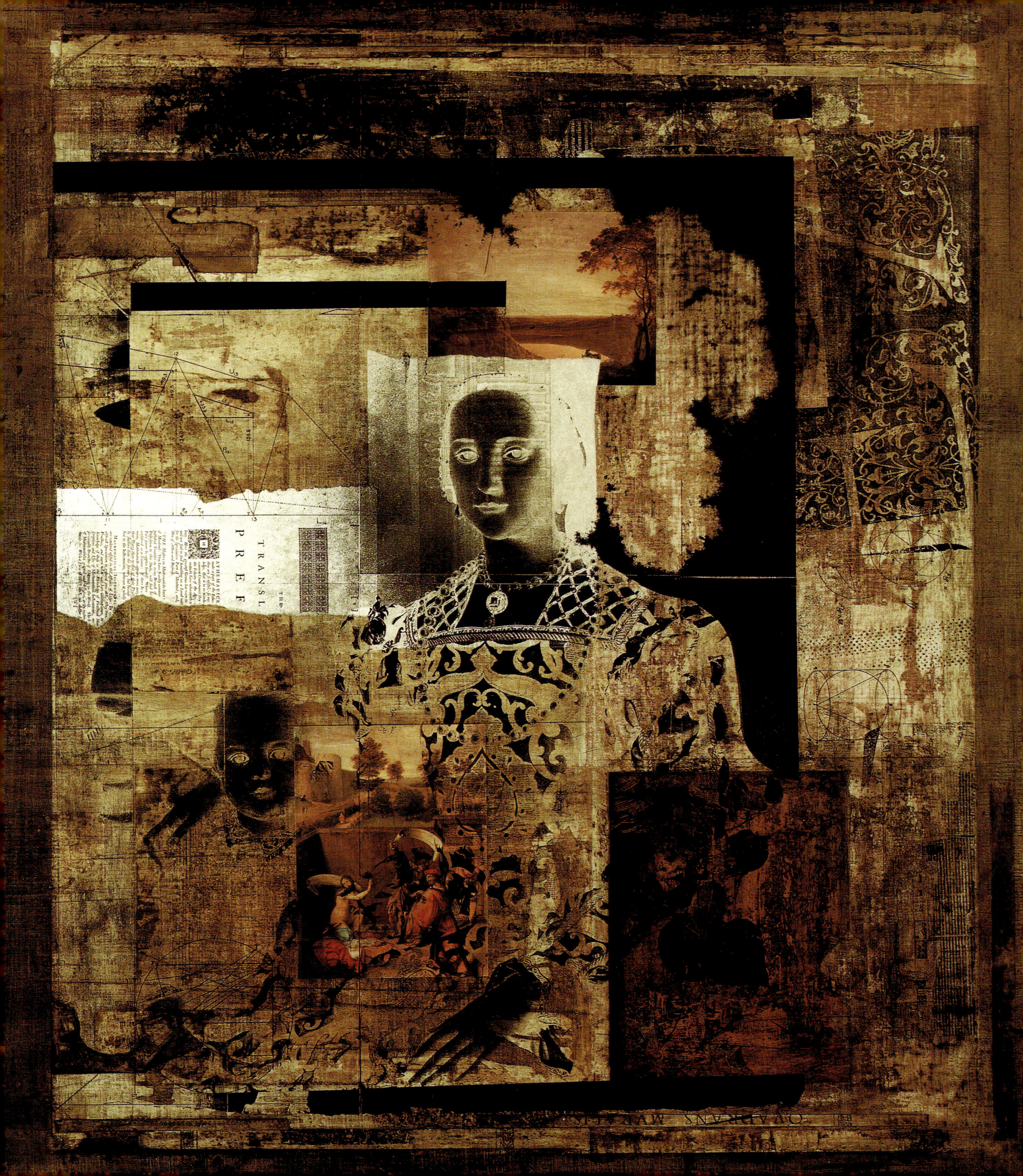

87 | VERTICAL L 1995

Collage painting, 53" x 35 1/2"

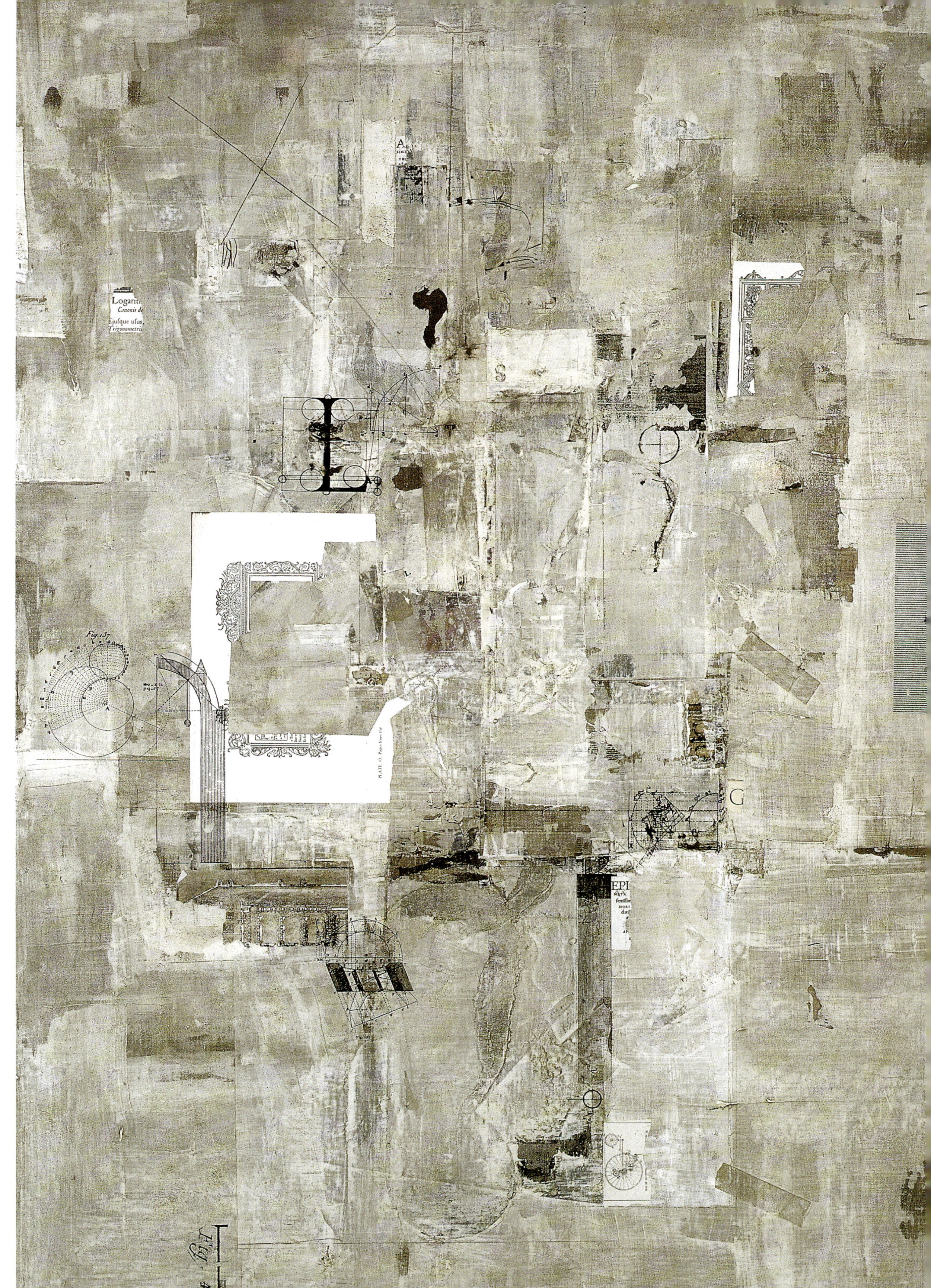

88 | THE FLOWERING TREE 1994

Mixed media collage, 17 1/4" x 13"

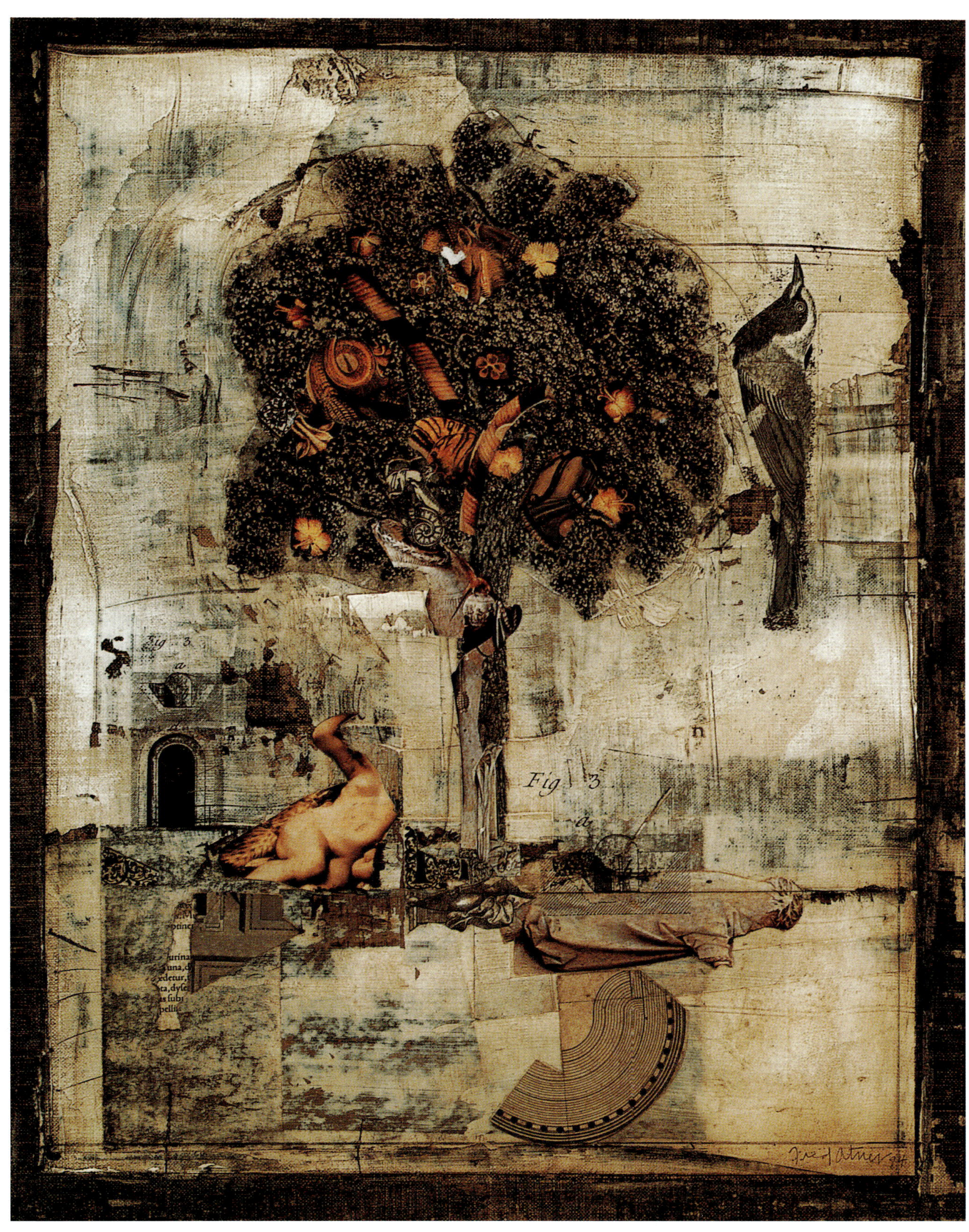

89 | PIERO 1992

Mixed media collage, 41" x 37"

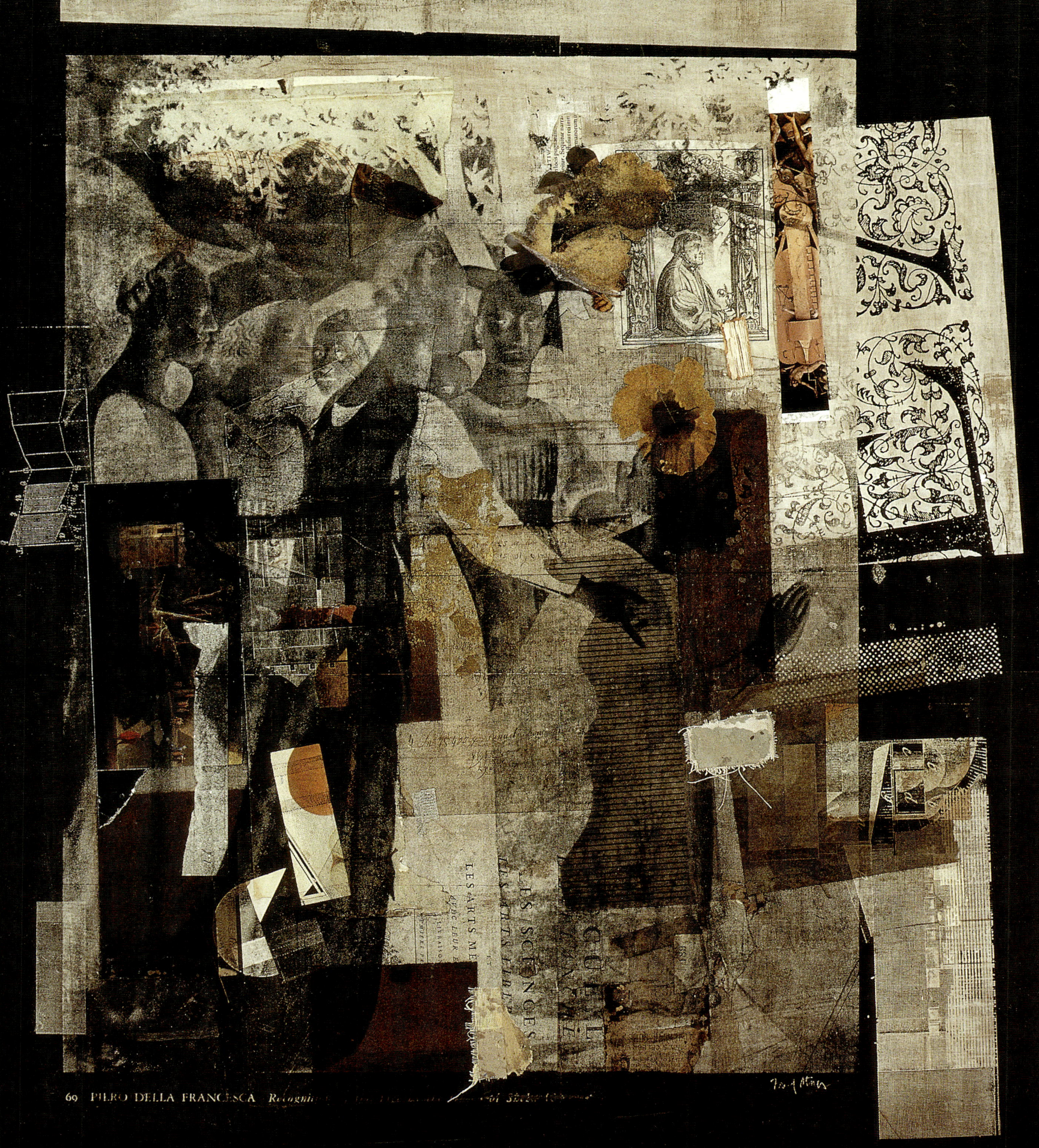

69 PIERO DELLA FRANCESCA
LES ARTS ME
LES SCIENCES

90 | THE TIMES MAN 1999

Mixed media collage, 40" x 31 3/4"

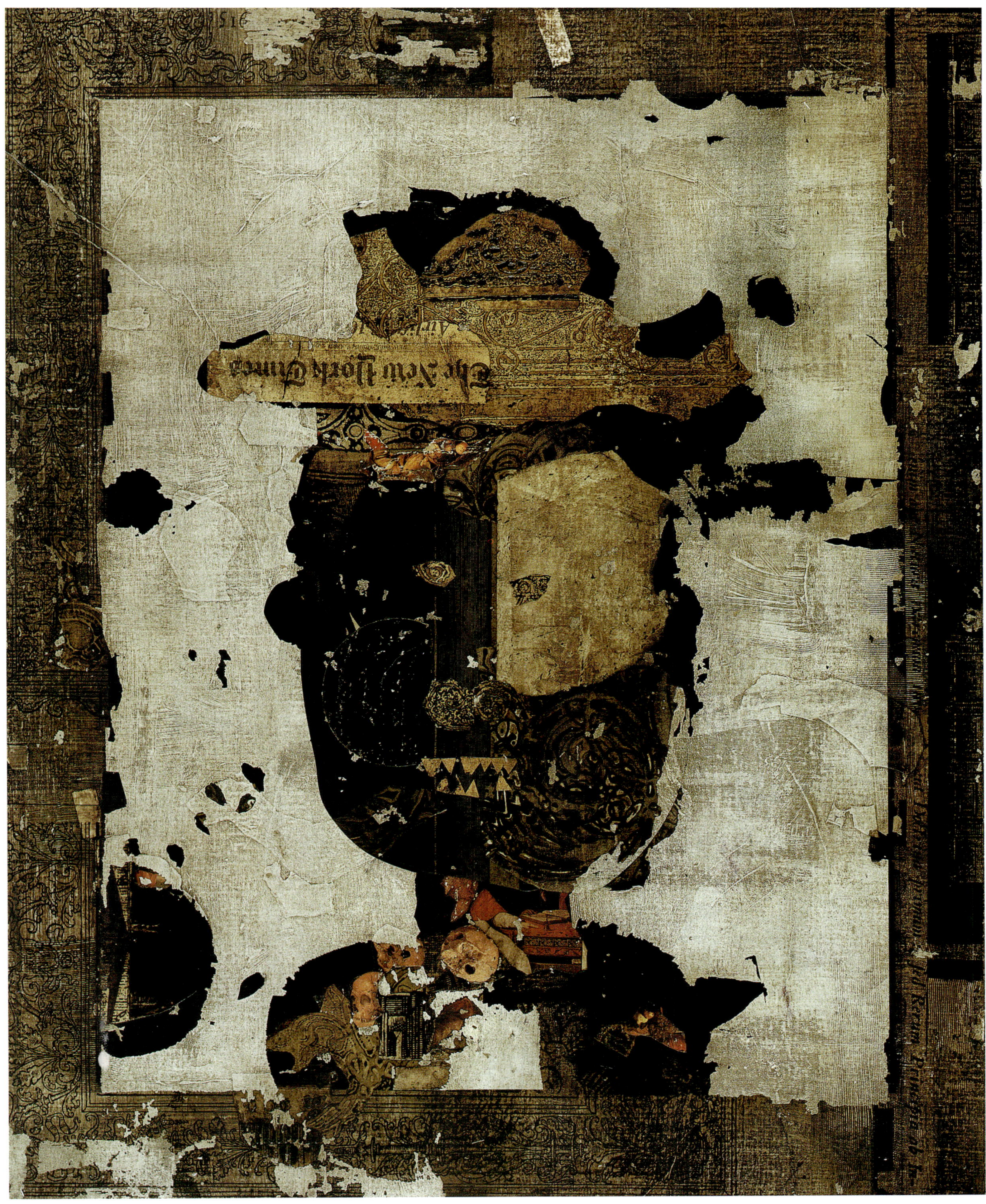

91 | JOURNEY TO SIYAH GALEM 1997

Collage painting, 20 5/8" x 22 3/4"

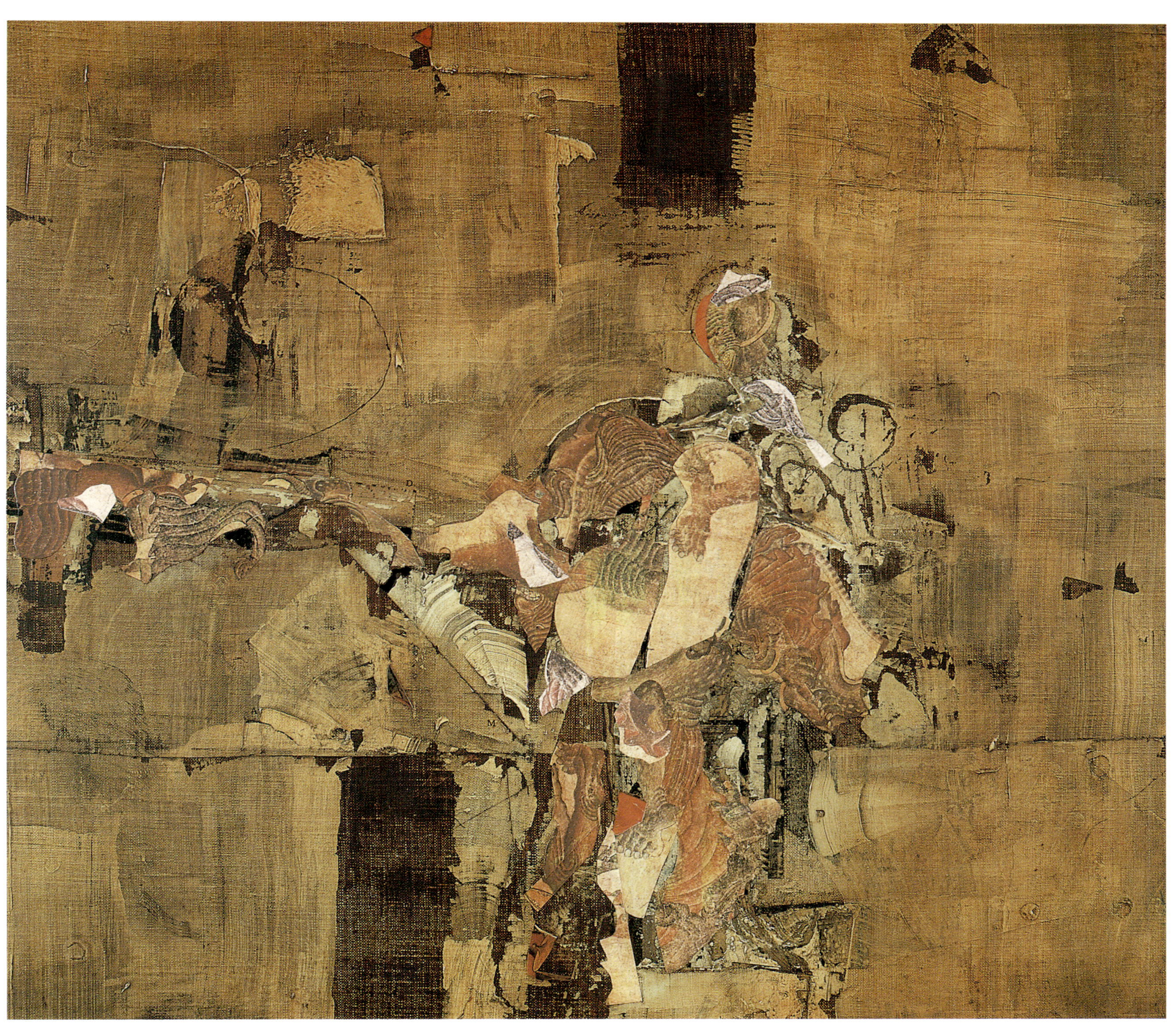

92 | UNTITLED 2000

Collage painting, 40" x 27"

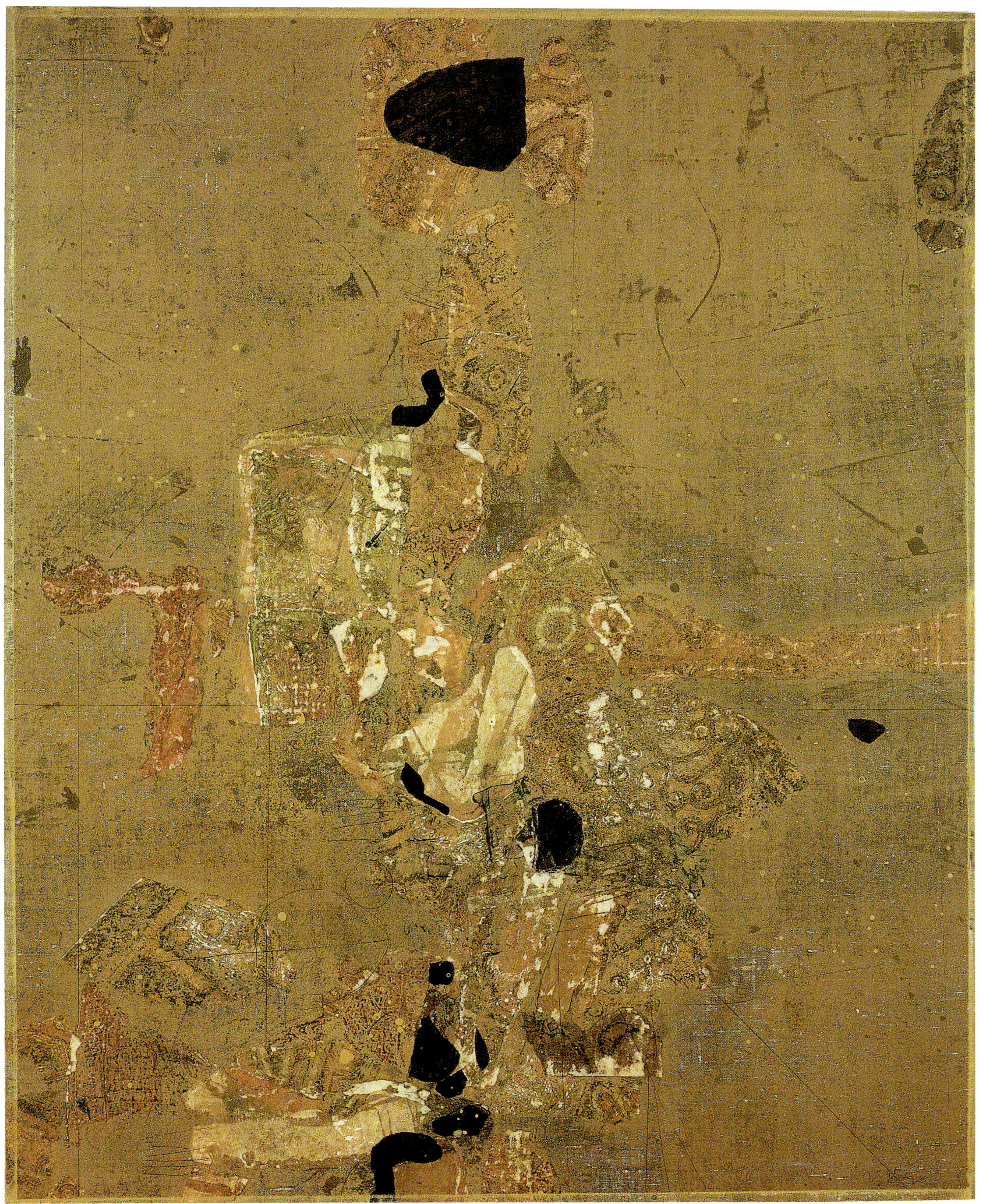

93 | THE CHALBURN 1999

Collage, metal, acrylic and oil stain on linen, 13 1/2" x 15"

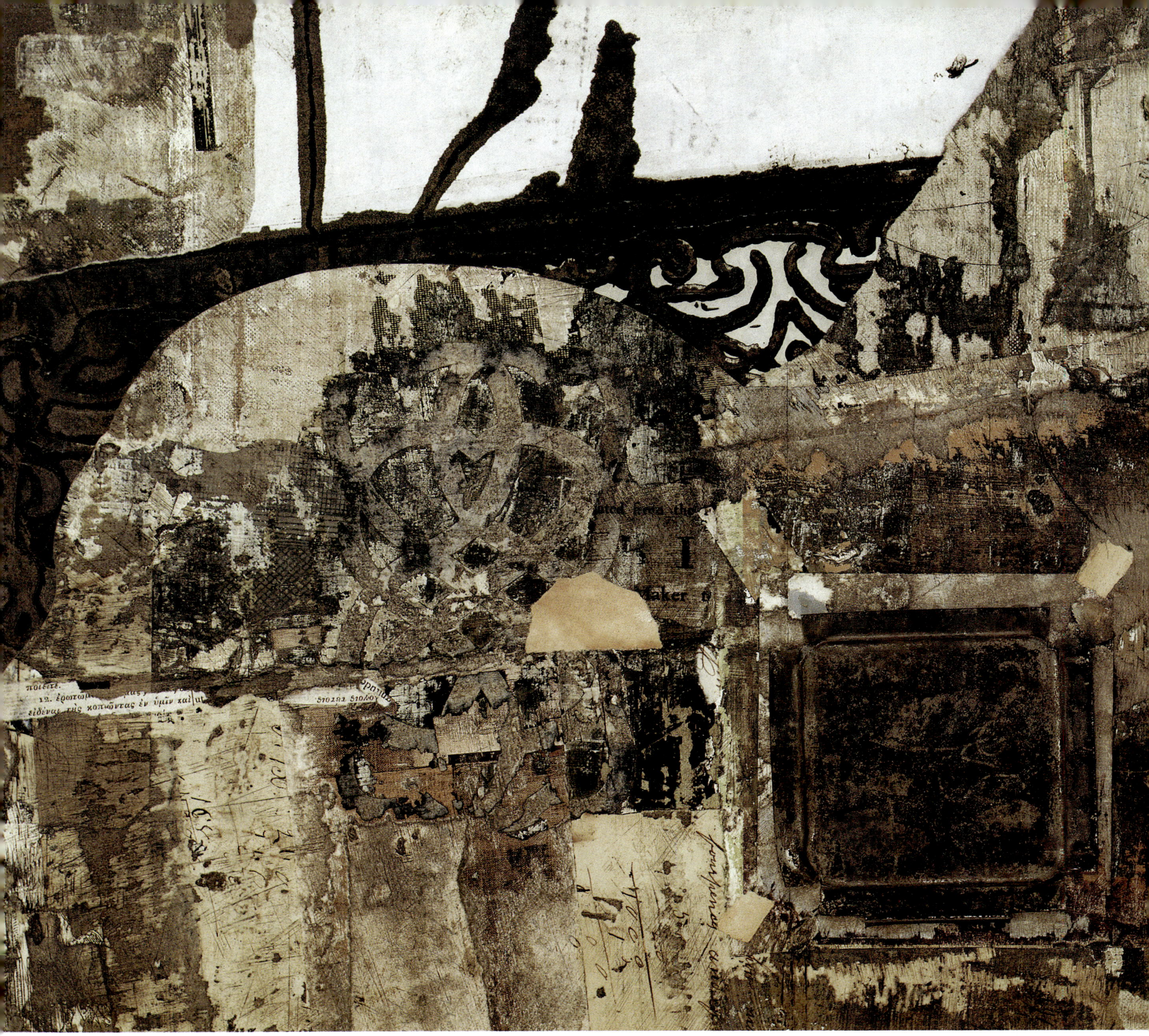

94 | WITZ 2003

Collage painting, 34 1/2" x 26 1/4"

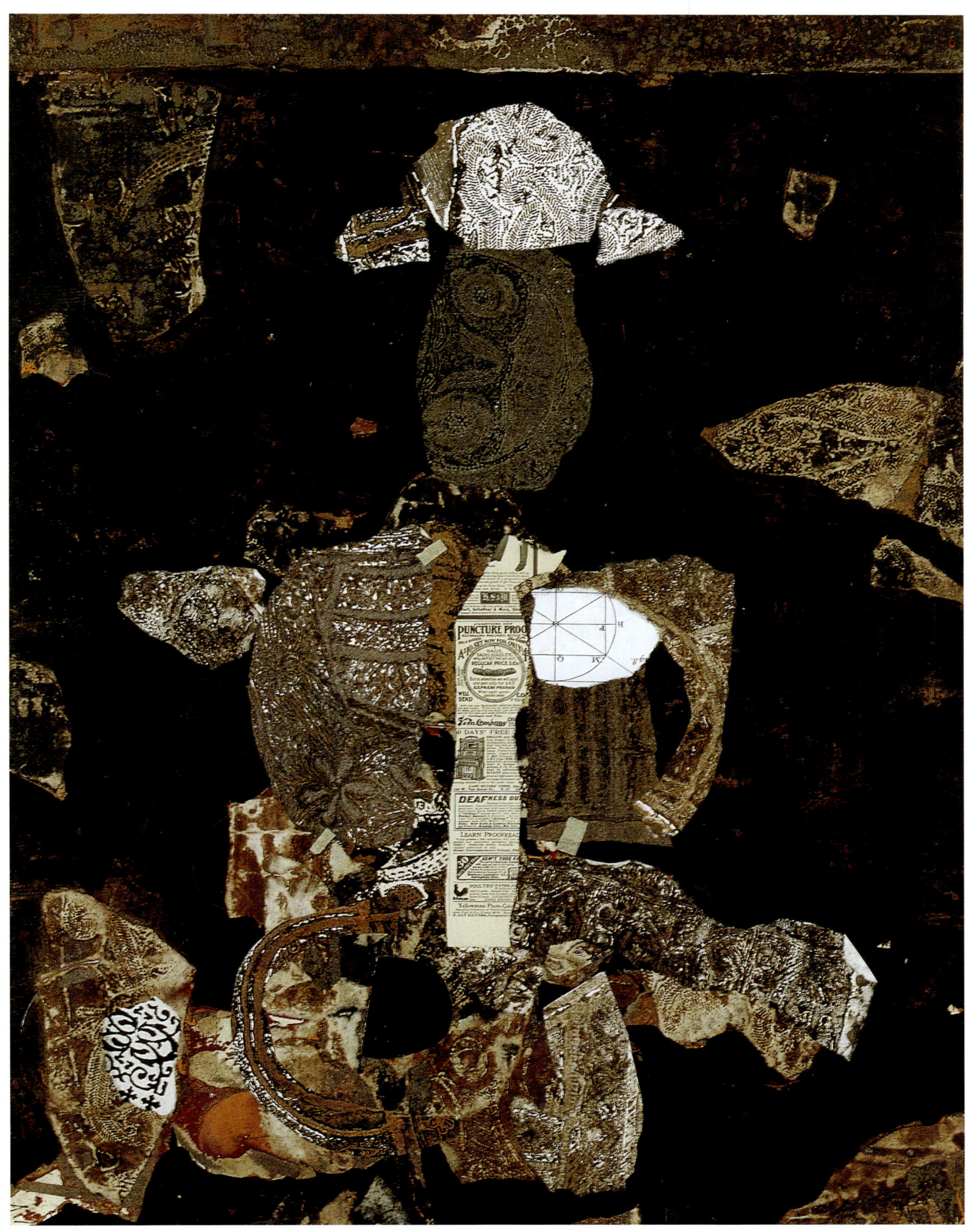
PUNCTURE PROO
REGULAR PRICE $10
EXPRESS PREPAID
WILL SEND
DAYS' FREE
DEAF
LEARN PROOFREAD
Yellowstone Photo-Col

95 | GEOMETRIC FIGURE 1997

Acrylic and collage on linen, 38 1/2" x 30 1/2"

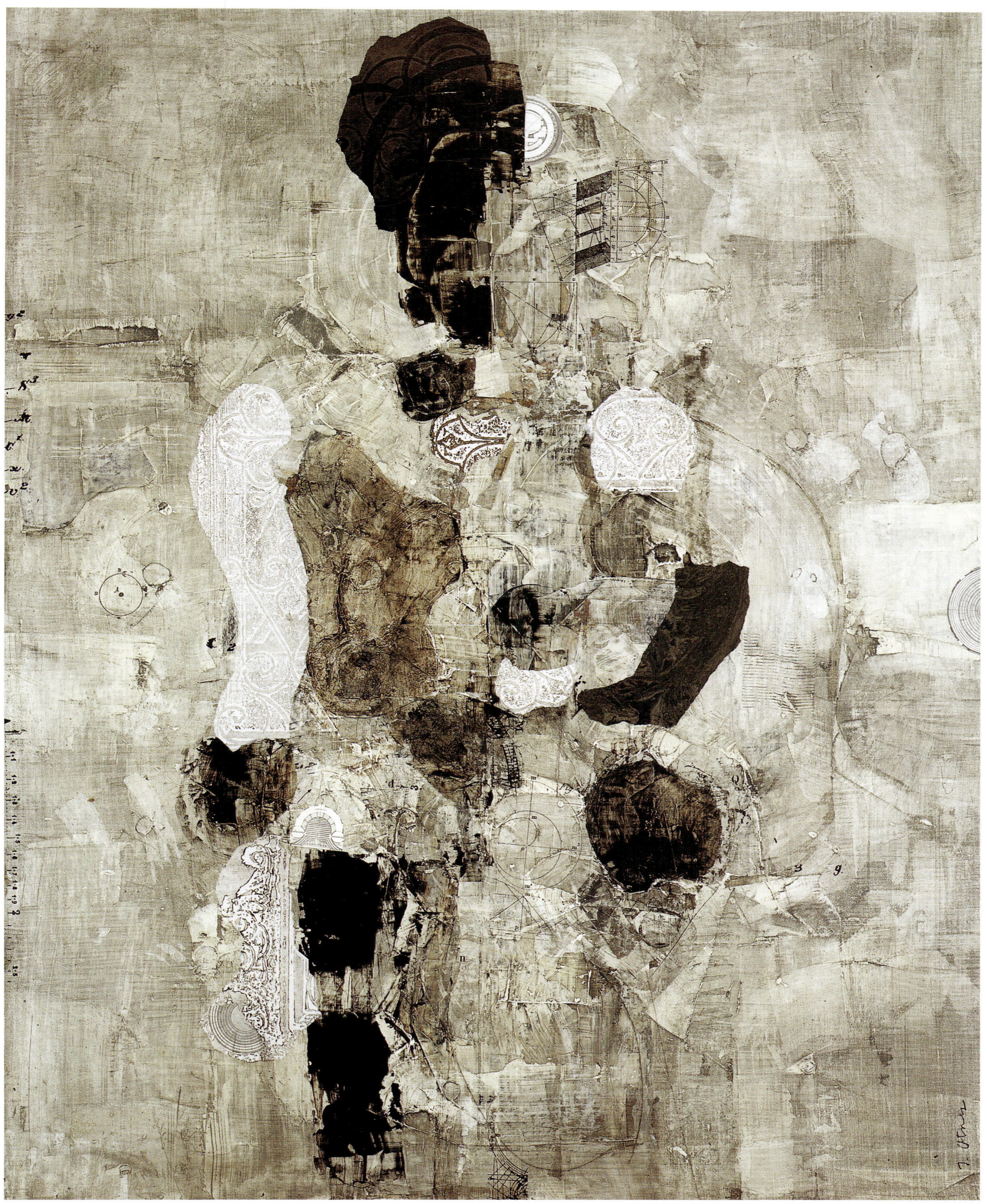

96 | THE VENICIAN 1993

Collage and assemblage, 16 1/2" x 18"

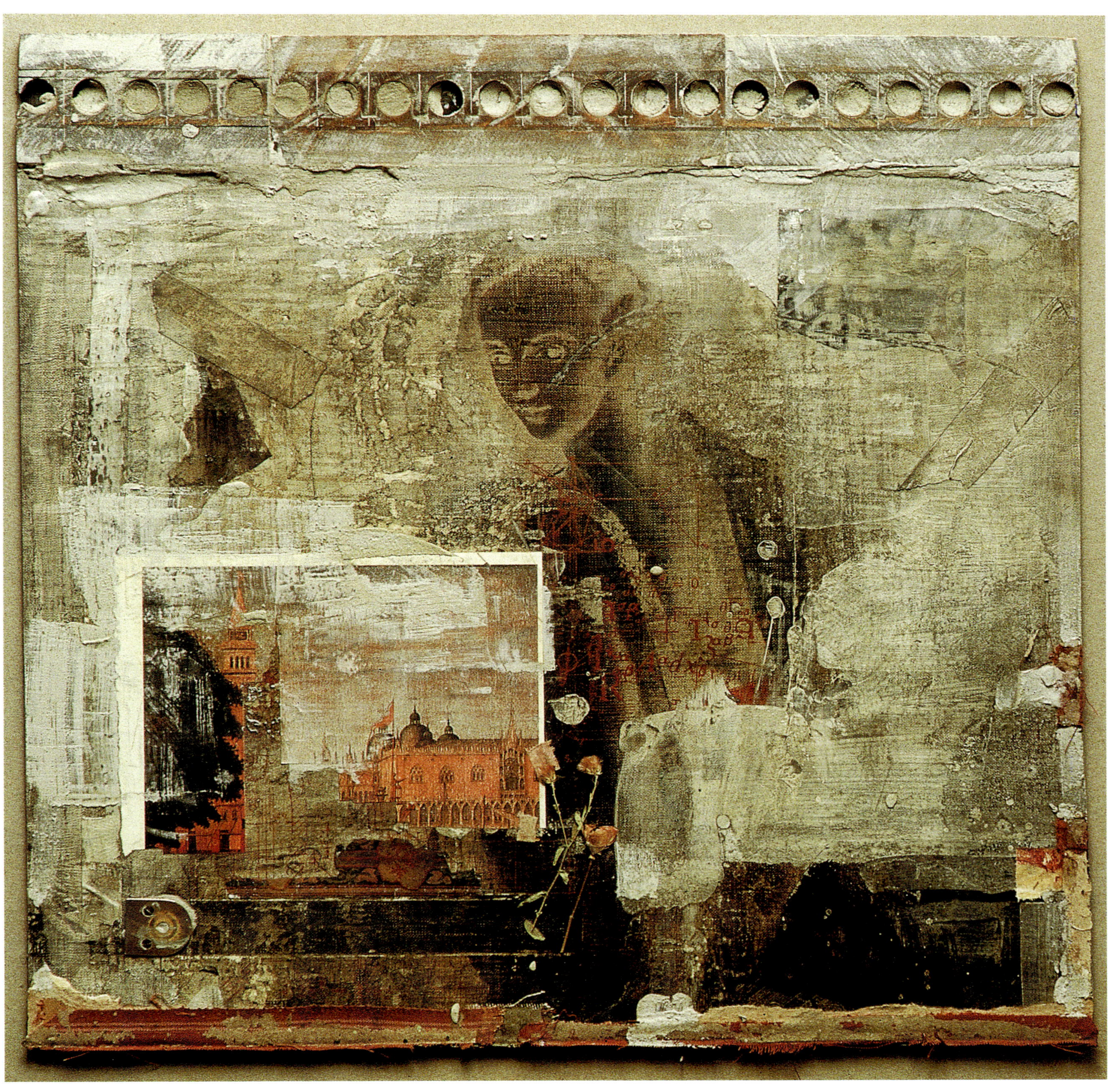

97 | THE PASCOLENE 2002

Mixed media collage, 28" x 26 1/2"

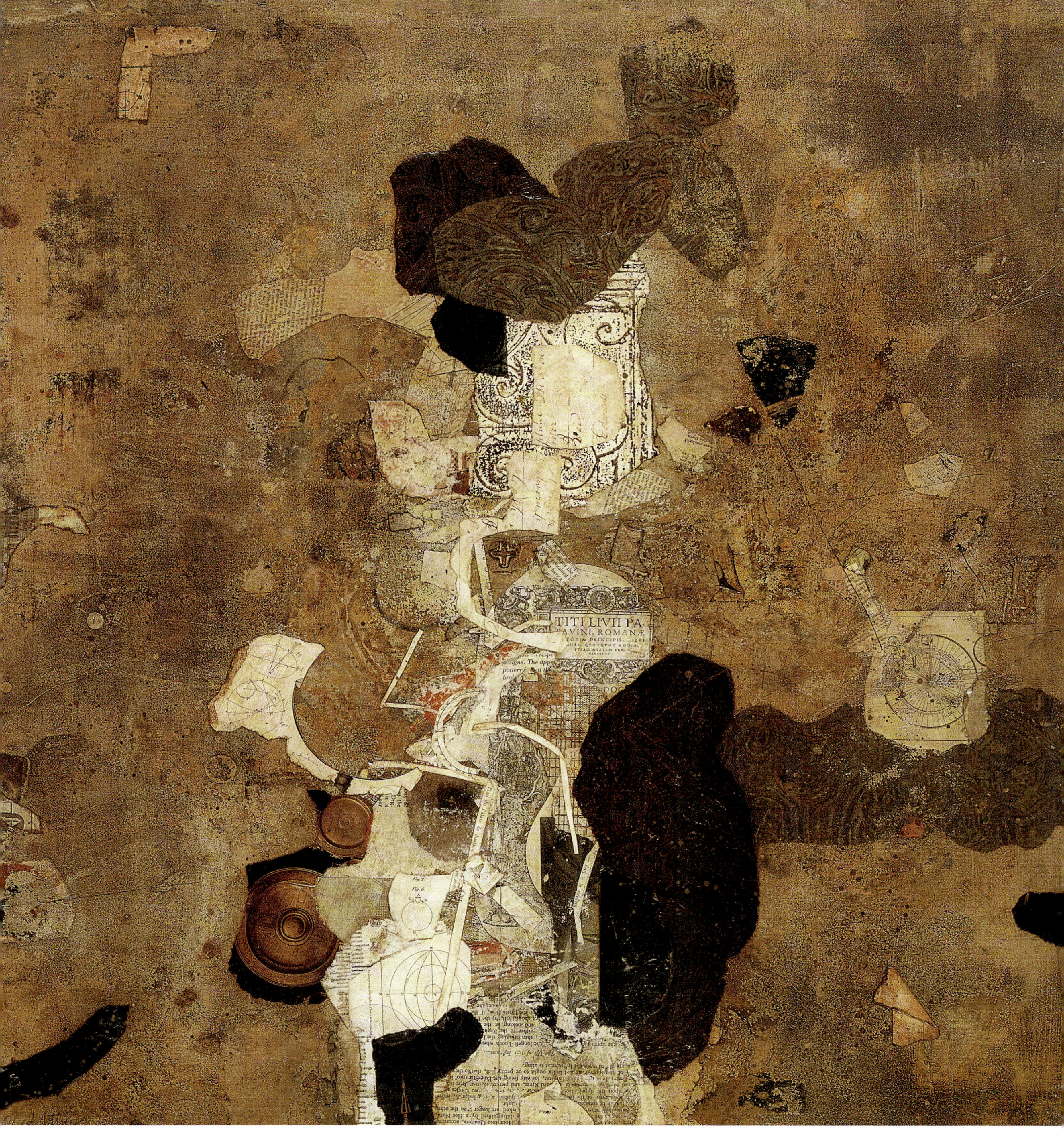
TITI LIVII PA
AVINI, ROMANÆ

98 | STARCK 2000

Collage painting on linen, 18" x 16 3/4"

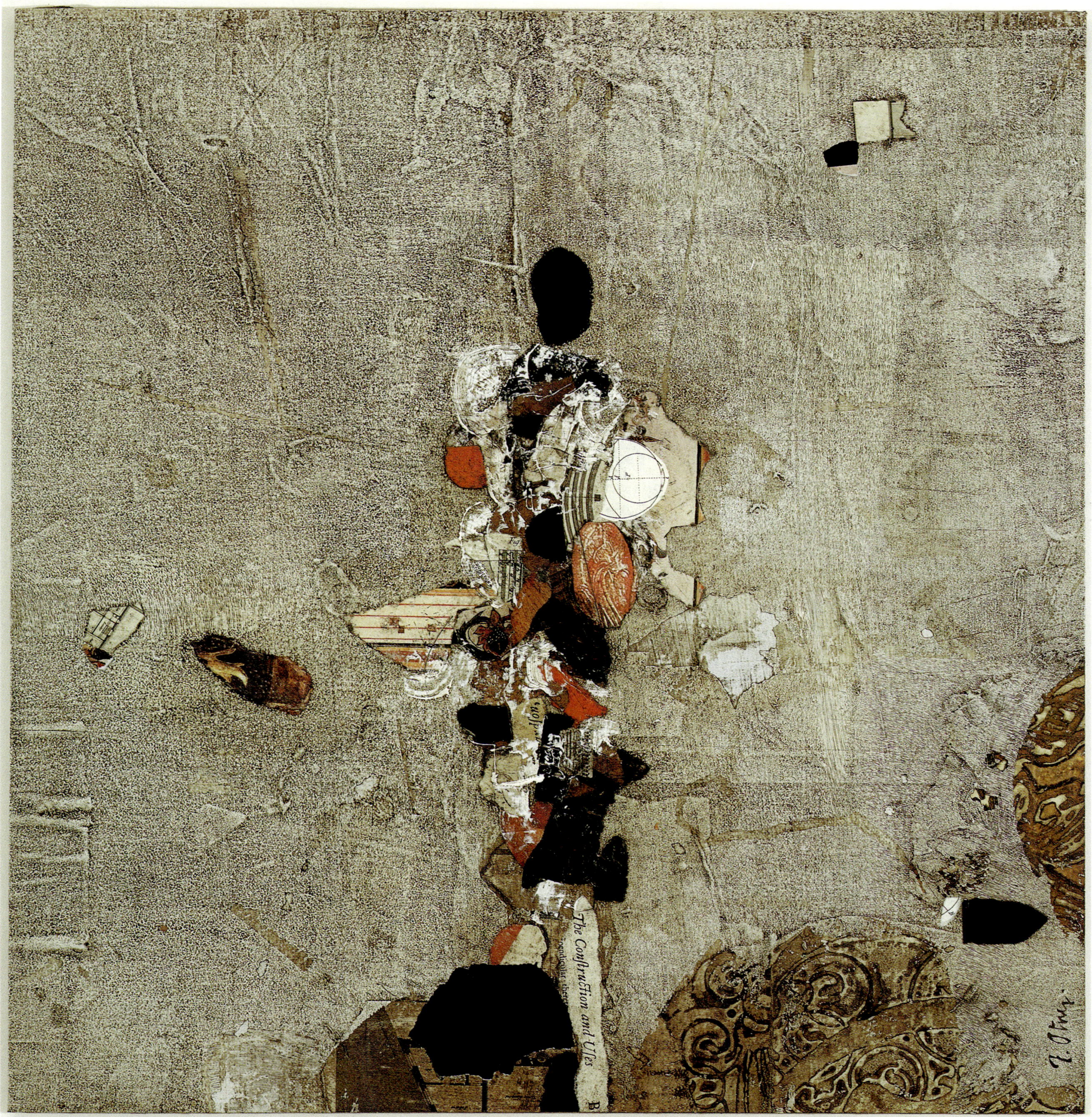
The Construction and Uses

99 | UNTITLED 2002

Mixed media collage, 43" x 41"

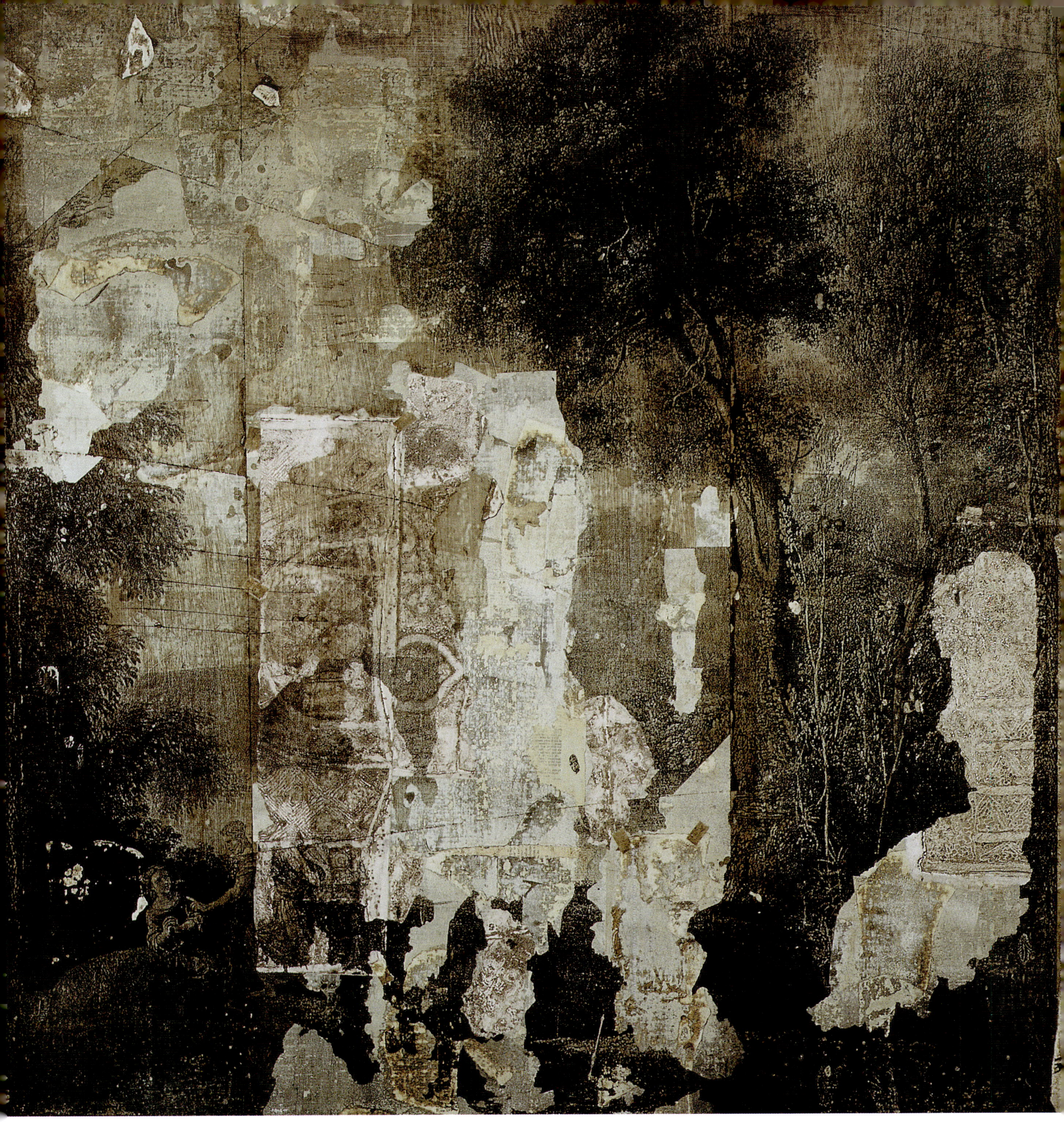

100 | SOLDIER BOY 1996

Mixed media collage, 40" x 47"

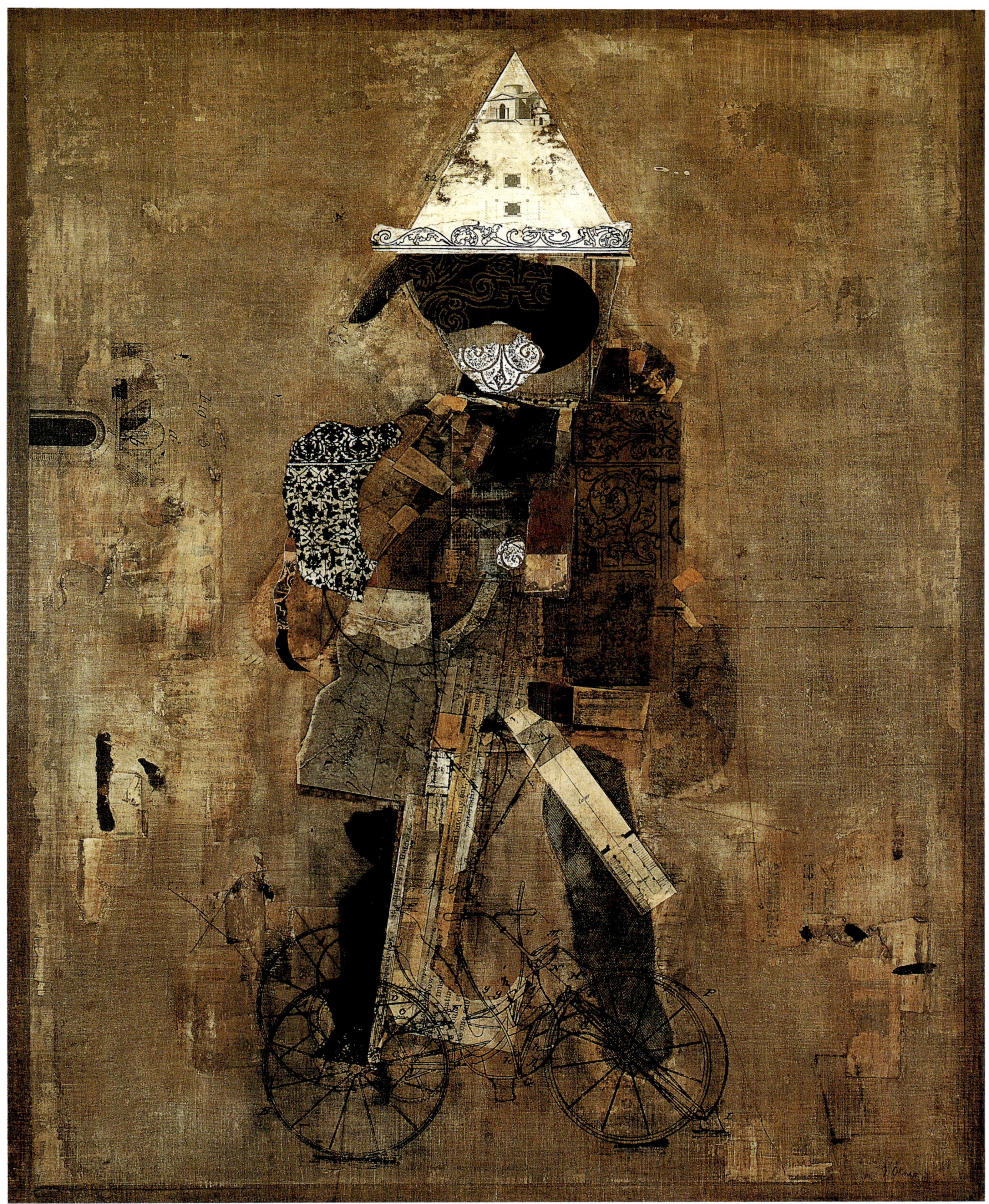

101 | UNTITLED 1996

Mixed media with tintype, 22" x 30"

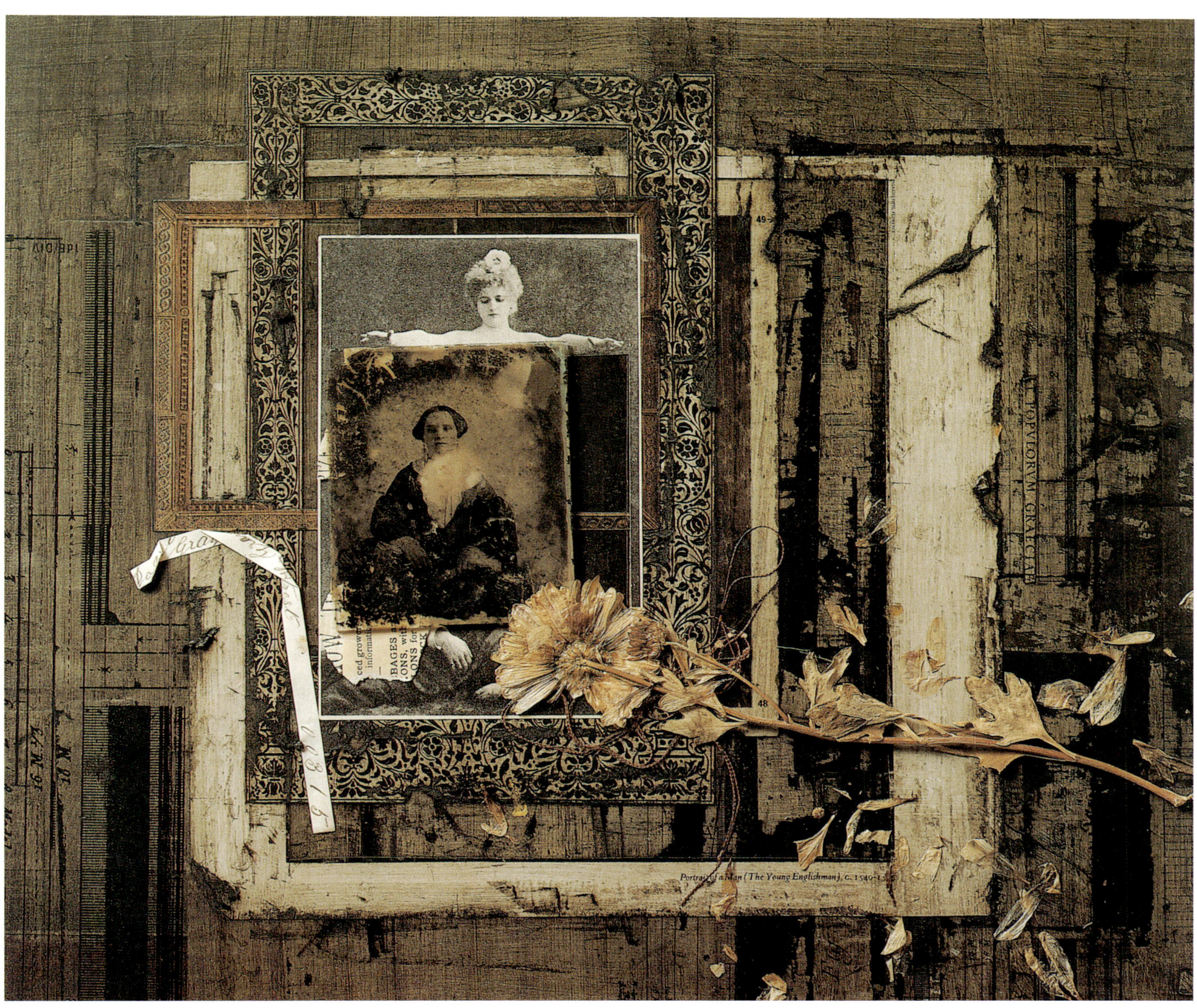

102 | UNTITLED 2000

Mixed media collage, 44" x 48"

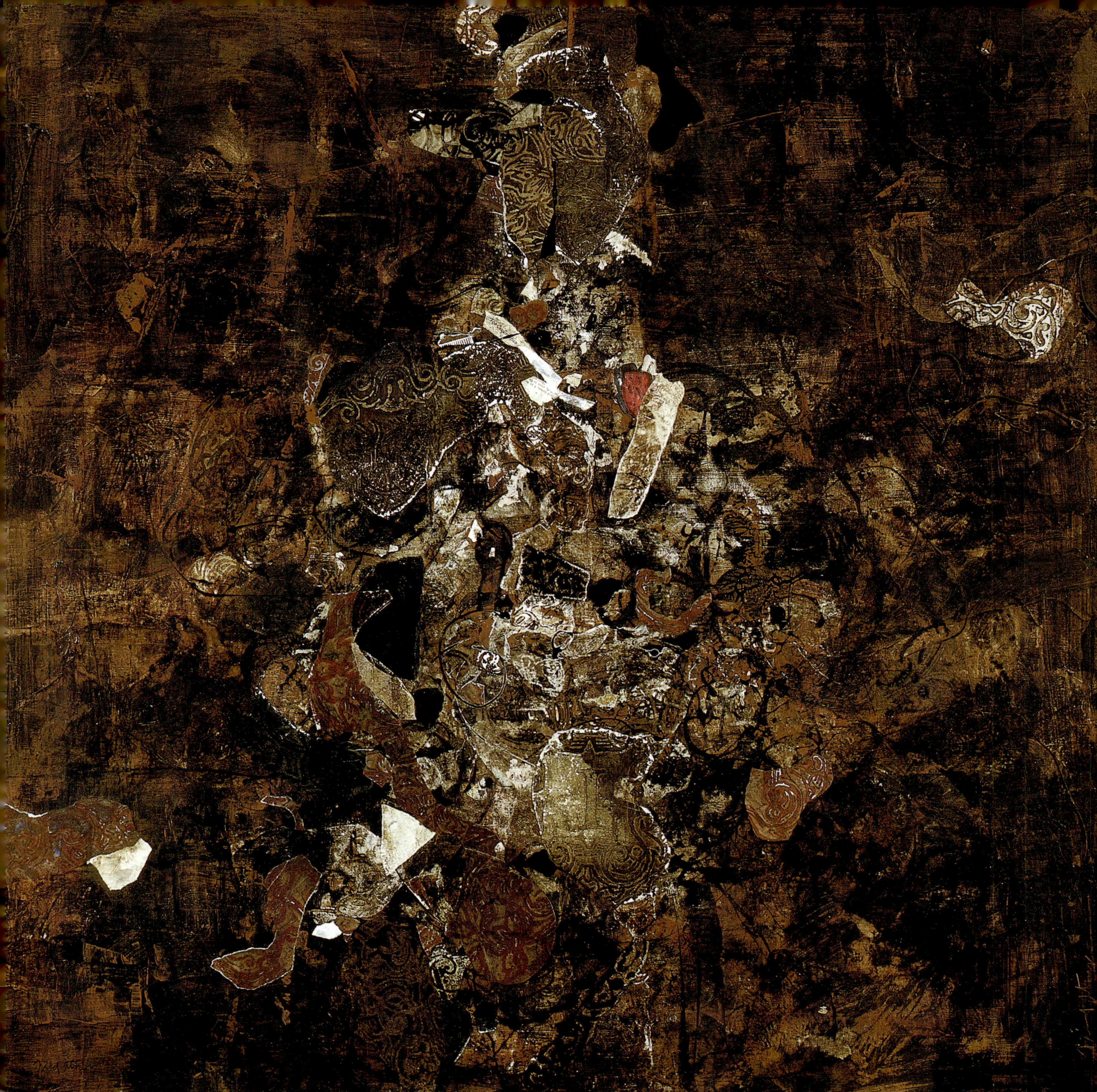

103 | UNTITLED 1997

Collage on linen, 24" x 24"

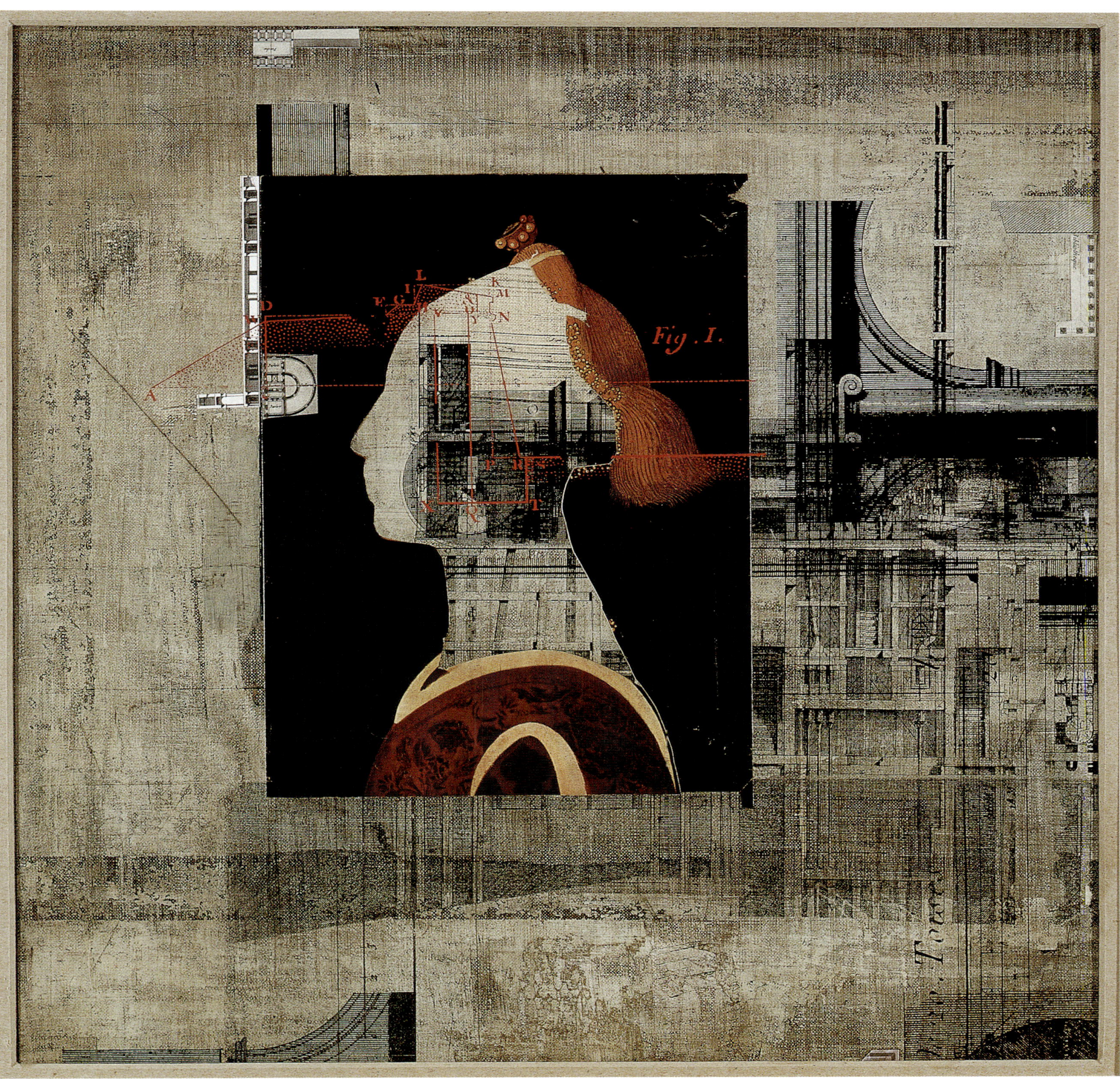
Fig. I.

104 | PALE FIGURE 2000

Mixed media collage, 60" x 48"

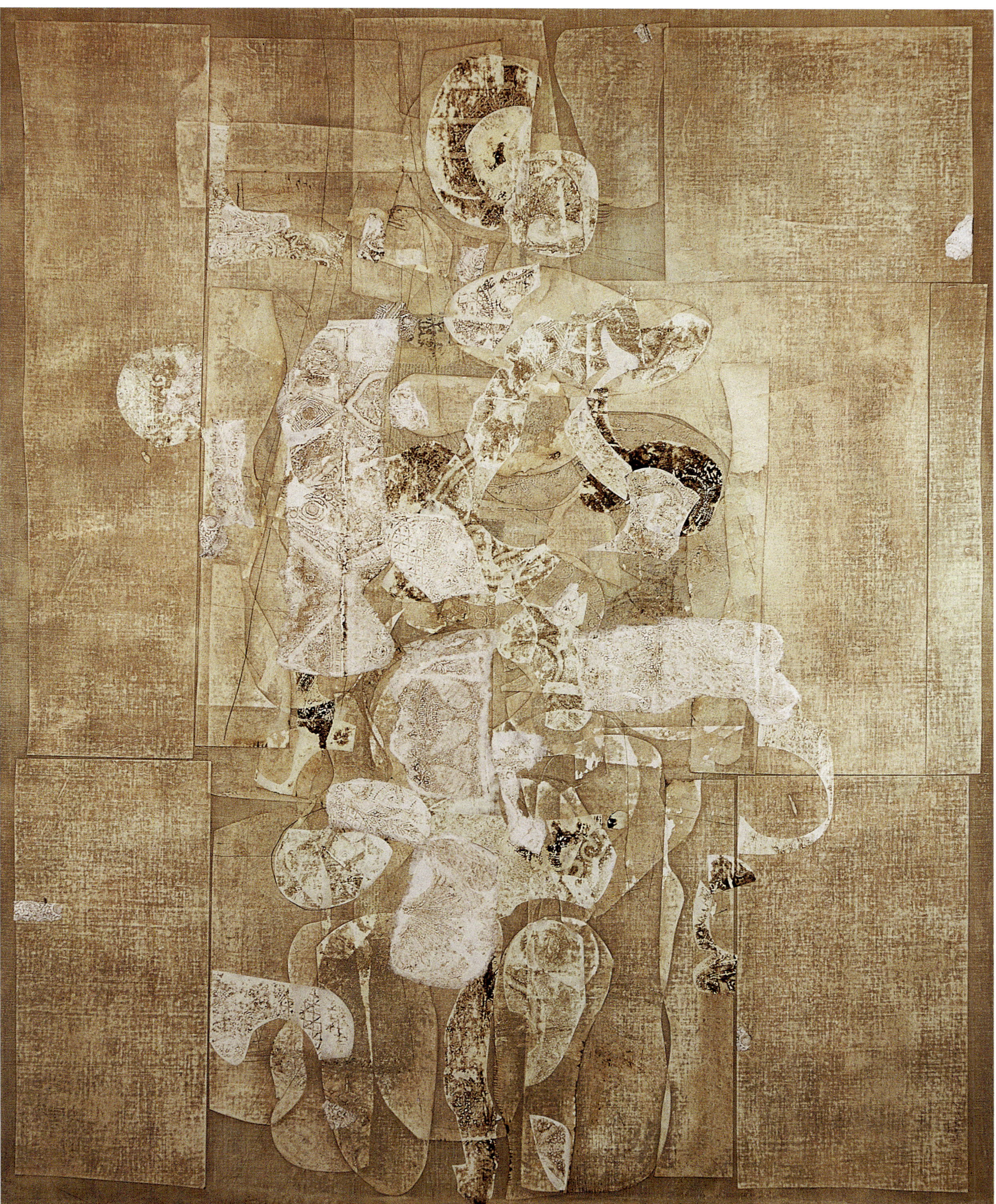

105 | DARK LADY 1996

Mixed media assemblage on wood, 18" x 18"

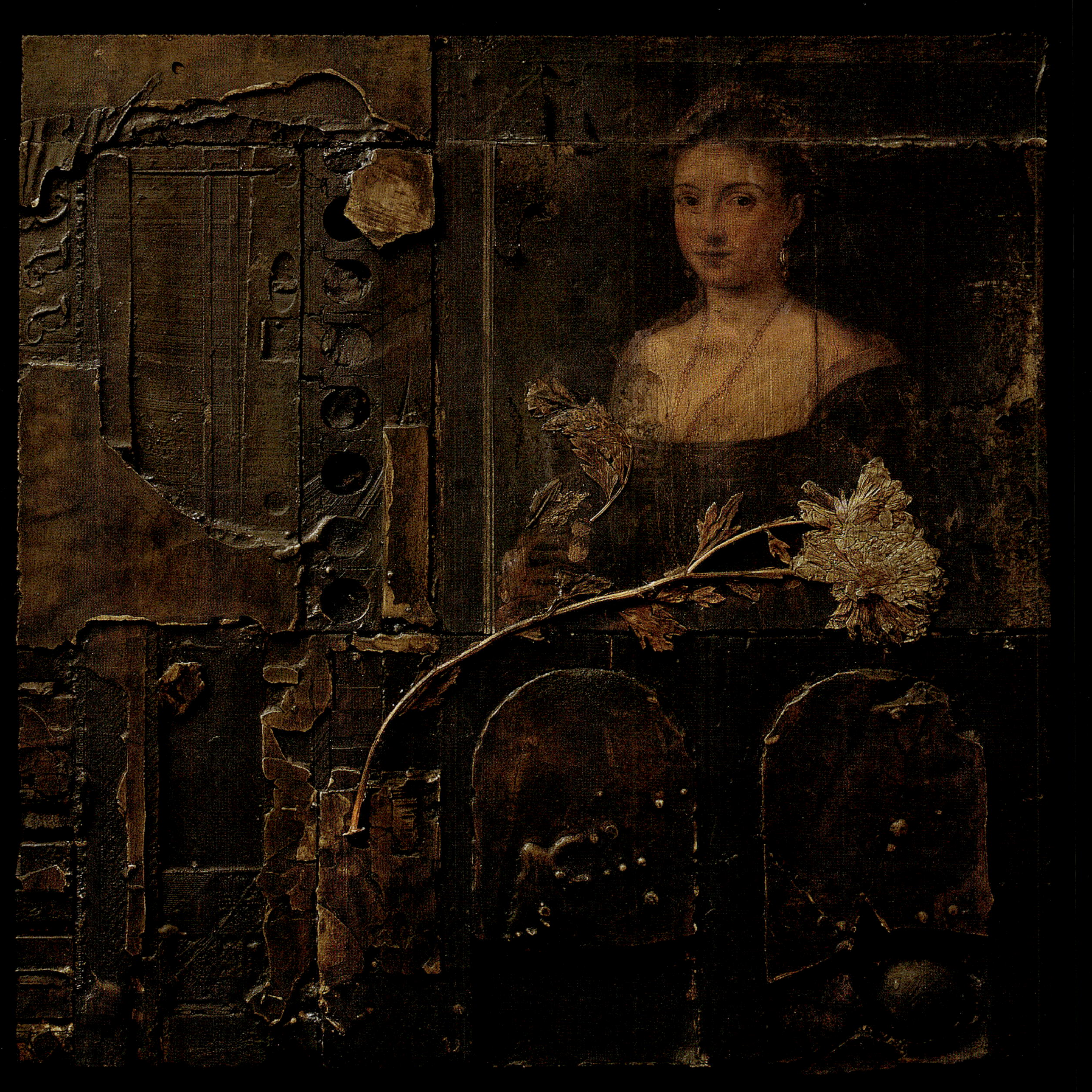

106 | FLANAGAN 1996

Mixed media on wood, 60" x 48"

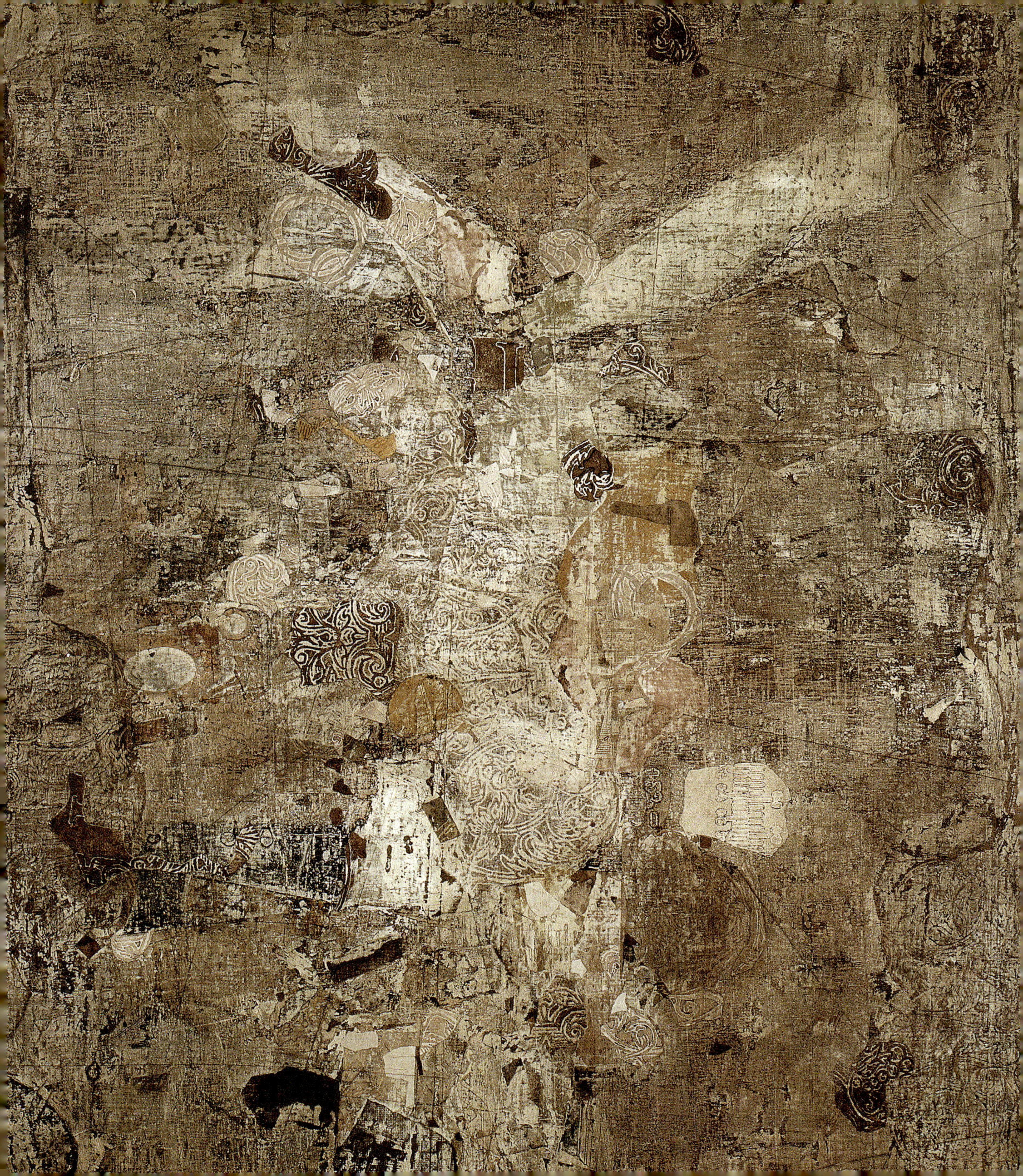

107 | OLDWEL 1995

Collage painting, 24 1/4" x 24 1/4"

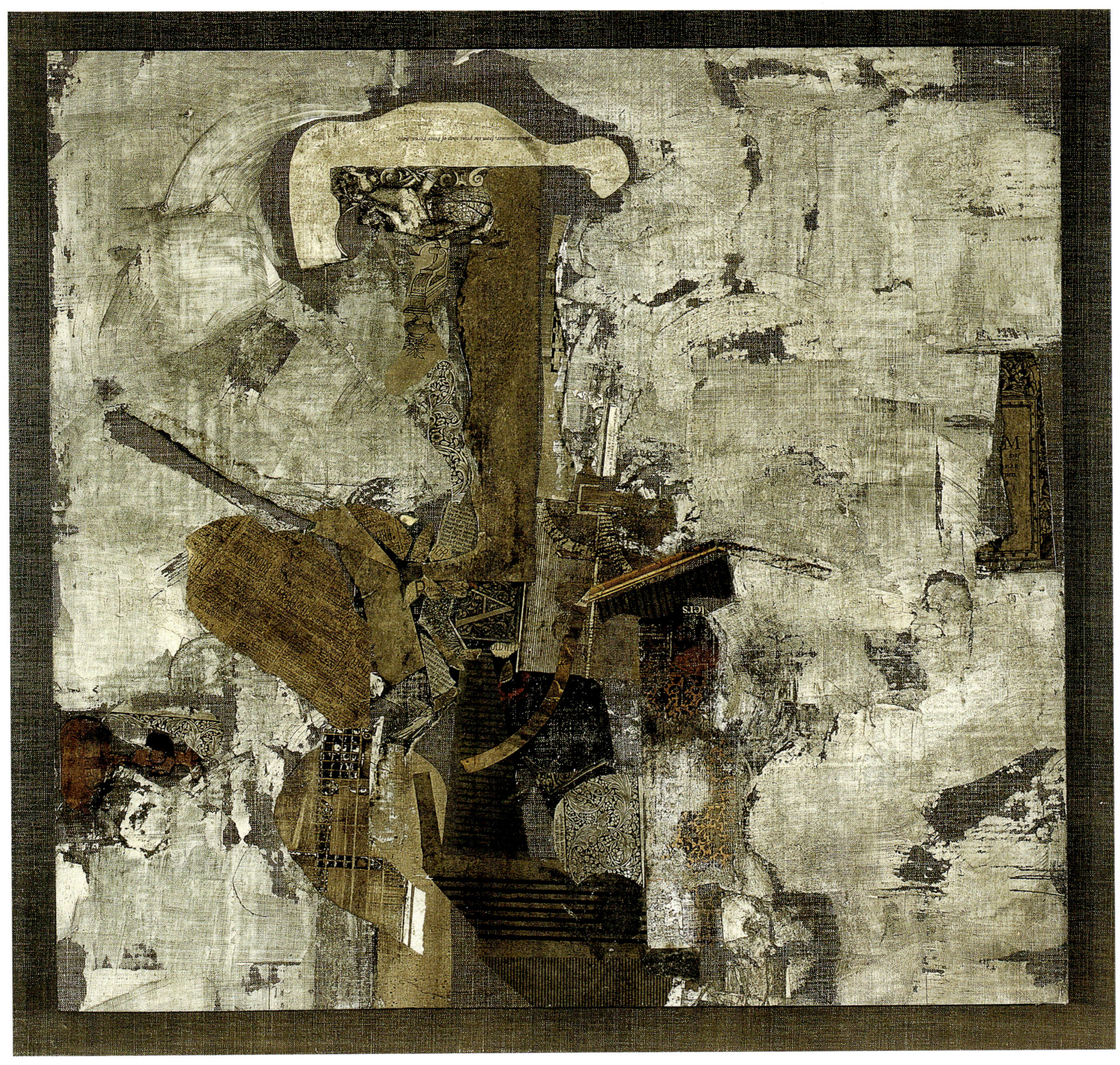

108 | REG'E FRACIX 2000

Mixed media collage painting, 40" x 32"

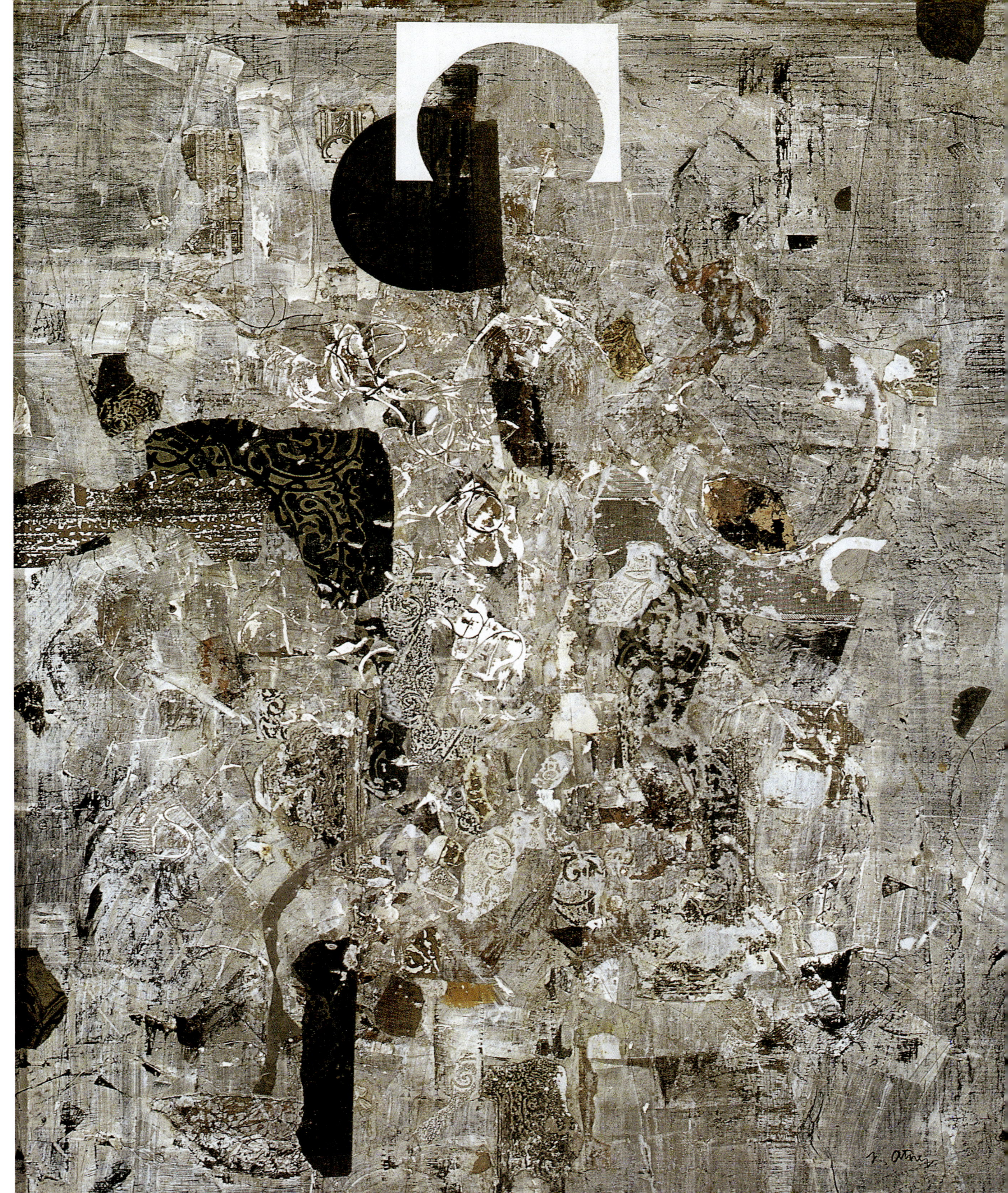

109 | DU T 1995

Mixed media collage, 26 1/2" x 25 1/2"

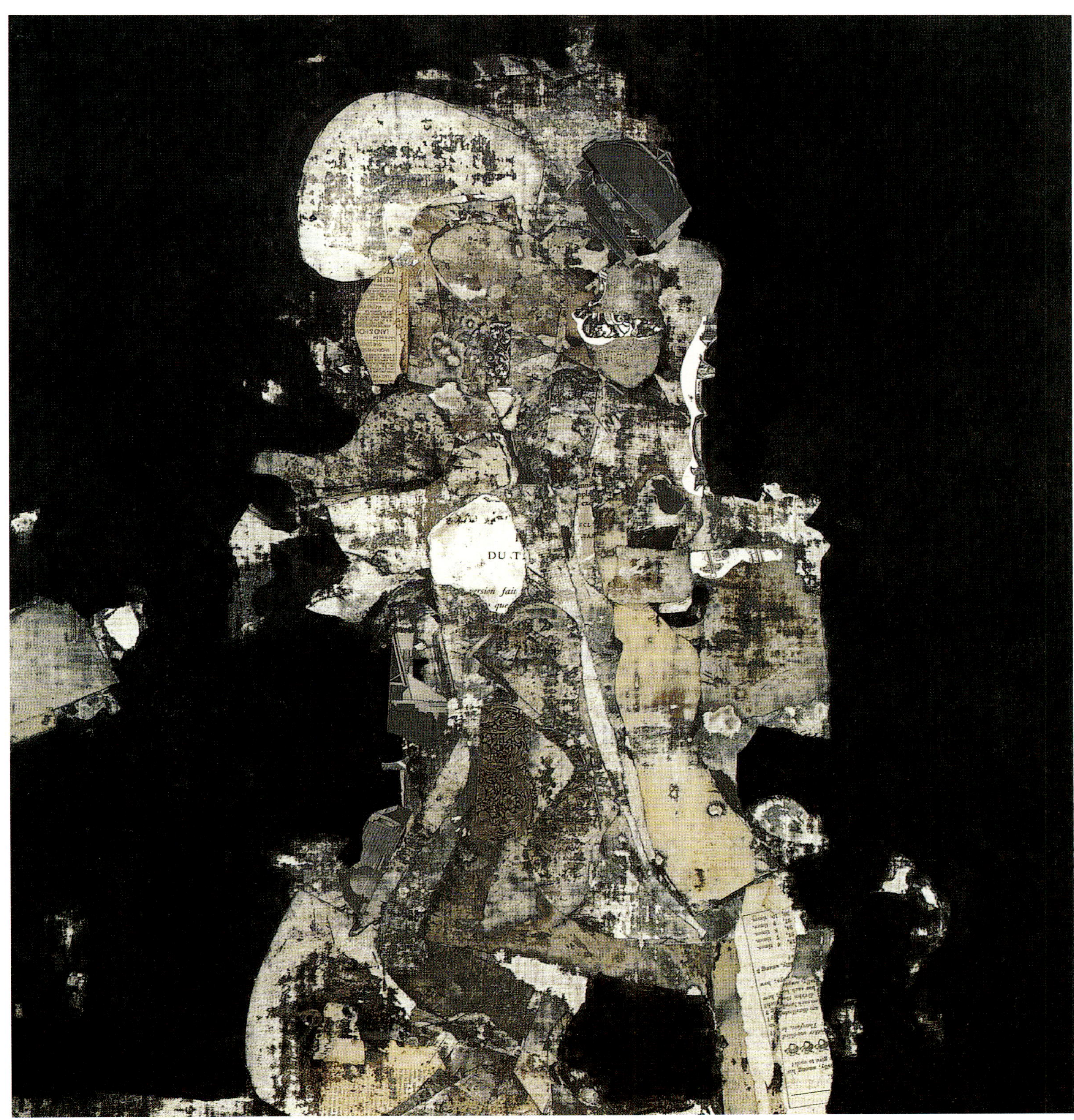

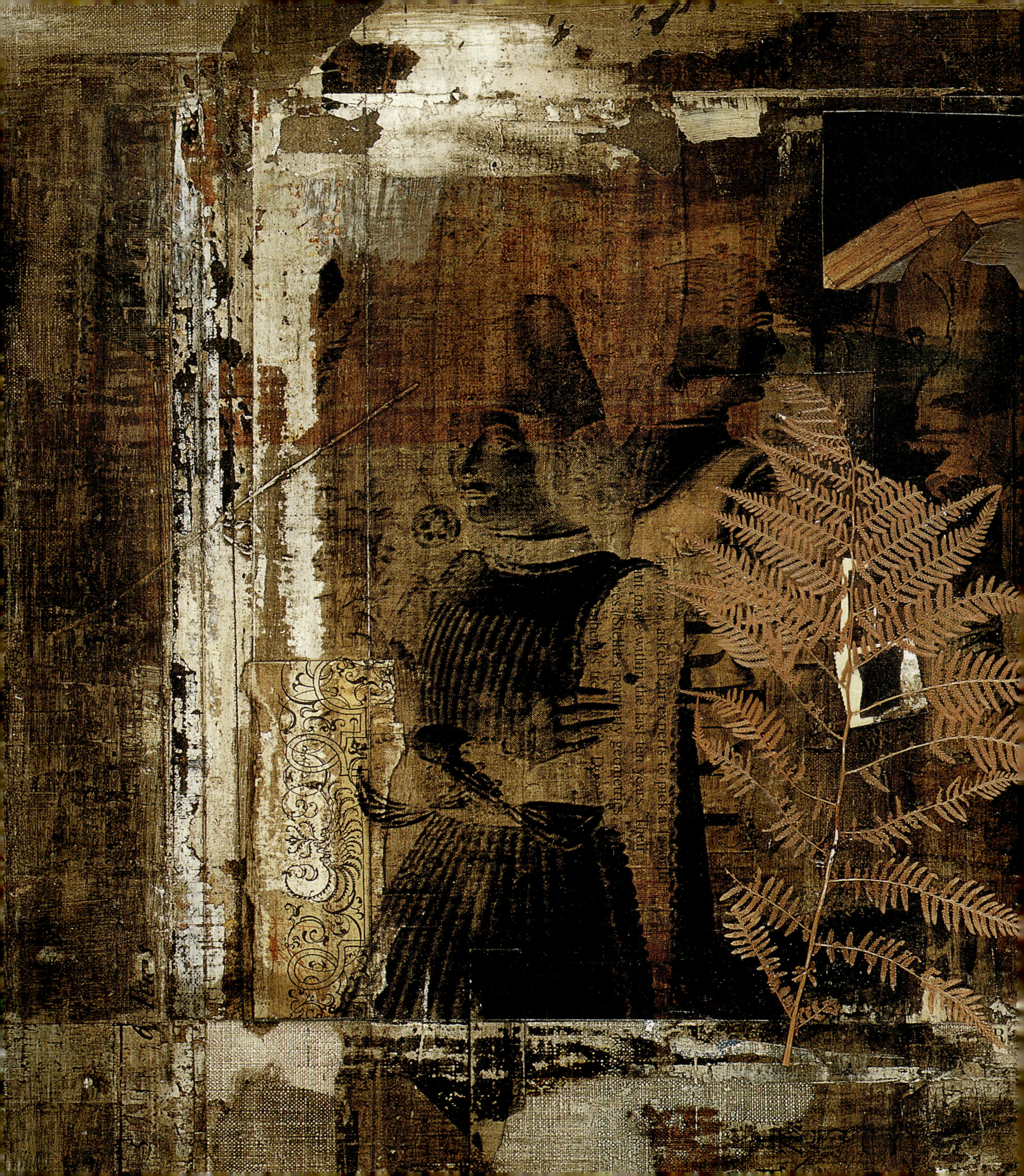
asked four experts to pick a
within the last ten years. Their
painterly geometric

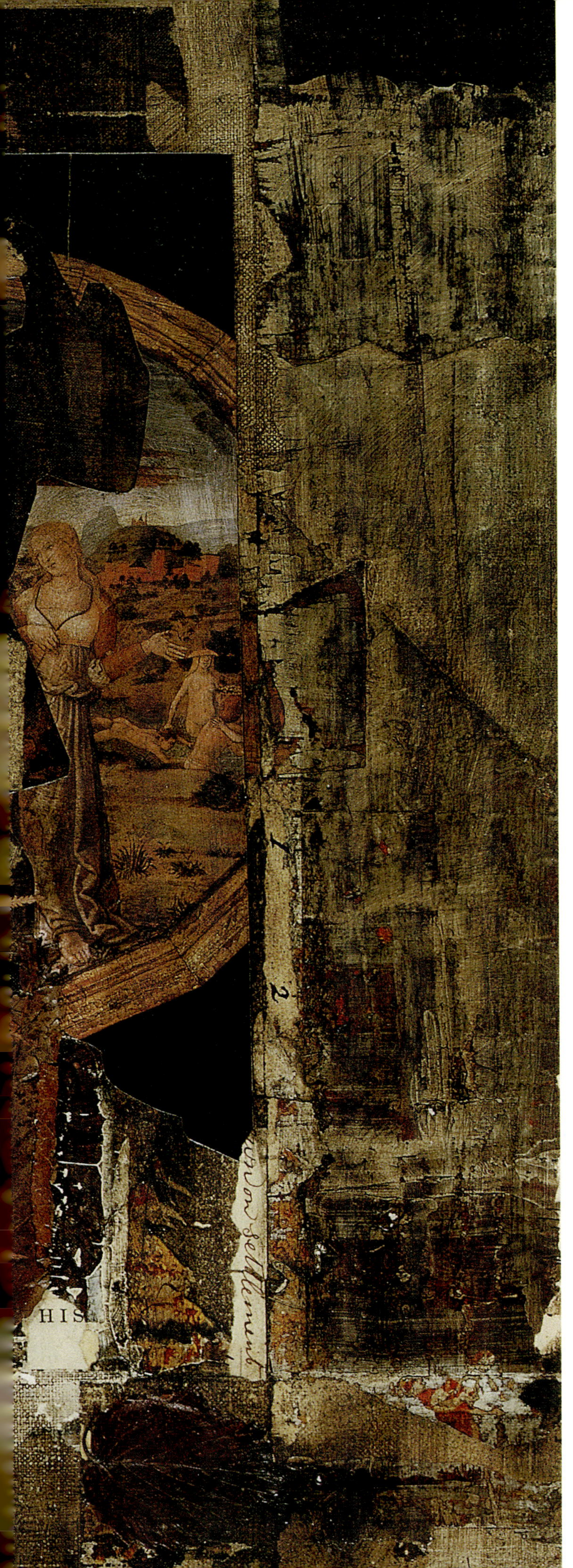

110 | THE SETTLEMENT 1992
Mixed media collage, 16 1/4" x 17 1/4"

111 | UNTITLED 1987
Mixed media collage, 18" x 24"

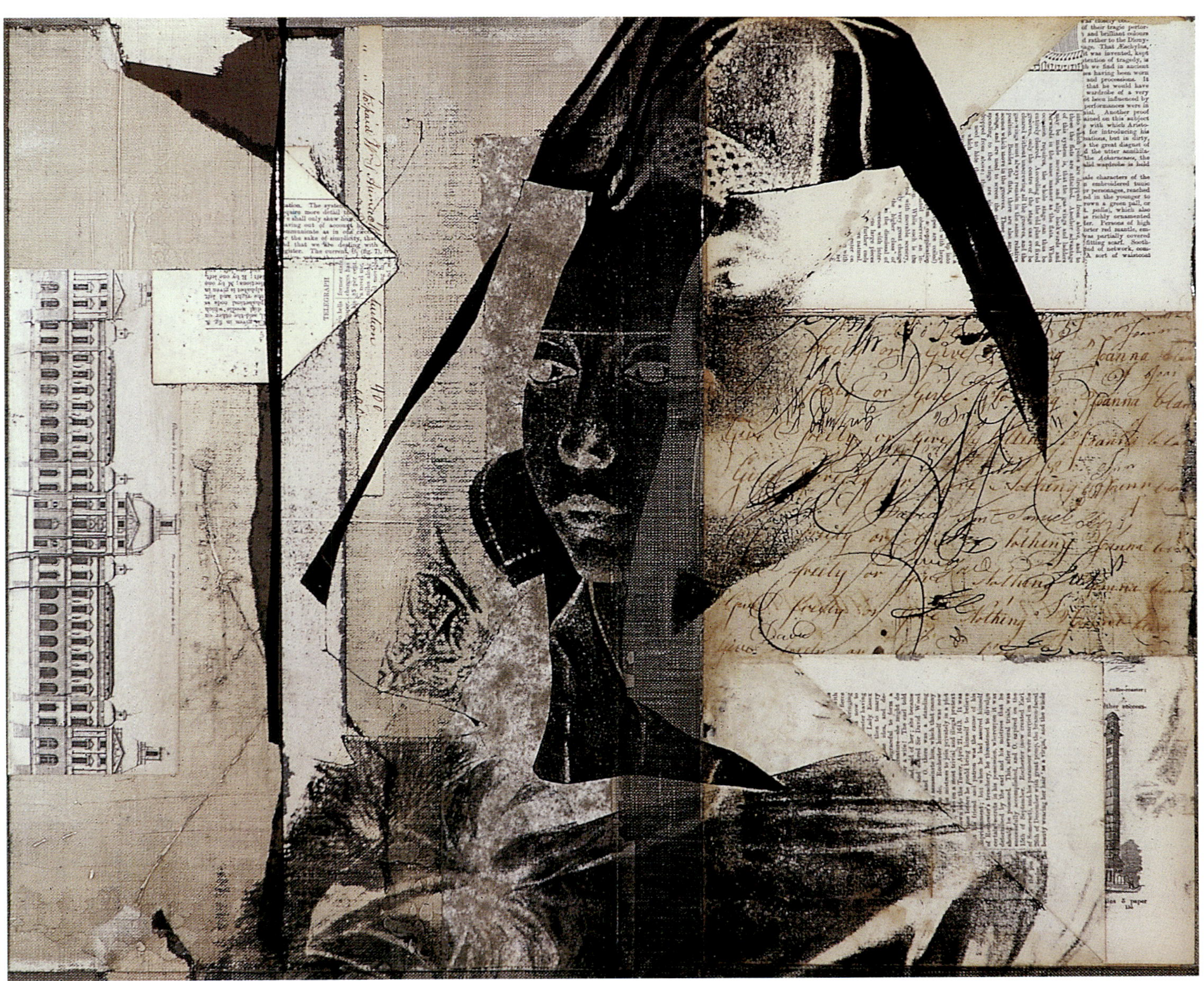

112 | MATTEO 2003

Mixed media collage painting, 31" x 28"

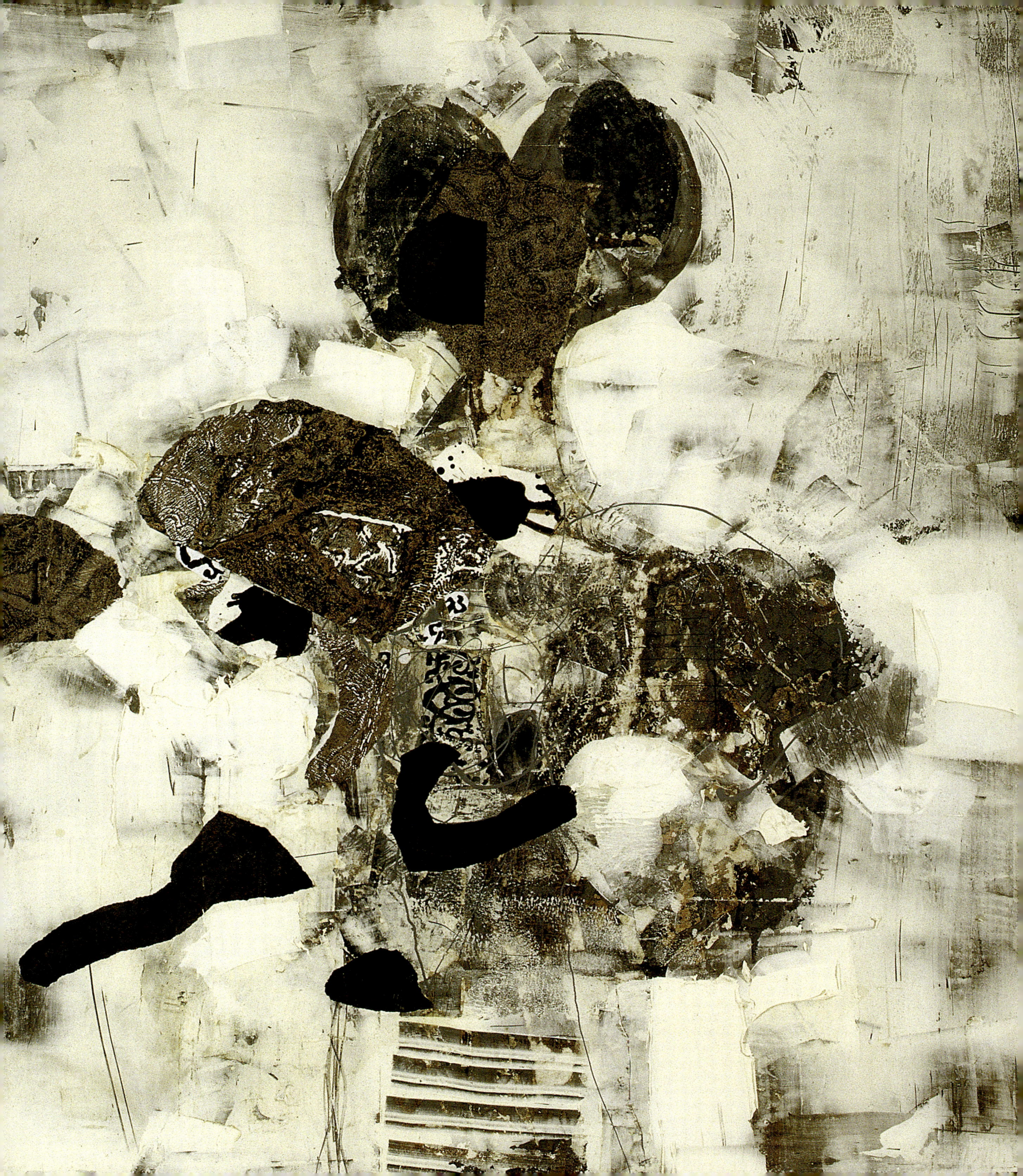

113 | UNTITLED 1995

Mixed media collage on paper, 13" x 18"

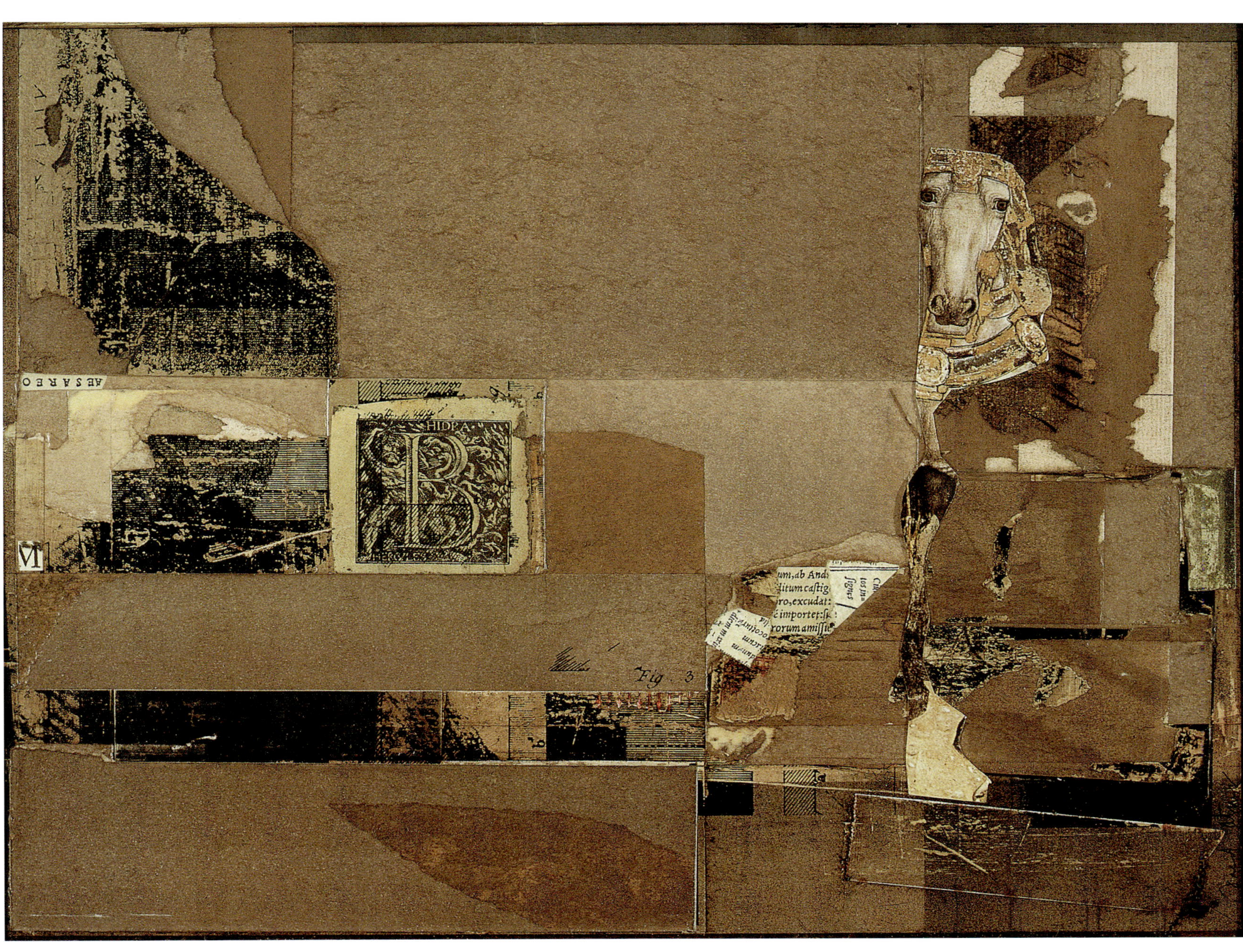

114 | DWELL 2000
Mixed media collage, 48" x 36 1/2"

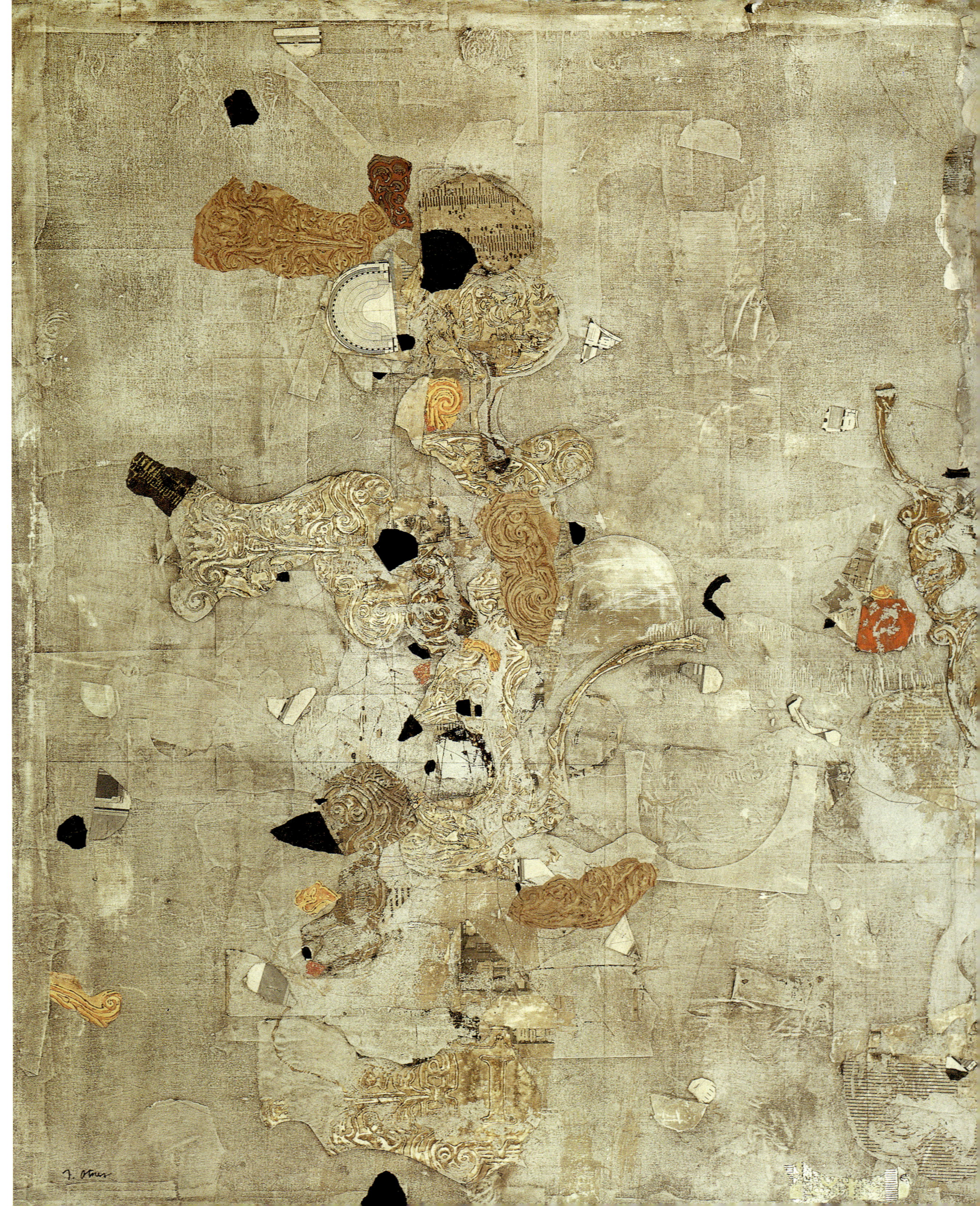

115 | ONOMICAL 1997

Mixed media collage, 47 1/2" x 42"

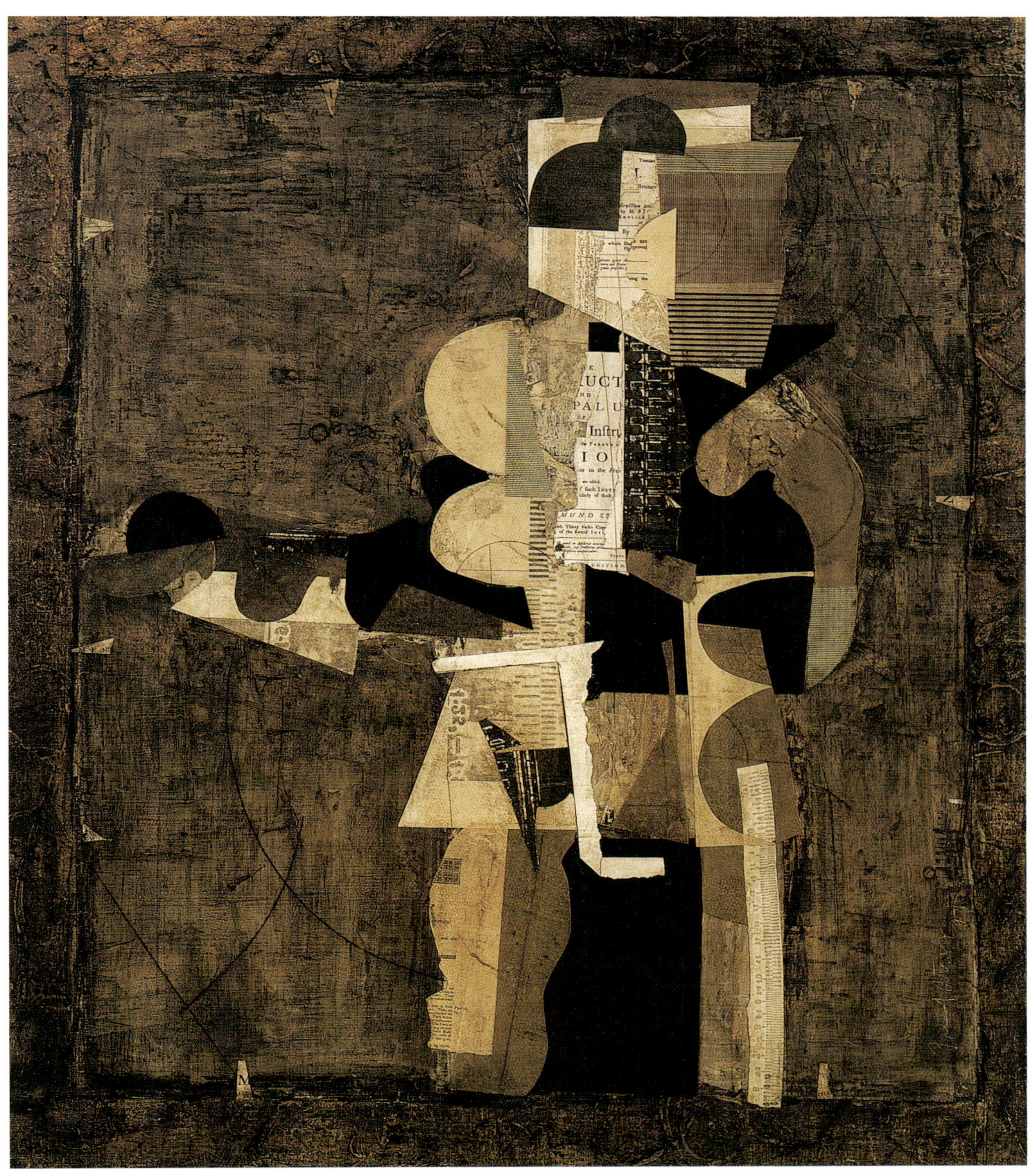

116 | THE FATHOM OR THE CHAIN 1998
Mixed media collage, 25 7/8" x 24 3/4"

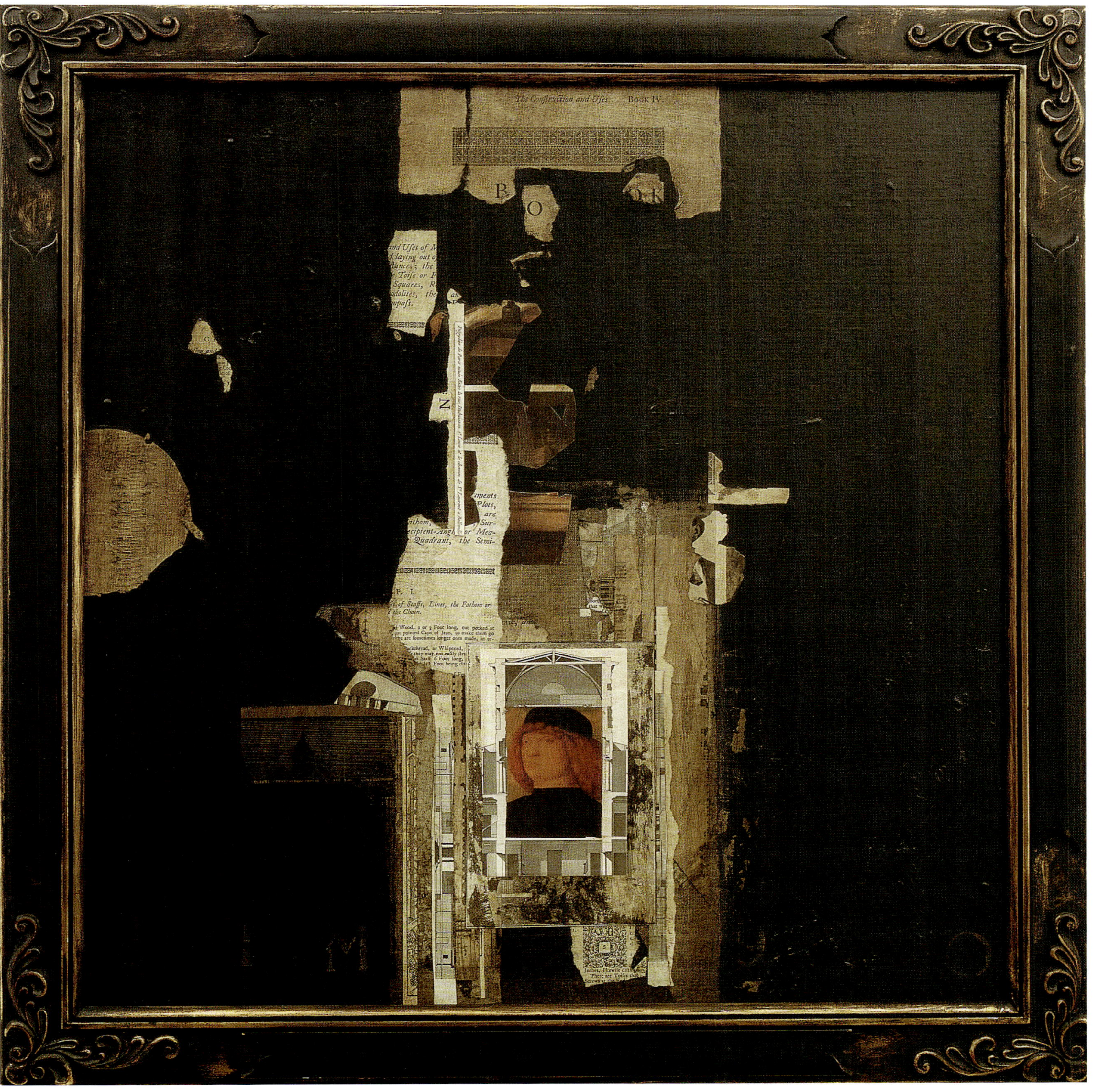
The Construction and Uses   BOOK IV.

117 | FAIRWEEK 1992

Mixed media collage, 21 1/2" x 21"

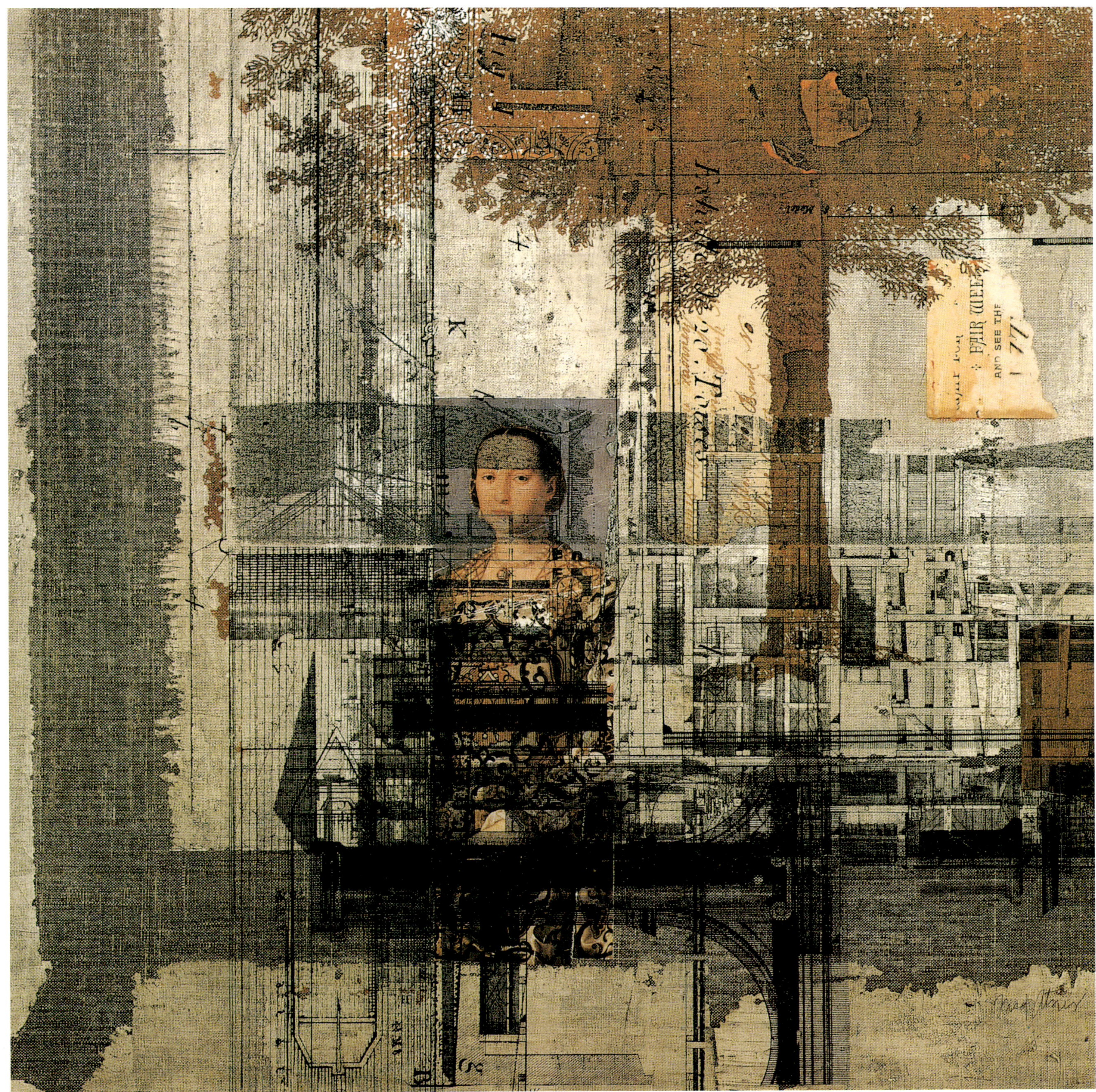

118 | OUGHTRED 2000

Mixed media collage painting, 47" x 37"

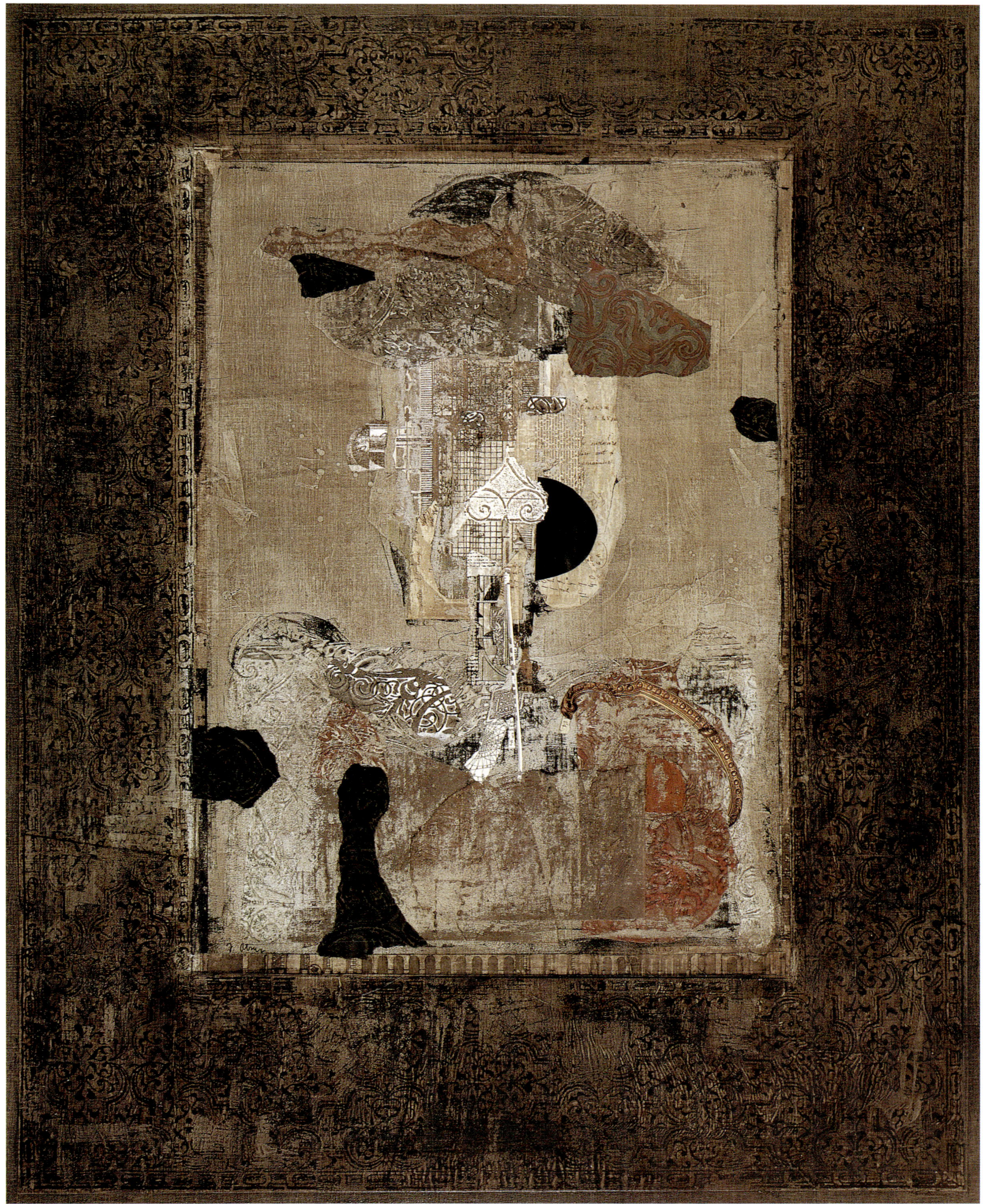

119 | UNTITLED 1994

Mixed media collage, 16" x 21"

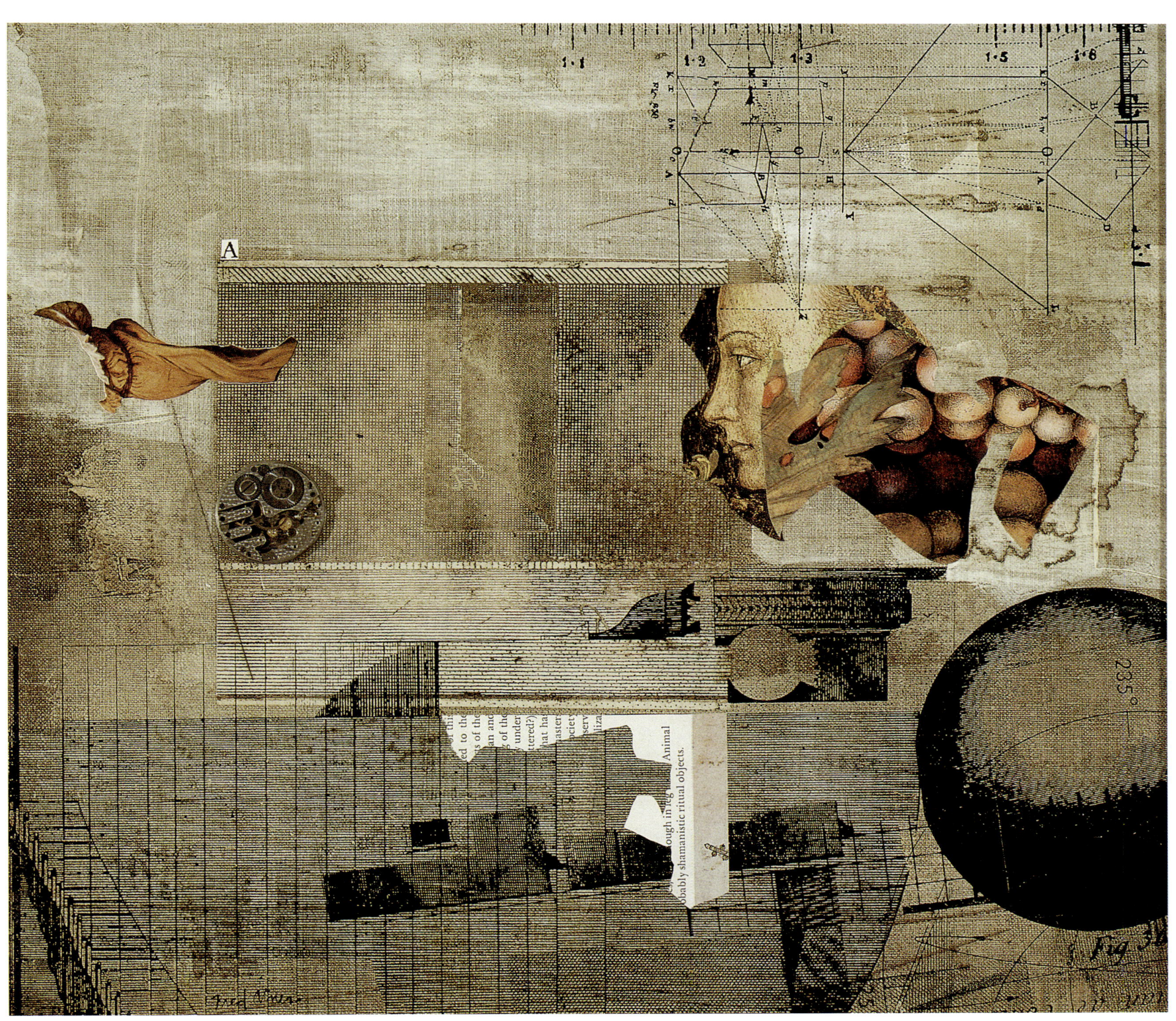

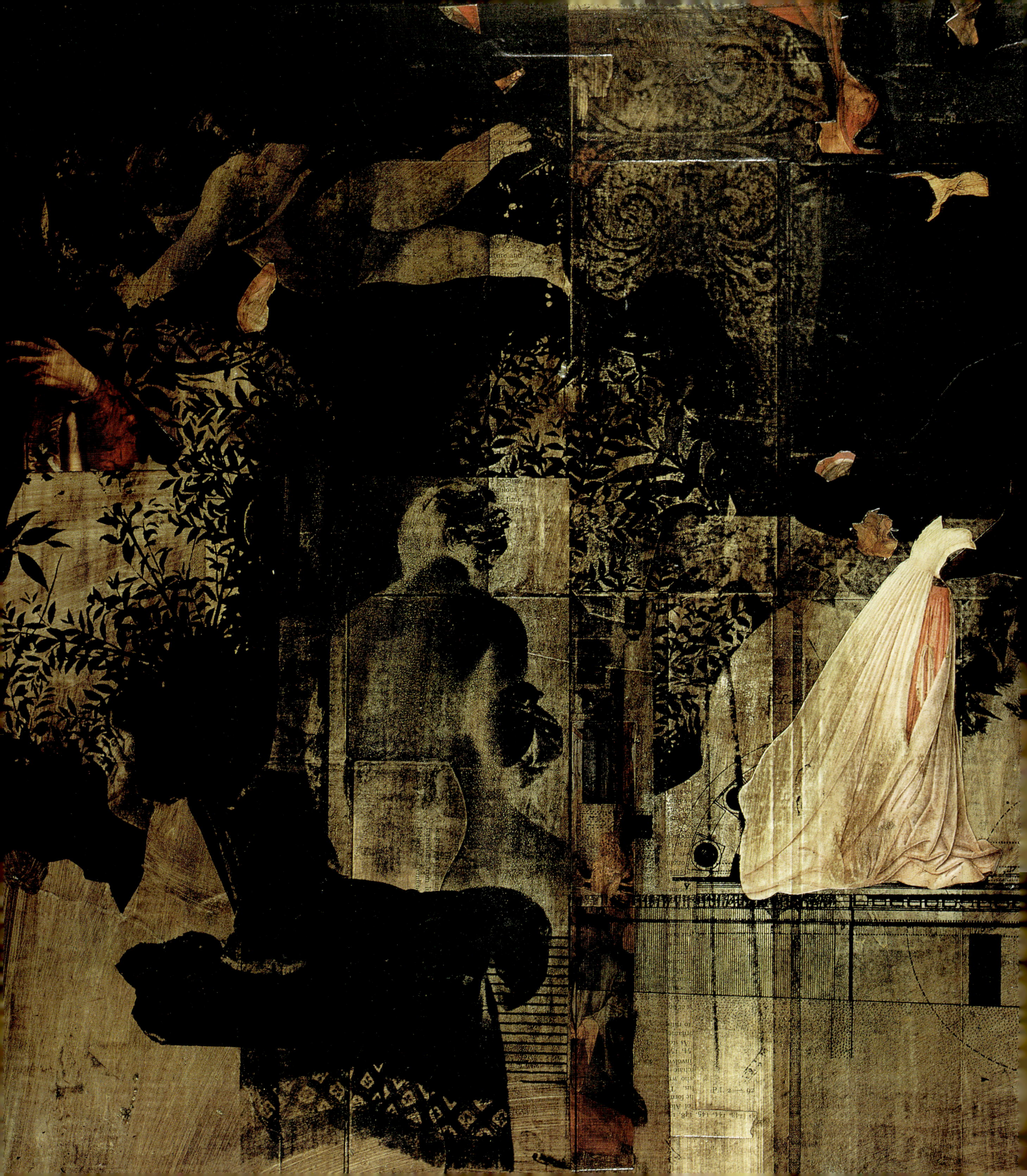

120 | NIGHT IN THE GARDEN 1996

Mixed media collage with photo transfer, 27" x 29 5/8"

121 | UNTITLED 1995

Plaster, wood metal and objects on wood, 20" x 24"

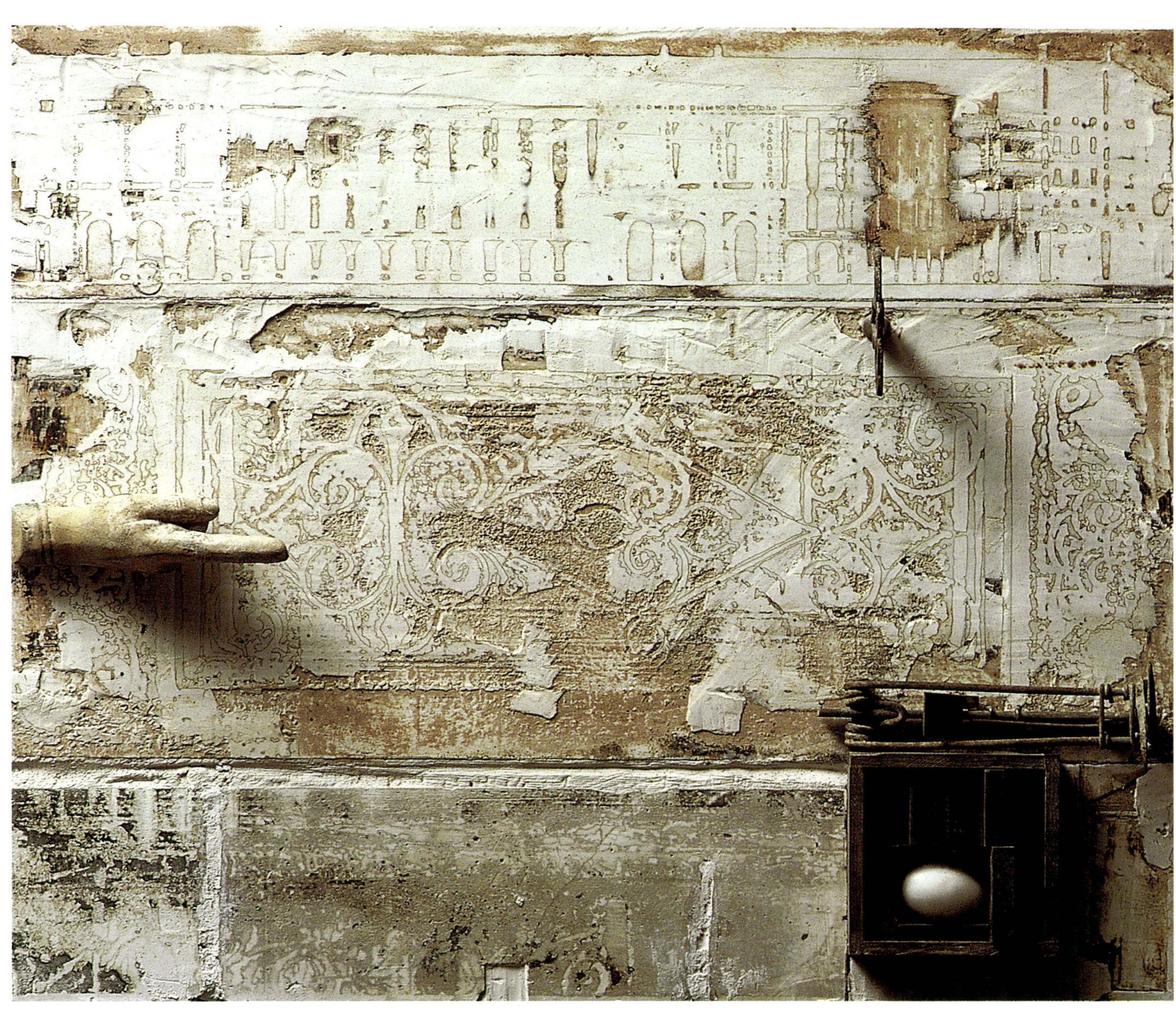

122 | RENAISSANCE TRAVELER 1996
Mixed media collage on linen, 24" x 19"

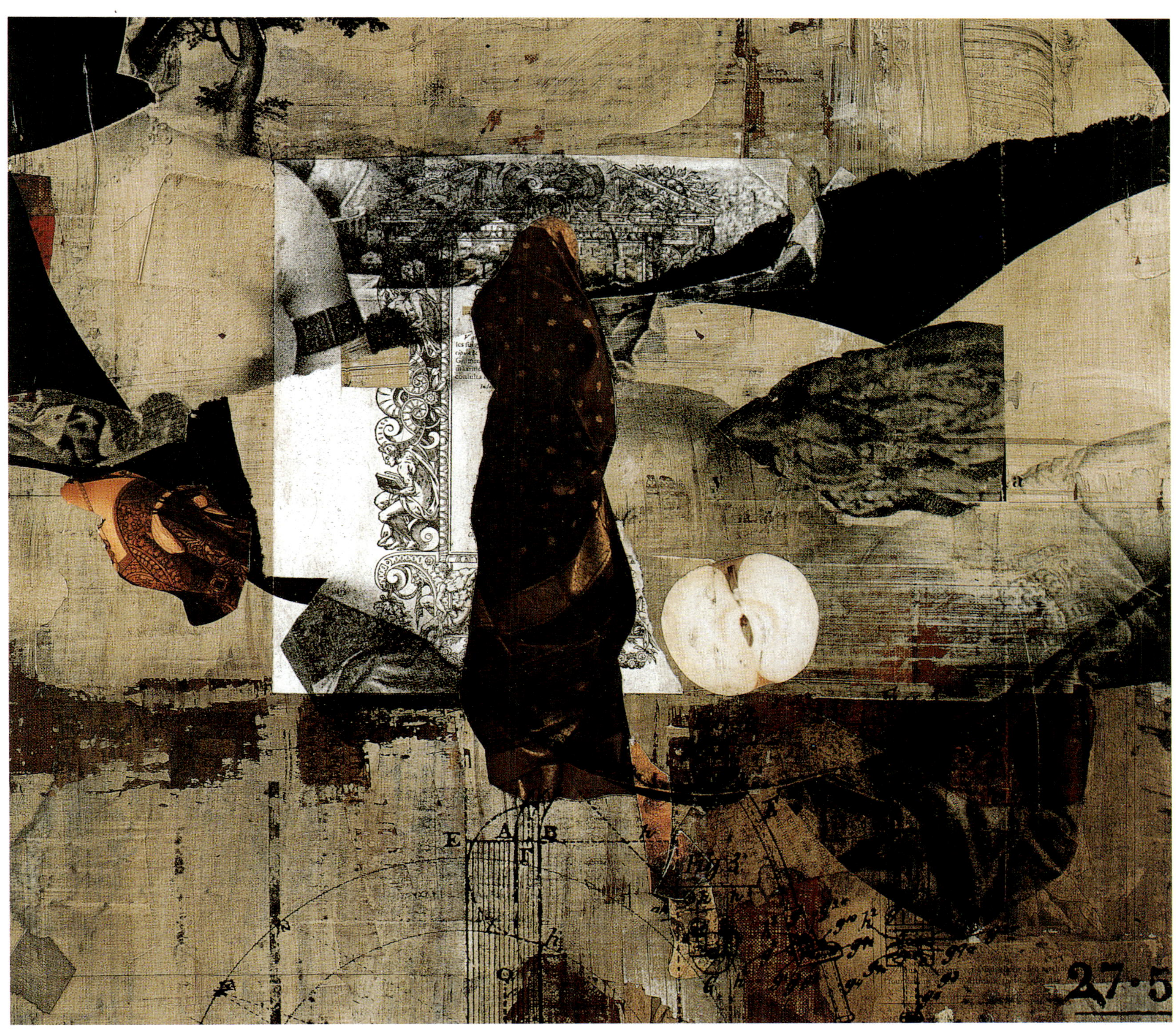
27·5

123 | A LITTLE TREE 1992

Mixed media collage, 19 1/4" x 14 1/4"

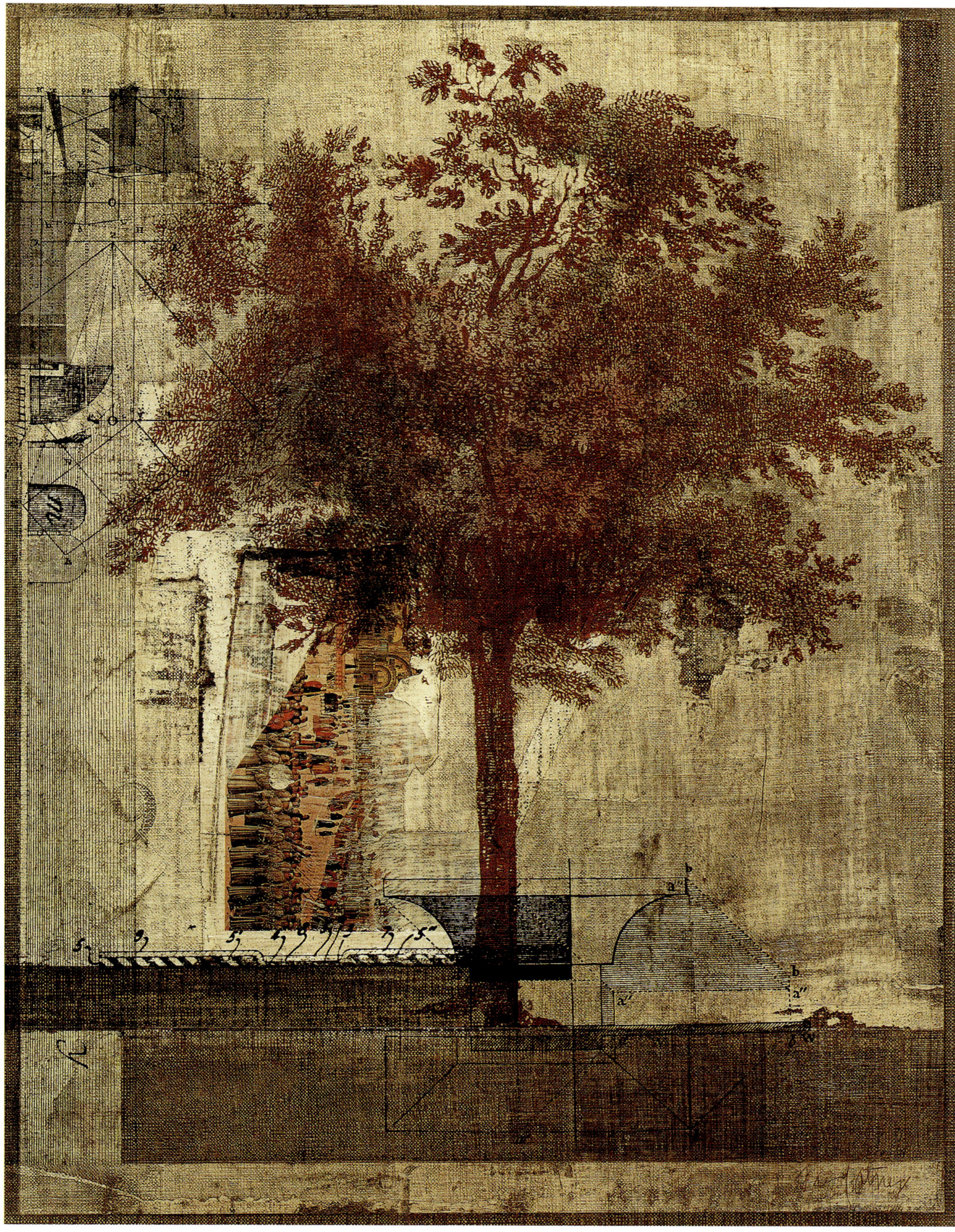

124 | QUADRANS 1998

Mixed media collage, 37 1/2" x 34 1/4"

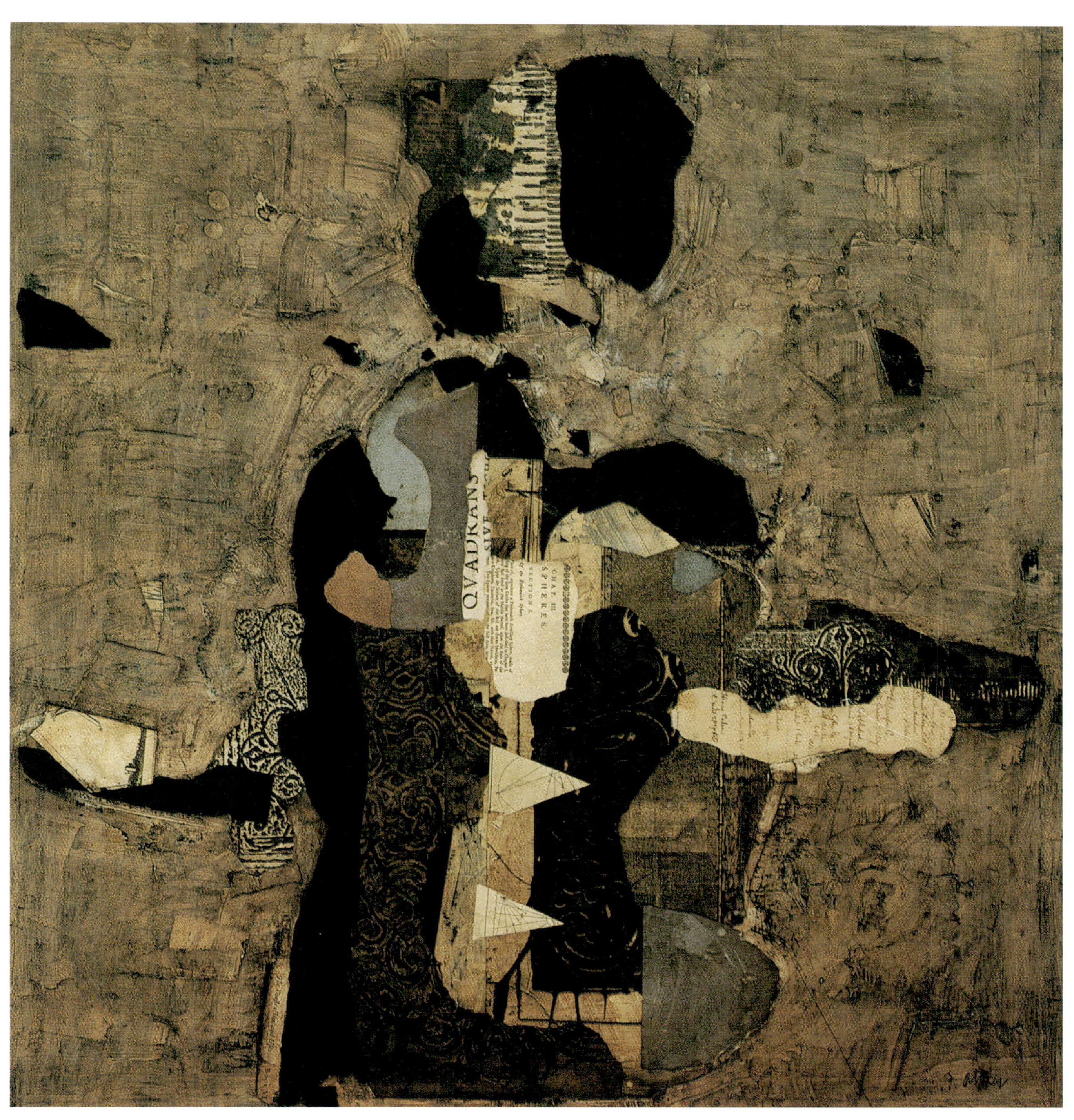
QVADRANS

125 | UNTITLED 1998

Mixed media collage, 18" x 30"

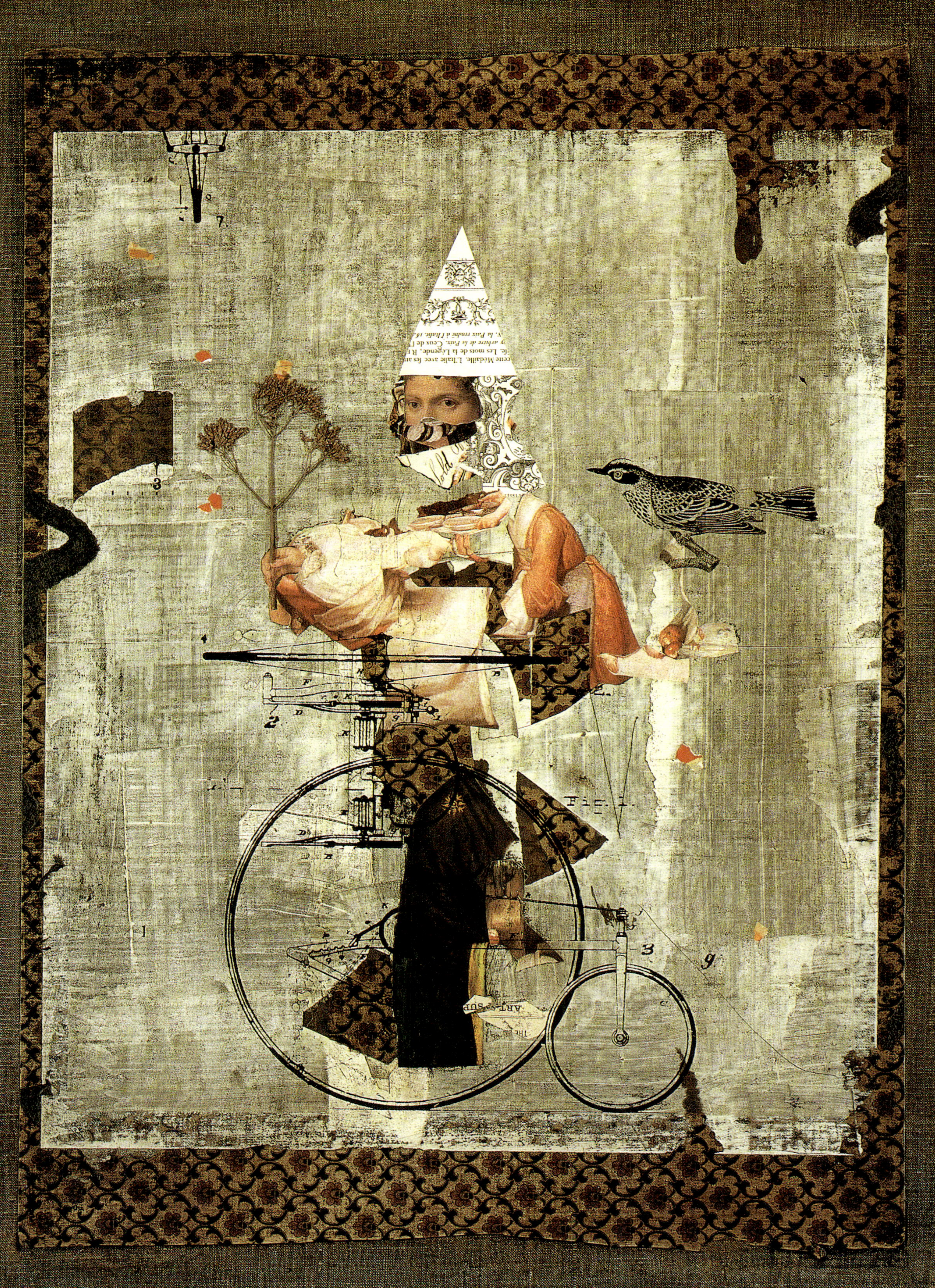

126 | UNTITLED 1998

Mixed media collage, 24" x 30"

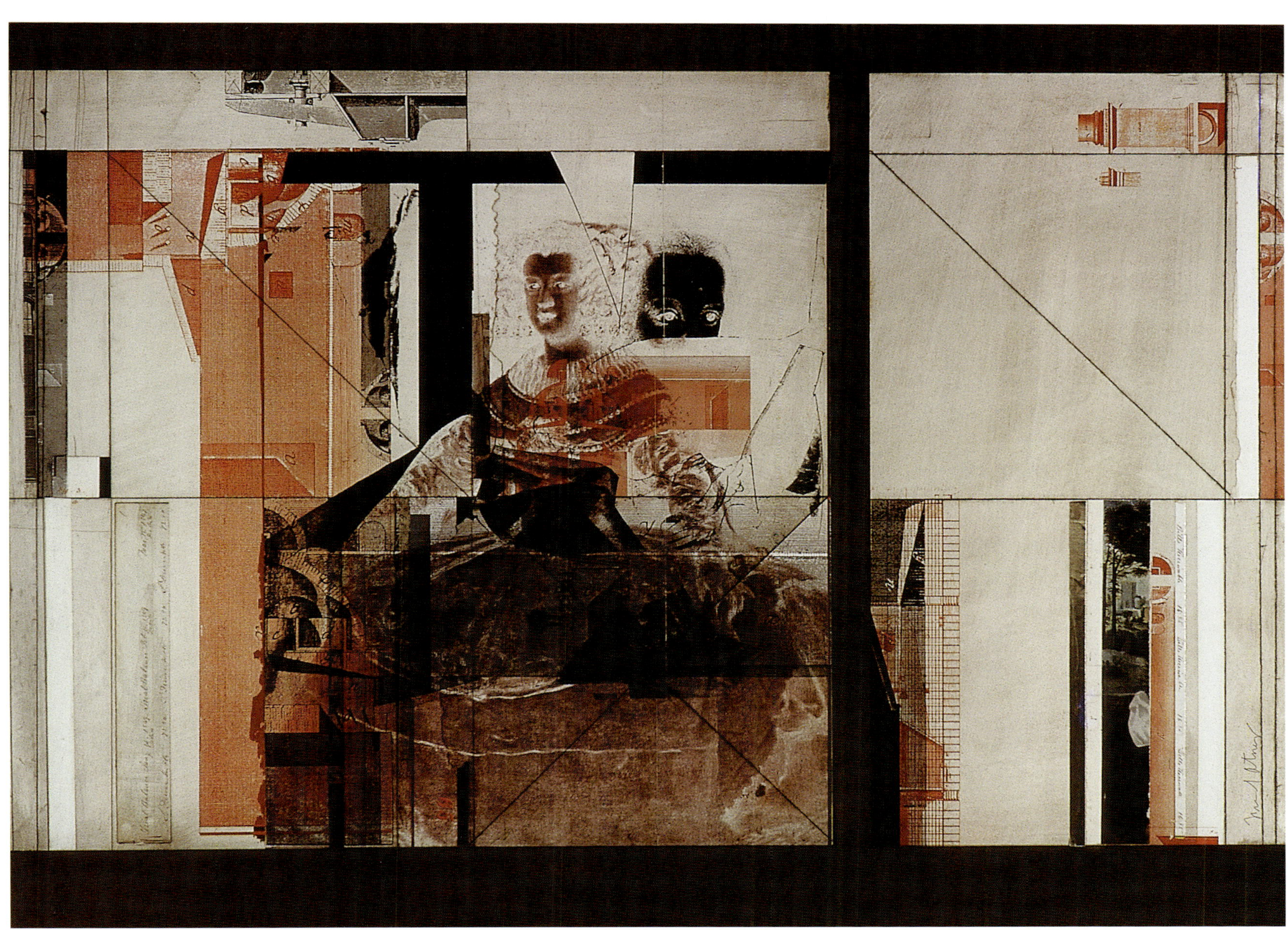

Chronology of Fred Otnes	1930	Born in Junction City, Kansas Currently resides in Redding, Connecticut
Education	1949-52	Studied at The Art Institute of Chicago & The American Academy
	1953	Moved to Connecticut
	1962	Began a 30-year association with Artists Associates, New York
Awards		Winner of over 200 Awards including Gold and Silver Medals from the Museum of American Illustration and The New York Art Directors Club.
Selected Exhibitions and Lectures	1980	Geigy Symposium, Honolulu, HI Texas Christian University, Dallas, TX University of California, Sacramento, CA
	1981	*Fred Otnes: Collage & Assemblage*, Hirshhorn Museum, Washington, DC
	1982	American Education Center, Reid Hall, Paris, France Rhode Island School of Design, Providence, RI Spokane Community College, Spokane, WA
	1983	East Carolina University, Gray Art Museum Gallery of Shinsai Bashi, Parco, Tokyo, Japan Sappora Parko Gallery, Tokyo, Japan University of Tennessee, Knoxville, TN
	1984	The Butler Institute of American Art, OH Columbus College of Art, Columbus, OH
	1985	Asilomar, Monterey, CA
	1987	The Workshop at University at Buffalo, SUNY, NY
	1988	20 + 1, Seoul, Korea
	1989	Art Center, Dayton, OH
	1991	Creation Gallery, Tokyo, Japan Kansas State, Manhattan, KS Kansas City Art institute, Kansas City, MO
	1992	*On the Cutting Edge*, Javits Convention Center, New York, NY Studio of Artists, Tokyo, Japan Tokyo Central Museum, Tokyo, Japan Umeda Museum of Contemporary Art, Osaka, Japan
	1993	John Slade Ely House, Center for Contemporary Art, New Haven, CT New England Show, Silvermine, CT Waterside Gallery, Stamford, CT West Harbor Gallery, Ltd., Oyster Bay, NY
	1994	*Positives and Negatives*, The Reece Galleries, Inc., New York, NY
	1995	Hamilton Gallery, Savannah College of Art & Design, GA
	1996	*Recent Work*, The Reece Galleries, Inc., New York, NY Rosenwald-Wolf Gallery, University of Arts, Philadelphia, PA
	1997	The Red Dot Gallery, London, England
	1998	Gomez Gallery, Baltimore, MD Irving Gallery, Palm Beach, FL *Collage Paintings*, The Reece Galleries, Inc., New York, NY
	1999	*New Collage Paintings*, The Reece Galleries, Inc., New York, NY
	2000	*Collage Paintings*, Cline Fine art Gallery, Santa Fe, NM
	2000	*New Collage Paintings*, The Reece Galleries, Inc., New York, NY
	2002	*The Otnes Collage Liagre Series*, The Reece Galleries, Inc., New York, NY
	2003	*Collage Paintings*, The Reece Galleries, Inc., New York, NY
Recent Group Exhibitions	1997	Milwaukee Institute of Art & Design, Fredrick Layton Gallery, Milwaukee, WI The Reece Galleries, Inc., New York, NY Southern Utah University, Braithwaite Fine Arts Gallery, Cedar City, UT
	1998	Art Institute of Seattle, Seattle, WA Brigham Young University, Department of Design, Provo, UT McDonough Museum of Art, Youngstown State University, Youngstown, OH The Reece Galleries, Inc., New York, NY Savannah College of Art & Design, Savannah, GA Western Illinois University, University Art Gallery, Macomb, IL *Selections: Collage*, Anthony Giordano Gallery/The Islip Art Museum, Islip, NY
	1999-00	*Intermission I, II & III*, The Reece Galleries, Inc., New York, NY
	2000	Irving Gallery, Palm Beach, FL
	2001	Society of Illustrators, New York, NY
	2003	Stremmel Gallery, Reno, NV

Commissioned Illustrations

Atlantic Monthly, "Who Do Men Say I Am: Historical View of Jesus," Cover and Illustrations, Dec 1986
Atlantic Monthly, "Homosexuality and Biology," Cover and Illustrations, Vol. 271, No. 3, March 1993
Atlantic Records, "The History of Rhythm & Blues," 7 Covers
Eugene O'Neil, Four plays, Franklin Library
National Geographic, Ten Paintings for 100th Anniversary Issue
The Selected Poetry of Blake, New American Library
Selected Writings of Walter Pater, New American Library
Short Stories of Guy de Maupassant, Franklin Library
Designer of Sixteen United States Postal Stamps

Selected Reviews

Harrison, Helen A., "A Range of Collage With Contemporary Touch," *The New York Times*, July 18, 1999, p. 14
Breienbach, Tom, *Artforum International*, May, 1999, pp. 180-181
Brown, Gerard, "The Art of Seduction," *The Philadelphia Weekly*, Feb. 14, 1996
Enriquez, Mary Schneider, "Fred Otnes," *Artnews Magazine*, Dec. 2000
Fennell, John. "Melding Technology with Tradition," *Step-by-Step Magazine*, Vol. 5, No. 4, 1988, pp. 42-53
Henry Gerrit, "Fred Otnes," *Artnews Magazine*, May 1994, pp. 160-161
Henry Gerrit, "Fred Otnes at Reece," *Art in America*, Oct. 1998, Vol. 86, No. 10, p. 138
Goodman, Jonathan, "Fred Otnes, *Art in America*, Dec. 2002
Kramer, Virginia, "Collage Professor," *Confetti*, Vol. 5, No. 1, pp. 26-31
Macleod, Chris, "From Whimsey to Wisdom: Fred Otnes at Reece Galleries," *Manhattan Spirit*, Feb. 12, 1998
McKanic, Arlene, "Fred Otnes," *Artnews Magazine*, Sept. 2002
Sozanski, Edward J., *The Philadelphia Inquirer*, Feb. 8, 1996

Individual Articles

Communication Arts, Vol. 15, No. 3, 1973
Confetti Magazine, May 1993
Creation Magazine, Japan, 1995
Design Magazine, Korea, 1995
Graphis, No. 188, 1976-77
The Greatest Illustration Show of America, Japan, 1992
Idea Magazine, Japan, 1993
Illustration in the Third Dimension, Hastings House
Northlight, March – April, 1976
Novum Gebrauchsgraphik, Germany, 1993
Print Magazine, March – April, 1975
Styling Magazine, Japan, 1991
Today's Art, Vol. 28, No. 5
Typographic, Vol. 12, No. 2
Who's Who in Graphic Art, De Clivo Press
World Graphic Design, Japan, 1991
Graphica, International Publication of Design and Graphics, Brazil, 1994
Pro-Illustration, Society of Illustrators, 1998

Public Collections

Aetna Insurance, Hartford, CT
American Express Co., New York, NY
Bear Stearns, New York, NY
Boston Consulting Group, Boston, MA
Bristol Meyers, New York, NY
The Equitable Companies, Hartford, CT
Ernst & Young, Los Angeles, CA
Exxon Corporation, New York, NY
General Electric, Fairfield, CT
Grupo Industrial Alfa, Monterrey, Mexico
Hutchinson Whampoa, Hong Kong
IBM, New York, NY
Interpublic Group of Companies, New York, NY
Marsh & McLennen, New York, NY
NASA, Washington, DC
National Academy of Science, Washington, DC
National Geographic Society, Washington, DC
National Parks Service, Washington, DC
Northern Gas, Omaha, NB
Pfizer, New York, NY
Phillip Morris Headquarters, New York, NY
Ronald Reagan Library, Los Angeles, CA
Twentieth Century Fox, Los Angeles, CA
Vastar Resources, Inc. Houston, TX
Viking Lines, San Francisco, CA

Special Thanks To:

Karen Gangel
Roger Mudre
Shirley Reece